FOUR KEYS TO
GUATEMALA

Biener

FIESTA DE SANTO TOMAS, CHICHICASTENANGO

Figures of St. Thomas, St. Sebastian and St. Joseph, each on red dais, ornately canopied with flowers, mirrors and plumes, leaving church to take part in ceremonial procession about the village.

FOUR KEYS TO GUATEMALA

BY

VERA KELSEY

AND

LILLY DE JONGH OSBORNE

REVISED EDITION

FUNK & WAGNALLS COMPANY

NEW YORK

Guatemala, C. A., 9 de Marzo de 1939

Visto el dictámen rendido por la comisión nombrada por esta Sociedad, en que manifiesta su conformidad del contenido del libro de doña Lilly de Jongh Osborne y señorita Vera Kelsey, titulado *Four Keys to Guatemala,* apruébase en todas sus partes.

[TRANSLATION]

Guatemala, C. A., March 9, 1939

Having examined the opinion prepared by the commission appointed by this Society, in which it finds itself in agreement with the contents of the book by Madame Lilly de Jongh Osborne and Miss Vera Kelsey, entitled *Four Keys to Guatemala,* it is approved in all its parts.

ACKNOWLEDGMENTS

Guatemala is rich in friends among her own and other peoples living within her borders. Out of interest in making the country known, scores have contributed generously of their observation and experience to the information in this book. We are deeply grateful to them all. And to those who, in addition, have given hours out of busy days to compiling material or checking our information against their more specialized knowledge, we are happy here to give all credit.

Colonial data—Sr. don F. Fernandez Hall, Professor don Joaquin Pardo, Sr. don Fernando Juarez Muñoz (all members of the Sociedad de Geografía é Historia), Sr. José Luis Reyes, Librarian.

Chichicastenango—Father Ildefonso Rossbach.

Fauna of Guatemala—Sr. don Alberto Fuentes Novella.

Flora of Guatemala—Sr. don Mariano Pacheco Herrarte, Mrs. B. B. Lewis.

Fishing and Hunting—Mr. Donald Hodgsdon.

Indian Etymology—Sr. Licenciado don Federico Morales.

Indian Music—Professor don Jesús Castillo.

Kekchi Indians—Mr. David Sapper.

Maya Sites—Carnegie Institution of Washington; Dr. J. Alden Mason, University Museum, University of Pennsylvania.

Modern Arts in Guatemala—Professor don Rafael Yela Gunther, Director, National Academy of Fine Arts.

Mountain Climbing—Mr. John Mario Willemsen.

Statistics—Sr. don Carlos Bickford, Director General of Highways; Colonel don Carlos Cipriani, Jefe Politico, Totonicapán; Sr. Licenciado don Ramón Aceña Duran, Huehuetenango; General sr. don Miguel Idigoras Fuentes, Jefe Politico, San Marcos; Colonel don Artemio E. Ruiz, Jefe Politico, Sololá; Sr. don Guillermo Schwartz, Director General of Statistics.

THE AUTHORS

CONTENTS

CONTENTS

ILLUSTRATIONS

xiii

[End papers, design reproduced from Guatemala textile. Jacket design, by George Switzer, inspired by *nacimiento* figures.]

FOUR KEYS TO
GUATEMALA

I

INTRODUCTION TO GUATEMALA

TO achieve an approximate idea of Guatemala as an area, imagine the United States concentrated within the boundaries of Ohio. In this small Republic's 42,000 and some odd—some very odd—square miles are found all the geographical features of the 3,000,000-square-mile Republic to the north: mountain ranges with 13,000-foot peaks, canyons 2000 feet deep, plains and deserts, lowlands and plateaus, great rivers and tiny streams, lakes, waterfalls, thermal springs, and both an Atlantic and Pacific seaboard. In addition, insert some 30 volcanoes, placing most of them like a picket fence along the Pacific coast.

Spread forests and jungles everywhere, splash color freely in flowers, in butterflies and birds everywhere too, but particularly along the coastal lowlands. Heat these lowlands to tropical temperatures; give the plateaus and highlands a perpetual spring with all that means in variable changes from cold to hot; chill the mountain regions, and, on winter mornings, top the mountains with snow and ice. Cover with electric blue skies and foaming white clouds.

That is the Land of Guatemala.[1]

Side by side on that land exist three civilizations. One day, perhaps, they will merge—here and there they can be seen merging today—but as yet their differences are more apparent than their similarities.

The first of these is Indian Guatemala, stemming from at least a millennium before the birth of Christ, complete with its own culture, costumes, customs and lore. The second is Colonial Guatemala, its heart the old capital of Antigua, but its cultural and rigidly conventioned social life continuing today in all parts of the

[1] See Notes 1 to 10.

country where the Spanish conqueror and the Spanish priest laid strong hands. Finally, there is the Republic of Guatemala, modern and progressive, economically and politically alert to changing conditions in a changing world.

Visitors to Guatemala are bewildered alike by the variety of scenic splendor and of the life spread before them. Residents— both Guatemalteco and foreign—cross the invisible boundaries from one Guatemala to another unaware that within the circle of a day they may have moved through a living history of civilization on the American continent.

Four Keys to Guatemala is an effort to open doors to the various and rich interest of a little-known country's yesterdays and today and to provide a background of understanding for its tomorrows.

INDIAN GUATEMALA

II

THE INDIAN AND HIS ANCESTORS

PRE-MAYA AND MAYA

FOR unknown centuries of the span of time when the Indians held full sway in Guatemala, nomadic tribes roamed the mountains and valleys, hunting and fishing. Eventually, each would disappear, leaving a few hardy descendants behind, and another tribe would rise to roam and disappear in the same cycle.

Sometime between 2000 and 1000 B.C., a wild grass—*teocintle*—growing on the plateaus of southern Mexico and northern Guatemala became the ancestor of the maize or corn. By 1000 B.C. its use was known to small nomadic groups called Maya living in the forests of what is now the Department of Petén, Guatemala. When they planted this seed, they planted also the first seeds of civilization on the western hemisphere.

With the means of providing food at hand, the Maya abandoned their nomadic life and settled down to farm. From this beginning grew a Maya Empire that spread beyond the forests to include western Honduras, British Honduras, the states of Chiapas and Tabasco in Mexico, and all of Guatemala of today. Hence derives Guatemala's title, "Land of the Maya."

Libraries, already written on the Maya, have as yet but scratched the surface of the tale to be told. Here it is sufficient to mention briefly those aspects of their life that influenced or are reflected in the life of the Indian of today.

For centuries the Maya crossed and recrossed their territories, erecting magnificent cities without the aid of animals or wheeled devices, creating a culture which proves them to have been the "most brilliant aboriginal people on the planet." [1]

When they had developed agriculture until they not only had sufficient food but reserves in great storehouses, the Maya turned

[1] Dr. Sylvanus Morley; see Bibliography.

their attention to the arts and sciences. Music and dancing became integral parts of all their ceremonies, religious and civil. They gave much time to architecture, painting and sculpture, decorating everything from pots to temple walls.

Writing, the invention which H. G. Wells calls "the true measure of civilization," they developed to a high point, perfecting an ideographic system that represents a much earlier stage than that of either the Egyptian or Sumerian, for they brought it to the verge of phonetics.

They devised a simple numerical system by means of dots and dashes which even today stands as "one of the most brilliant achievements ever conceived by the mind of man." [1] They had a system of arithmetic 2000 years before mathematics came into general use in Europe, at least 1000 years before the Hindus developed their system; their knowledge of the use of zero antedated that of the Arabs by a millennium.

Their calendar computations are among the most complicated known to scientists. In fact, they had various calendars, based on the movements of Venus, the moon, and certain constellations. The two principal ones interlock like the cogs of a wheel. One divided the year into eighteen months of twenty days each and an extra period of five. These five days became a time of solemn ceremony and gay fiesta whose spirit and ritual are observed in the Department of Alta Verapaz today. (Holy Week, page 41.) The other calendar, known as the Tzolkin or ritual calendar, is also still in use by the Quiché and other highland tribes (page 35).

Well-built roads joined their cities and the shrines to which in time of famine, pestilence and other disasters they flocked to petition their gods. Mounds and stone altars were erected along them that travelers with flowers and incense and sacrifice of animals might ask of the gods a safe journey. Over these roads Maya merchants ventured to all parts of Central and even South America, trading their textiles, ceramics, feather work, carved jades for the cacao beans, bells, stones and other small objects prized as money. As they went they spread knowledge of the Maya and his culture.

In religion they were polytheistic, with a long roll of major and

[1] Dr. Sylvanus Morley; see Bibliography.

minor deities, each of whom had his own highly conventionalized symbol in their art and writing. Most revered was Kukulcán, whose symbol, the plumed serpent, still is found everywhere in sculpture and decoration. He was their God of Wisdom and Nature, their Law Giver and progenitor of a new religion that did not demand human sacrifice.

A superstitious people, they believed in all manner of omens, good and evil, and in the divine power of witch doctors to cure the sick with incantations and medicinal herbs. They buried their dead in a sitting posture and with them the implements of their craft and regalia of office.

Their social life was complex and highly moral, based on the clan system. They reverenced age, and old men joined the nobles, priests and warrior chiefs in the highest of their clearly defined social castes. Their laws were strict. Death punished adultery and severe penalties were imposed for damage to property and other crimes. Children were carefully trained in the arts. And in special schools the girls were taught to cook and weave, the boys to till the soil. At an early age marriage was arranged for them by their parents.

Between the fourth and seventh centuries, Maya civilization reached its zenith. After that flamboyance crept into every phase of life, resulting in decadence and disintegration. Then for some reason—disease, changing climate, earthquakes, soil exhaustion and, in the Petén, because of the loss of water supplies and transportation routes due to silt filling their shallow lagoons—they began to abandon their largest and most magnificent cities and to turn back toward the north from which originally they had come. Like the nomads, they left scattered groups of their people behind. Soon the forests reclaimed their cities and shrines.

On the peninsula of Yucatan they settled to build new and enormous cities where they lived until the twelfth century. Then intertribal wars, invasions of Aztecs and other tribes from the Mexican highlands, and the sterility of the arid lands of the peninsula brought weakness and decadence. And again some of them trekked south to the land of Petén. This time they entered the region around what is called today Lake Petén-Itza.

On an island in this lake they established their principal city, Tayasal, where they lived more or less at peace until the close of the seventeenth century. There in 1697—much to his surprise and theirs—Martin de Ursua at the head of an army of Spanish soldiers came upon them. Beaten and despoiled, the Indians who survived scattered and fled, and the Maya as a people and an independent culture were lost to Guatemala.

POST-MAYA NATIONS

For very good reasons little authentic information concerning the Indian from the exodus of the Maya to the arrival of the Spaniards is available. The Conquistadores destroyed every vestige of Indian culture they could find, and killed off the ruling houses, the priests and warriors in order the more easily to impose their own culture and to forestall any leaders rising against them. After the Conquest, Indian chroniclers of several nations set down their records in their own tongue, but already the teachings of the Spanish priests had become so ingeniously interwoven with their own that these records too are unreliable.

In general, it can be said that out of the mixture of pre-Maya and Maya descendants remaining in Guatemala, new peoples began to develop. These in turn, mixing bloods with later invasions drifting down from the north, developed additional new nations. Through them all ran a thread of their Maya heritage.

The invasions were the result of three great migrations which left a legendary home in the north called Tulán, in a legendary year given as 1035 A.D., and wandered southward. The first of these—led in the beginning by a Chief Gucumatz—after years of hardship reached the shores of Lake Atitlán. There it divided into three nations.

One, the Maya-Quiché, took the northwest shores; the second, or Cakchiquel, the northeast, and the third, the Tzutuhil, the south. The second migration—the Mam nation—settled in the highlands near what is now Huehuetenango. And the third, the Rabinaleros, turning to the southeast, preempted the region known today as Verapaz.

Too many nations flourished prior to the coming of the Spaniards to mention them all here. Following are the chief tribes, important both for their contribution to pre-Columbian history and for their still active influence and participation in the Guatemala of today.

The Maya-Quiché Nation

This tribe took its name from the chieftain who led them as a separate people away from the great migration with which they had come to Guatemala. His name was Nima-Quiché (*Qui* = many; *che* = trees). They selected as the site of the capital of their domain, the present Santa Cruz del Quiché. And because they found there traces of an earlier people, they named it Gumarkaaj, "Place of Old Sticks."

The site was a natural fortress surrounded on all sides by deep ravines, accessible by only one causeway, but they made it impregnable with an enclosing wall and watchtowers. Within this fortress dwelt the nobility, priests and warriors; outside on the forested hills and plains lived the common people in thatched huts as do their descendants still. From this fortress the Quiché armies marched out to conquer the tribes from Lake Atitlán to Verapaz.

So vast grew their territory, so great their power and numbers, that their Chief could no longer rule them alone. Reserving for himself Supreme Command, he divided the nation into twenty-four branches, each with its own chief. The result was that the nation grew more rich and powerful than ever as each clan vied to conquer and win favor in the eyes of the Supreme Command. In this they were aided by their deities—Tohil, Agüilix and Jacagüitz —who, pleased with the splendid temples erected to them, gave victory to the arms of the Quiché.

Again the ruling Chief was forced to divide his empire. To his eldest son he gave the conquered territory of the Cakchiqueles, and to his second son the conquered kingdom of the Tzutuhiles, reserving for himself the mighty Quiché realm. This division, according to Indian records quoted by the Spanish chronicler, Fuentes y Guzmán, was made at a time when "three suns [stars] stood together in the sky"; from this some declare that it was made on the night that Christ was born and the shepherds followed three bright stars.

The Quiché triumphs in war were their own ruin—and pre-Columbian Guatemala's. They paid no heed to the warnings of the priests and sorcerers that

> "Men who are clothed, not naked like thee, well armed; men who are cruel will arrive tomorrow or the next day. These will destroy your edifices which will become the habitat of the wild fowl and mountain lions. The grandeur of this Court will cease to be."

And they saw no significance in the message sent them by Montezuma, King of the Aztecs, warning that white men, fully clothed, had arrived in the empire to the north. As a result, when the Spaniards descended, the Quiché lacked the allies with whose aid they could have defeated them. Every nation was their enemy.

On a memorable day in 1524, the Quiché, 70,000 strong, marched out of their fortress to join other Quiché armies on the plains near Quezaltenango and annihilate the white invaders. And they might have succeeded had they followed the fighting style of the North American Indian. But they clung to their traditional strategy of massed armies, and their arrows and spears were helpless against bullets and swords and that fear-inspiring phenomenon, the horse. When in a hand-to-hand conflict between Tecúm-Umám, leader of the Quiché, and Pedro de Alvarado, commander of the Spanish, the Indian was killed, the Quiché admitted defeat at arms.

They had one more weapon, however—their fortress. To this they invited the conquerors to arrange the terms of surrender. The Spanish, eager to seize the wealth of this fabulous city—which they called Utatlán—agreed, and Alvarado and all his men marched across the causeway. But, inside, the capital "looked more like a place where robbers lived," Alvarado wrote his King.

Not a woman or child was in sight. And the causeway, the one means of exit, he discovered, had been undermined, ready at a blow to crash into the ravine. On the pretext that his horses must have grazing ground, Alvarado hastened to march his forces out again.

When he learned that the Quiché had planned to destroy the causeway and burn him and his men alive, he ordered the Chiefs of the Quiché to be burned and the fortress razed. So fell the Quiché Nation. Succeeding chieftains were merely Spanish puppets, their people scattered and broken.

In 1815, Anastasio Txul, the last of the line of the ruling Quiché house, was crowned in San Miguel Totonicapán and attempted to raise his people once more. He was imprisoned and the dream shattered. Today the town of Santa Cruz stands on the site of the old fortress-capital, and in Chichicastenango and the surrounding country the last descendants of the Maya-Quiché people carry on their old social and religious customs while they farm, raise cattle, and weave their tribal textiles. Their Maya heritage is still evident. Wherever an important and prosperous Indian is found, in him is found, too, a descendant of the Maya.

Cakchiquel Nation

The name is derived either from the staffs cut from a redwood tree (*cak* = red; *chiquel* = trees) which the warriors carried, or from the fact that they are believed to have stolen the sacred fire from a temple (*cak*, also meaning fire; *chiquelep*, thieves).

When first the Cakchiqueles settled on their new territory about the present city of Tecpán, they devoted themselves to planting the fertile valleys to corn, to building a well-fortified capital, and to setting up a court that would do justice to their ruling house. The capital they named Iximché, or Corn Plant; the court, Patinamit, or First City of the Kingdom, sometimes known as Tecpán-Quahtemallán (Court of the Royal House of Guatemala). This ruling house was Xahilá, Clan of the Bats.

The capital completed, they declared war, and from then until the Conquest, they fought continuously. Chiefly they fought their blood-brothers, the Quiché and Tzutuhiles, but they descended on other tribes too. In time they acquired much territory, riches and power, were, in fact, second only to the Quiché. And in the war that followed the placing of a Quiché chief on a Cakchiquel throne, they were on the point of defeating the Quiché when the Spaniards arrived, saved them the trouble, and changed the course of history.

Although the Cakchiqueles refused to aid the Quiché against the Spanish, their canny chief—Sinecan Belejebcat—was much alarmed at the fate of Utatlán. At the same time he saw in the defeat of his foe an opportunity to make his own nation supreme. Therefore, he sent emissaries with gifts and messages of peace to Alvarado and an invitation to visit Iximché.

When Alvarado arrived, he found the Cakchiqueles preparing for war, but war with the Tzutuhiles, they explained, and asked his aid. And with his aid they eliminated their second most powerful enemy. Pleased, Alvarado established his first headquarters or capital at Iximché. Because it was founded on St. James' Day, July 25, 1524, he called it Santiago de los Caballeros (St. James of the Knights).

One of Alvarado's chief aims in invading Guatemala—to secure treasure—was not being realized. In spite of the fact that the Cakchiqueles had provided him and his men with everything needful "as if they had been in their own homes," he demanded jars filled with gold and silver, including the drinking cups and crowns of the chiefs. "If you do not bring me the precious metals in all your towns," he threatened, "choose then, for I shall burn you alive and hang you." He cut the gold ornaments from the ears of three chiefs and ordered, "I want the gold here within five days."

While the Indians were trying to gather what gold their people had, one of their priests became inspired. "I am the lightning; I will destroy the Castilians," he prophesied. "I will destroy them by fire. When I beat the drum, let the chiefs come forth and go to the other bank of the river." And he named the day on which this should be done.

On the day appointed, the Indians deserted Iximché, but the miracle did not come to pass. Shortly Alvarado and his men were on them, killing and scattering them among the forests and destroying all their villages, making of the one helpful and friendly tribe a bitter enemy.

Tzutuhil Nation

Even with the aid of the Cakchiqueles, Alvarado found the Tzutuhiles a more difficult foe than either the Quiché or the Cakchiqueles when he fought them later. Unusually tall and well set up, they were fearless warriors and resourceful. They had not

only built a strongly fortified capital on the promontory that juts
into Lake Atitlán between the volcanoes Toliman-Atitlán and Santa
Clara-San Pedro, but fortified and garrisoned other strategic points
and supplemented them with a large fleet of dugout canoes.

This capital they named Atziquinahay in honor of their ruling
clan, House of the Eagle. It topped the steep hill now familiarly
known as "Child of the Volcano" that lies at the foot of San Pedro.
More than 300 feet high, ragged with outcroppings of lava, it
enabled the Tzutuhiles to boast that no enemy had ever approached
their capital, much less taken it. Here lived the royal house and
priests who attended the altars. The common people, *el populacho,*
lived where the village of Santiago Atitlán now stands.

As a result of their prowess in war, the Tzutuhiles had acquired
almost all the rich area surrounding the lake and great sections of
the Pacific lowlands. Here they grew cotton and cacao and *achiote,*
a red dye in demand by Indians of many tribes for painting their
bodies and coloring food. From the exchange of these products
they had also acquired much gold and silver.

Alvarado found his approach to this rich and strongly entrenched
capital barred some distance away by a steep volcanic ridge over
which his cavalry could not pass. Between this ridge and the lake
was a flat gap and on its farther side a peninsula, Tzanyuyú, meaning in the Cakchiquel tongue, "nose of the mountain." Here the
Tzutuhiles, for some reason making no use of their fortress-capital,
had stationed themselves.

Unwilling to descend the ridge in the face of their deadly weapons, Alvarado sent forward his crossbowmen who killed enough
Indians to bring the rest charging into the open. After a long and
furious battle, the Indians broke before the gunfire and fled for
their fortress. The Spaniards, pursuing, killed them by scores, and
the Cakchiqueles, arriving at this moment with 300 canoes, killed
those who attempted to swim to the little island now known as
Teachuc, said to mean "where the glory departed."

Visitors to Santiago Atitlán can see today the curiously shaped
hill that was once the citadel and place of sacrifice of the Tzutuhiles
and the ruins of their pyramids, courts, terraces and altars. Tradition says that beneath the hill runs an underground passage, built

long ago as an avenue of escape to the mainland, and that in the hill is buried the vast treasure hidden there when word came that the Spaniards had reached the lake.

Mam Nation

Another powerful and warlike people, the Mames, grew out of the second great migration. They are believed to have settled in Guatemala before the Quiché. Perhaps for this reason they are called Old Men, though the usual explanation is that they were so nicknamed because they stuttered when they tried to pronounce the names of their Quiché enemies. Their ceremonial center was given the Quiché name, Zaculeu, between the 12th and 15th centuries.

To defend their territories, the Mames also built a strongly fortified capital on the hill-encircled plains known as Las Lagunas y Gambote. From this fortress to the Zaculeu River they built a subterranean passage through which reinforcements and water could be brought into the city in time of siege, and for it named their capital Chinabajul, "in the hole of the shrewd and distrustful mole."

The Mames were constantly at war, chiefly with the Quiché, but it was the Cakchiqueles who brought about their downfall. They filled Alvarado's ears with accounts of the riches of the Mames and their dangerously increasing power. Busy fighting the Quiché, Alvarado had heard little of the Mames, but in 1525 he sent his brother, Gonzalo, at the head of a large force of Spaniards and Indian allies against them. After four months of hard fighting, the Mames were defeated though not without first inflicting severe losses on their conquerors.

Sacatepéquez Nation

Two centuries before the Conquest, a section of the Cakchiquel nation revolted and set up an independent government under the name of Sacatepéquez, "Hill of the Weeds." Establishing themselves in the territory between the Piscaya River and the Valley of the Snake, they began incessant warfare on their old Cakchiquel brothers and on neighboring tribes. In time they became one of the dominant nations, controlling the area that is today included in the Department of Sacatepéquez and part of the Department of Guatemala.

While the Cakchiqueles and Sacatepéquez were having their worst troubles—shortly before the Conquest—Indians from the Pokomán nation living in the overcrowded lands of Cuscatlán (now El Salvador) asked permission of the Cakchiqueles to settle on the fertile plains between them and the Sacatepéquez. Not displeased at the idea of having a buffer state between themselves and the troublesome Sacatepéquez, the Cakchiqueles consented. Whereupon the Pokomanes constructed an almost impregnable fortress capital on a hilltop (near the present San Martín Jilotepeque), named it Mixco, and started war at once with the Quiché and Cakchiqueles.

In Alvarado, the Cakchiqueles saw an opportunity to crush the Sacatepéquez—though this time they did send envoys to warn them first to cease their depredations. The Sacatepéquez reply was to murder all the envoys but one and send him back with their defiance. Whereupon the Cakchiqueles, with Alvarado's aid, succeeded in subduing the Sacatepéquez and garrisoning their largest settlements with Spaniards and Indian allies.

To the aid of the Sacatepéquez went the Pokomanes and their allies, the Chinautlas. Once more, if the Indians had stood together, the Spaniards could have been defeated. Again and again, with great losses to his Mexican allies, Alvarado's forces were driven back from Mixco's lofty hill. He succeeded only in killing off most of the Chinautlas.

Angered, the Chinautlas sent gifts of green plumes, textiles and gold to Alvarado to say that they would surrender. More, they promised that if he would not announce their surrender until he had defeated the Pokomanes, they would help him to do it. When Alvarado with gifts of looking-glasses and other trinkets signified his consent, they told him that even if the fortress could be captured, the Pokomanes couldn't be, as they had a subterranean passage to the river by which they would escape. Alvarado promptly placed forces at the river entrance to this passage, and when the Pokomanes, retreating at last, emerged, the Spaniards fell upon them. Unaccustomed to open-country warfare, they were easily

defeated and the survivors transported ten leagues to found the
Mixco of today. The ruins of their fortress capital are now known
as Mixco Viejo.

Rabinal Nation

Developed out of the third of the three original migrations, the
Rabinaleros took root in the region divided now into the Departments of Alta (upper) and Baja (lower) Verapaz. Near the site
of the village of Rabinal they erected their fortress-capital, Min-
pokom. Their common people, however, did not live together
near by but in isolated huts scattered about the thickly wooded
valleys.

The fertile, well-watered soil, the mines, quantities of game and
gorgeous-plumed birds whose feathers were in demand by many
tribes not only made the Rabinaleros prosperous but roused the
greed of other nations. Defending their territory against continuous attack, the Rabinaleros became the fiercest and most invincible
fighters in the country. The Quiché were their most potent enemies, and with them the Rabinaleros fought one war that is said
to have lasted through an entire century. The fame of their blood-
thirsty gods, who demanded the living sacrifice of every captive,
and their terrible methods of warfare were sufficient to win them
the alliance of neighboring tribes.

So invulnerable had they become that even Alvarado and his
victorious armies were powerless against them. Driven back time
after time, he at last named the country Tierra de Guerra, Land
of War, or, in the tongue of the Rabinaleros, Tezulutlán, and
abandoned further attempts to conquer it.

The Spanish priests, however, could not allow so many souls to
remain ignorant of the Christian God. Under the leadership of
Bartolomé de las Casas, the friars of the Dominican Order made
a pact with the Conquistadores. If for a period of five years, they
promised, Alvarado would not permit a single armed man to enter
the Rabinal territory, they would undertake to win these unconquerable people to the Spanish Cross and Crown.

So in 1537 began the peaceful conquest of the Land of War.
Las Casas with the aid of three other Dominican friars—Pedro de

Angulo, Luis Cancer, Rodrigo de Ladrada—entered the territory unarmed. Though they suffered hardship and privation, they traveled everywhere, preaching and teaching by means of simple songs and stories.

By 1538 conversion of the Indians to Christianity was making headway, because, as the priests admitted, of the high moral principles of these warriors. They even, after some opposition, gave up their traditional habits of living and consented to gather in villages centered about small churches. The first of these villages was Rabinal.

The Rabinaleros, in fact, took their new religion so seriously that they almost defeated the work of the friars. One of the converted Christians (christened don Jorge) was a powerful chief, engaged to be married to the daughter of the chief of the Cobanes, another strong tribe in the Land of War. On the day of the wedding, don Jorge, with his followers bearing gifts, met the Chief of Cobán, his daughter and their people, also gift-laden, at a river bank.

The Chief of Cobán was not a convert, and among his offerings to the groom were many pagan gifts. These don Jorge refused to accept. Enraged, the Chief of Cobán and his warriors fell on the new village of Rabinal and destroyed it and its church. The Dominicans, discouraged, were forced to abandon for a time the founding of other villages.

At the end of five years, however, the invincible Rabinaleros and their allies were peaceful Spanish subjects, living in Christian villages. The King of Spain, to show his pleasure, changed the name from Tierra de Guerra to Verapaz, Land of the True Peace.

THE INDIAN TODAY

The powerful ruling clans and nobility, the warriors, priests, artists and astronomers of the post-Maya nations were almost wiped out by the Spanish conquerors. It was the plebeians, the common people, who survived the slaughter. And during the 400 years since, they and their descendants, to survive unrelenting oppression, have had to evolve a new way of life.

Hence the taciturn and secretive Indian of today, expert in concealing his thoughts and emotions, traditions and rituals. Out-

wardly all he asks is a bit of ground to grow his corn, a thatched
hut, a few chickens, a pig and a dog and the simple tools of his
crafts. Inwardly he lives a complicated existence among the spiritual teachings of Christian and pagan priests and the superstitions
derived from nature by every primitive people.

Serious, peaceful, orderly, with little humor, he is moral according to his code, loyal and honorable with his own people. Only
now emerging from the tidal wave of colonial civilization, he is
forced to face the onrushing crests of modern machine civilization.

Against this new conqueror, he has one powerful protector—his
costumbres. The word is variously translated as customs, conven-
tions, manners, habits, traditions, and it implies them all. The
nearest equivalent is the Englishman's phrase, "It isn't done." And
costumbre is the opposite of this: *it is done.* Few Indians any
longer know why it is done; it is sufficient for them that such is
the *costumbre.*

These *costumbres* are infinite, guiding every act of life from birth
to death. In general any *costumbre* is representative, but none is
typical, as each tribe has its own way of observing them, and within
each tribe, each clan or division, and within each division, each
family, depending on its mental, spiritual and financial capacity.
And now, the *costumbres* are being modified and changed almost
from day to day under the pressure of modern conditions.

Against this fortress of *costumbres,* modern civilization breaks
and breaks again, undermining a section here, sweeping away another there, falling back defeated elsewhere. Meanwhile the Indian
watches this new world. Some are destroyed by it, some fall willing captive. Others prefer to die rather than submit to it; still
others are determined to be its conquerors.

That the fortress must crumble eventually is inevitable. Whether,
when it falls, the Indian will emerge as Indian or *ladino,*[1] is a
question about which *ladino* Guatemala is thinking much, saying
little. If present-day signs are to be trusted, he will be *ladino,* and
the Indian of today like the Maya of yesterday will be lost to
Guatemala.

[1] Incorrect but popular term for all citizens of Guatemala not professedly Indian
(page 255).

III

HIS *COSTUMBRES*

RELIGION

RELIGION is the primary motivating force of the Indian's life, as much a part of him as his breathing and as continuous. This is as true today as it was before the arrival of the Spanish priests.

As one sees him in the churches, he is a devout Catholic. Elsewhere he is equally devout in his worship of the *Dios Mundo,* God of the World, or *Hurakán,* the Heart of Heaven. God is everywhere, he believes, in trees and mountains, river, air, sun, sky.

Hypersensitive to the fact that his life is in the hands of supernatural powers, the Indian takes no chances. He worships the litany of pagan gods left him by his forefathers. He pays homage to the all-powerful Christian God imposed on him by the friars of Spain. As a result, in the most sacred of pagan rituals or Christian services, he plays safe by including some devotions for the deity whose presence at that particular time is not admitted.

The "pure" Indian tribes that have not permitted either their blood or their *costumbres* to be contaminated, use the symbols of the Christian faith as a guise under which to worship their pagan gods. This is not difficult, as much of the symbolism of the Catholic Church is already familiar to them through their Maya heritage. The cross, for example, signified many things to the Maya —the four winds of heaven, the four directions, everlasting life. Elaborate ceremony, incense, prayers, music, images as symbols of deities were known to the Indians long before Christianity arrived on horseback.

The Spanish priests likewise adopted symbols of the Indians and gave them Christian meanings, took over old pagan rituals and developed Christian ceremonies as counter attractions to the pagan.

This practice was not and is not original with the Church in Guatemala. In Europe, centuries ago, the Church made many compromises with pagan faiths to gain influence over rites it could not stamp out.

In time pagan and Christian ideology blended until now neither priests nor Indians can define sharply where one religion ends and the other begins. Nor can one say of ceremonies and pilgrimages, "This is purely pagan, that truly Christian."

On the steps of the portico of a Catholic church, the Indian will kneel to pray to his pagan god, to burn candles and incense; then he will rise and enter the church to pray to the Christian God, burn candles and incense. And when the sacred figures of the Church must be arrayed in their best for the processions and ceremonies of saints' days and Holy Week, the Indians reverently dress them in Indian costumes.

If there is a distinction in their conception of the character of Christian and pagan gods, the belief of the Kekchi tribe in what happens after death may illustrate it. When a man dies, they say, his spirit is taken under the kindly wing of the pagan god, Tzultáca, who retraces with him all the roads the Indian traveled in life in order that he may see how he sinned on earth. The Indian's spirit then goes before the Christian God, "the God of the Cross," who judges him and imposes punishment. When he has expiated his sins, he is free to enter the heaven where Tzultáca presides.

Every day of the week and every moment of the day the Indian is in direct contact with both Christian and pagan deities. Shrines are everywhere, along the roads and on the summits of the highest mountains and elevations; hidden in the deepest forests are stone altars. About the cross, whether Christian or pagan, the Indian places flowers and sprigs of pine as he prays for a safe journey or gives thanks for one completed. Although he attends mass in the Catholic Church on Sunday, he can also be found there on any day at any hour, praying, burning candles, kissing the feet of the saints, and, if the matter is especially urgent, pouring a little *aguardiente* (popularly called White Eye) over them.

To the Indian the figures of Christ, the Virgin and the saints or the stone images of Tojil, Tzultáca, Jefe Dios are real and present. He speaks to them directly and in a loud voice, confiding his requests for favors, for dire punishments on his enemies, his thanks for prayers granted. And if they have not been granted, he is just as frank in voicing his displeasure.

Recently an Indian was overheard declaiming angrily to a saint who had let him down: "Last week I burned a candle to you, a large candle, to ask for only a simple thing. You took the candle but you did not grant my prayer. Very well. That is the last candle I will ever burn to you." On the altars in their homes stand small stone images or photographs of gods or saints. To them the Indian also confides his needs, especially for rain for his corn. And it is not unusual, if his request brings too heavy downpours, for him to beat the figure or place it out in the rain.

Each village has its own church—and great village cross—under the authority of a ladino priest. If the community is large enough, the priest resides there; if not he makes periodic visits to preach, marry, baptise. Indian attendants or *chajales* are appointed each year by the elders of the village to serve him.

The church itself, however, is in complete charge of the Indians. And in connection with the church is a system of *cofradias* (organizations or brotherhoods) made up of both men and women; each *cofradia* serves a single saint and takes its name from that saint. Members of the *cofradias* carry out every duty and responsibility for keeping the church in order and staging the ceremonies and processions of the church calendar. In the *cofradias* the religious, social and political life of the community are linked, for it is the elders of the village who elect from the families of the upper classes the heads of the different brotherhoods to serve, usually for one year.

Homes of these leading families consist of several houses, arranged in a quadrangle about an ample patio. One house is set aside for the use of the *cofradia*. There the figure of the saint the brotherhood serves is kept, and ceremonies in its honor are held throughout the year, and on the saint's own day a fiesta.

In this *costumbre*, too, pagan and Christian paths cross. Before the Conquest, the images of Indian gods were hidden during the greater part of the year in hills and caves and forests where prayers and sacrifices were offered them in secret. Even now, figures of the Christian saints only return to the church on important holy days to take part in the services and to be carried in procession.

The occasion when the newly elected *cofrades* enter office is an important ceremony in itself. Among the Mames, for example, the retiring *cofrades* enter the *cofradia* first and seat themselves on a bench, their faces to the wall. One at a time the new *cofrades* enter, dancing; in some villages each wears a wreath of flowers to denote the office he is to fill. The corresponding, outgoing *cofrade* rises and dances with him until the new official has danced to the bench and seated himself, face to the room, and the retiring officer has danced himself out the door.

To be elected an officer of a *cofradia* is a very real honor. Only the most venerable and wise men and women are so chosen, for their responsibilities, religious, social and political, are heavy.

It is also the head *cofrade's* duty to pray daily in the church for his people. This too involves ceremony. Each morning, the head of each *cofradia,* accompanied by a servant, enters the church vestry. In the corner rest a number of long staffs, and in the antique colonial treasure chest are silver ikons, symbolic of the various saints of the brotherhoods. The servant fixes the ikon of his master's *cofradia* to a staff and with a solemn bow presents it. The *cofrade* accepts it as solemnly. When all are ready, *cofrades,* the priest if he is in the village, and the servants march in procession to the altar.

SUPERSTITION

Occasionally when a highway passes a hillside cave or giant ceiba tree, visitors to Guatemala will see before it a row of three or more wooden crosses. They are a sign that there a witch doctor plies his trade and conducts his various rites.

These witch doctors—variously called *brujo, shaman, zahori*— have various functions. They are medicine men when they heal by medicinal plants [1] and incantations. They are magicians when

---

[1] Note 10B.

they cause sickness or curses to fall on man or beast. They are fortunetellers and soothsayers when they reveal the future. And they are a form of priest when they advise or direct purely Indian ceremonies or act as intermediary between god and man, praying on behalf of the man, allowing the words of the god to pass through their lips to the suppliant. And it is to their interest, whatever their capacity, to see that the web of superstition which binds the Indian at every turn is kept in good repair.

Some of them serve in only one capacity; others practise in all fields. A few of these witch doctors are men to whom by word of mouth the secrets of the race have been confided—the rituals and significances of symbols and ceremonies. Frequently they are self-appointed; sometimes the office passes from father to son. The majority are men, though occasionally a woman practises. Usually they have some pronounced physical defect, crossed eyes, a caul, lameness, or they may be very ugly. Esteemed, and needless to say feared, they also are distinguished by special costumes and a small bag in which they carry red beans, bits of looking-glass, broken pottery, and other properties of their trade.

Their counsel is sought on every occasion for community and individual problems. When a man has an enemy on whom he desires vengeance, he turns to a witch doctor as a matter of course. For the *brujo* can achieve that most loathsome revenge—insert a toad into the enemy's stomach. In the highlands when preparing such a curse, the witch doctor makes an image in wax or mud of the man to be afflicted and places it upside down beside a candle also upside down and burning. The man so cursed can seek a remedy, of course, by employing the services of another witch doctor. But if the *brujo* placing the curse upon him has gone to such lengths as to sprinkle image and candle with salt, the victim has no chance whatever to escape his fate.

In Jacaltenango a very special type of witch doctor thrives. Known as *ilum k'inal* or "time watchers," they are believed to possess some potent power in their eyes by which they can protect a man or object simply by looking at it. They are employed to protect communities and individuals from every kind of disaster. To their skill is attributed the fact that during the construction of the

Quezaltenango railway fewer Indians from Jacaltenango were killed than from any other village.

One curious and deep-seated superstition stems from antiquity: the *nagual*. According to this belief, each Indian's spirit has a counterpart in some animal; his life is irrevocably identified with that of his animal guardian. The *nagual* of Tecúm-Umám, who led the Quiché armies against the Spanish, was the quetzal, the beautiful bird now used as Guatemala's symbol of liberty. And the legend is often encountered that when Indian chief and Alvarado met in hand-to-hand conflict, Alvarado really killed the quetzal which appeared at that moment above the Indian's head.

As the Indians of Alta Verapaz travel the trails, they are careful when approaching a hot spring to gather faggots to place beside it for the god who boils the water. In return for this courtesy, it is hoped, the god will refrain from heating the Indian's blood and so causing fever. Indians tiring anywhere on the trail will cut a branch from a tree and switch their legs with it to acquire sufficient strength from the deity in the tree to continue. Or, in the highlands, they will remove the sandal from the right foot and so leave weariness behind. If certain snakes are encountered or if a star bursts over a man's house, some member of his family will die. The eclipse of sun or moon is a major calamity from which anything up to the end of the world may result; therefore, to aid the heavenly body to escape its doom, whole villages turn out with drums and pans, rockets, shouts and other noisemaking devices to drive the enveloping shadow away. There is no end to the superstitions, as will be seen in the following pages.

BIRTH

Like all people conscious that their roots are buried in antiquity, the Indians have a strong sense and need for maintaining the continuity of the family. Children, whether boys or girls, are welcomed, and their birth is attended with much ceremony.

For this event the witch doctor is as important a factor as the village midwife. Both are called when the child is about to be born. In some villages, the midwife bathes the mother in the *temaxcal,* or vapor bathhouse (page 58). The witch doctor prays steadily, calling on the gods to protect the child, to give it long life and good fortune. Among the Quiché, the witch doctor, if the mother is very ill, will split open a black chicken and allow the warm blood to flow over her head and breast. The moment the child draws its first breath, the witch doctor takes it under his protection.

In Todos Santos in the highlands, the midwife hangs the umbilical cord of the child on the outside of the house to remain for twenty days, on each of which mother and child are bathed in the *temaxcal*. Also on each day the witch doctor prays for long life, good health and particularly for protection from the Evil Eye. While doing this he passes burning candles over the baby's head in the sign of the pagan cross.

At the end of twenty days, the umbilical cord, hairs from the child's head and geranium flowers are carried in procession to some pre-Columbian ruins near the village which the witch doctor has hallowed for his own rites. There these relics are buried while the witch doctor pronounces solemn words over them and covers them with a large stone. Should anyone deliberately touch that stone thereafter, bad luck will fall on the child.

As soon as possible after birth, the child must be christened. From both the teachings of the Catholic Church and the precepts of his ancestors, the Indian believes that if a child dies without a name, its soul will never join the forefathers.

Names are chosen in various ways. In many villages, one name is taken from the particular date of the Tzolkin Calendar on which the child is born. His other names may be chosen from those of his ancestors or from the patron saint of the community. In several villages children born during the year to members of the tribe living at a distance are brought back to the home church on its saint's day and all christened at once with the saint's name. When in doubt, however, one is safe to address an Indian man as José and an Indian woman as Maria.

Godmothers and fathers are as essential as they are esteemed. A well-brought-up child will fall on his knees to kiss the hand of a godparent and remain there until given permission to rise. And never will a godchild be so thoughtless as to step on the shadow of a godparent. In return, the godparents assume many duties. In one village they masticate the first solid food the child eats to signify that they not only wish him well but that they will help him over the hard spots of life.

In Alta Verapaz, the *cacique* or head man of each village is asked to stand as godfather to a boy born to a member of the lower classes. This he is glad to do, for tribal law requires that the boy, when he reaches working age, must work for his godfather, even pay off his debts if necessary.

To cement this bargain, the godfather gives the baby, for his christening, a cap, handkerchief and shirt, all embroidered with tribal designs. And the wife of the *cacique* takes the child to church for the christening (one of the few times in his life he will enter a church for a real Catholic ceremony). Girls are christened with very little ado.

As soon as the boy is of age to work, the godfather announces that it is now time for him to prove his duty and devotion. Should the boy refuse or his father object, the full force of tribal law may descend upon the family. The christening gifts, grown, too, with the years, must be returned in the shape of a cow, a piece of land or an entire crop of corn. If the godfather still remains unappeased, the boy's father may have to surrender his hut and land and move elsewhere to start life again.

MARRIAGE

In spite of the fact that marriage is not included in the three great functions of Indian life—birth, work, death—the *costumbres* are varied, colorful and prolonged. Anywhere from one to eight years may be necessary to complete negotiations for the betrothal and for the wedding festivities to reach an end.

When the son of a family in Quezaltenango reaches marriageable age—fourteen to eighteen years—his father seeks out a *tertulero* or go-between to find him a suitable wife. This is a comparatively recent custom; long ago fathers betrothed their children in infancy or shortly afterwards as did the Maya.

This *tertulero* must be a resourceful fellow. To prove it he is sometimes required to jump over a high wall as a sign that he will so leap over any obstacle to accomplish his mission. When he has found a suitable bride—a girl under sixteen years of age—he and the young woman's father begin the interviews concerning the price to be paid for her.

These arranged satisfactorily, the young man calls at the girl's home, accompanied by quantities of *repuesto,* loaves of bread, chocolate and *aguardiente.* Everything must be carefully counted and weighed so that if the marriage falls through the bride's father can return the exact equivalent to the groom. If the groom is too poor to pay the entire dowry before marriage, he must arrange to pay it on the installment plan. Such payments may continue for years; sometimes for life.

Betrothal festivities continue for an entire week. An ox is killed, and all the poor of the village are invited to the feast. Here the sponsors or witnesses of the bridal pair are named. At the conclusion of the feast, the woman sponsor takes the bride home to make sure that she knows how to cook, sew, weave and manage a house. The prospective groom must prove to his father-in-law that he can till the soil, provide wood, water and other necessities for his bride. If either fails to satisfy the judges, the marriage is called off.

After a marriage ceremony, performed by a village priest if one is at hand, a feast follows. So much food and drink is served to the accompaniment of loud and continuous music that the guests fall asleep. Now the bride must brew strong coffee and prove her worth by preparing tortillas from the hardest corn that can be found. If the guests do not find these to their taste, they are privileged to beat the bride before they go home.

During the feast, the groom cuts food into bits and feeds them to his bride. These she must accept to signify her willingness to accept whatever he gives her later, no matter how little it may be. The young couple are also not only required to eat as much as possible of the feast but to take home in a large clay jar whatever is left over. This they must eat before it spoils; if not, their marriage will not last long.

One of the bride's chief items is the wedding sheet—*siquicul*—which she has woven herself. When the feast is over, the god-mother places this on the bridal bed; then she and the elder women of the village stand watch while the newlyweds retire. The god-mother's last duty is to pour a potion for the bride from a special, long-necked clay jar. This potion is called *adormeciendo la novia* —"putting the bride to sleep." Peace thus assured, the women leave, locking the door on the outside.

Early the next morning the mother of the groom unlocks the door and the wedding sheet is passed out to her. If this proves the chastity of the bride, all is well. Rockets are fired and mother and sisters of the groom assist her to prepare breakfast.

In villages in the Cuchumatanes Mountains another system pre-vails. The father of the young man who is reaching marriageable age selects three potential brides whose names he places before the village witch doctor. This sage makes involved calculations and arrives at a choice. That decided, witch doctor, father and a com-mittee of village elders call on the father of the young woman.

Carrying a clay dish in which copal is burning, the witch doctor enters the house first and solemnly breaks an egg over the burning incense. The delegation, kneeling, raise their voices in prayer and announce the purpose of their call. The father of the young man then offers the father of the girl a brimming cup of *aguardiente*. If the girl's father accepts it and drinks it in one draft, he gives his consent to the marriage.

Weeks and months of negotiations follow until the nature and extent of the price to be paid for the bride are agreed on. The price is determined by the quality of the young woman, and, as usual, much stress is laid upon her chastity. For a really good bride, $25.00, plus five sheep, 500 pounds of corn, turkeys, possibly a pig and other food, is reasonable. Meanwhile the prospective bride, lest she run away, is never allowed to take her water jar to the village well alone.

When the price is settled, the village elders sacrifice a rooster in gratitude to the gods, and the two fathers exchange phrases to the effect that they are now *compadres*. The son without further cere-mony takes the bride home and married life begins. If for any reason the bride does not like her new home, she can return to her father, but in that event he must return the exact price paid for her.

In Santiago Atitlán, young people are allowed a little more voice in the matter. Through an elder of the village, the young man asks the father of the girl for her. If he consents, the young man waits on the shore of the lake in the early morning for the young woman, jar on head, to trip down for water. When he sees her coming, he covers his face, and jumping up, seizes her arm while he declares his intentions. To learn her answer he must try to break her water jar. If she makes little effort to protect it, or better still, succeeds in breaking it on his head, she accepts him. Whereupon he uncovers his face so that she may know her future husband, they return to the village, and the festivities begin.

Because of the high cost of weddings—and occasionally because of the scarcity of priests in remote villages and fincas—marriage ceremonies are going the way of many other Indian customs. Most Indian couples today either marry without benefit of clergy or through a ceremony presided over by a village elder or witch doctor. Couples appear on specified days, in groups of from five to twenty couples, before the Intendente (Mayor) of their respective villages or towns, and he performs the civil ceremony without charge. It is significant that couples insisting on the ceremony are always members of pure-blood tribes.

Rings or other tokens are seldom exchanged or used. In San Martín Sacatepéquez, the happy couple scratch each other's faces until they are a mass of welts. And in certain other villages the groom immediately beats the bride to show her that he is to be master of the house.

Young men, as a rule, will not marry outside their own tribe or social class in their tribe. And the custom of the groom taking his bride to live in his own home is still generally followed. For this reason daughters cannot inherit property. Occasionally a rich family with a marriageable daughter will offer a price for the son of a poor family as her husband. As this means that the young man must live with the girl's people, such offers are seldom accepted.

If the wife proves unable to bear children, the husband may either return her to her home (in which case her father must return the price paid for her) or he may take a second wife. This sometimes works out most happily, the two wives caring for the house and children.

In recent years legal divorce has offered a solution to Indians who can afford it. The husband usually remarries and the children of his first wife are placed in charge of grandparents or godparents.

DEATH

The last event of an Indian's life is not a sorrowful one to him and his. Frequently one sees members of a family nodding and smiling as they walk behind the small casket of a child to the cemetery. The child, they say, will now not only escape the tribulations of this life but join the forefathers in another world much happier than this.

Adult Indians are fatalistic on the subject. Death is a journey like any other occasion that takes a man from home; the only difference is that from this one he does not return. A family will grieve that father or grown son has reached the time of departure, but accept it realistically and go on with their lives as before. Although great respect is paid to age and the wisdom age represents, sometimes when an old man becomes ill and no remedies have power to aid him, he will be assisted toward death for his own sake. There is no period of mourning and no mourning costume.

In fact, death and the funeral provide one more opportunity for ceremony and fiesta. The more esteemed the man in life, the more food and drink and rockets will speed him on his way. For the head of a village, the ceremonies may continue from twenty-four to forty-eight hours after his funeral. When the funeral is over, the departed will scarcely be thought of again until All Saints' Day.

Long ago an Indian was well equipped for his journey to the next world. Into his tomb went ample treasure, food, clothing, official regalia and the implements of his craft. Treasure is no longer buried, only regalia, tools, and such necessities. In Quezaltenango a *jicara* (gourd) of milk is buried with a baby to nourish it en route, and a little broom is placed beside a small girl so that she may grow up to be a good housekeeper.

The Kekchi people bury a complete outfit of clothing with a man as well as his cane or staff of office, umbrella, bag, cigars and matches, a candle to light his road and a rosary to prove to the "God of the Whites" that he is a good Christian. His woolen poncho or blanket is omitted (or any object made of an animal product) as this might acquire teeth in the other world and bite the spirit. Great care is taken to see that nothing is forgotten, as the spirit might return in anger and haunt the family in its sleep. Should something be overlooked, it is enclosed in the coffin of the next person buried in that community with a request to his spirit to deliver it to its owner in the other world.

Both of necessity (outside the cities) and as a sign of respect, the coffin is carried on the shoulders of men of the family or village elders to the cemetery. In Almolonga it still is the custom occasionally for professional women mourners to follow the coffin, tearing their blouses to shreds, pulling their hair down about their faces as they scream and cry. And when every so often the bearers place the coffin on the ground, they jump back and forth across it, shrieking.

The witch doctor, of course, has a role in the ceremony. It is his privilege to turn the coffin round and round at the grave to fool the devil and give the spirit the right direction toward heaven. When family and friends leave the grave, he remains to pray. For these services he must be paid ten cents, a bottle of *aguardiente,* a string of beads, and a fat hen.

November is the month of the dead, and on All Saints' Day ceremonies reminiscent of Decoration Day in the United States years ago take place. Among the ancient tribes of Guatemala, yellow was the color signifying death, so now *flores de muerto*— flowers of the dead—are hung in doorways and their yellow blossoms arranged in the form of a cross on the graves with candles burning among them.

Throughout the day, and all night in many villages, the church bells toll incessantly. Indians will stand in line for hours to get a turn at tolling for the dead of their families. In this way they acquire merit with the gods. Afterwards they light a candle for each of their dead in the church and at the graves.

At this time, too, food is placed at the head of each grave for the spirit of the departed. Later, children slip in and steal it, a custom highly pleasing to the bereft families, for if the food did not disappear, it would be a sign that the spirit did not like it.

The officers of the *cofradias* are in charge of the preparation of this food for the dead, which is called *cabecera*. One dish, something like a conserve, is made of pumpkin and black sugar. Another, *fiambre,* consists of all sorts of vegetables, meat, fish and fowl. In the *cofradias* is a dark room from which, while the Indian is buying his *cabecera,* the voice of his dead may be heard talking with a friend. What he has suffered since last All Saints' Day, wails the spirit, because of the poor *cabecera* he received! How can a relative who does not provide him with good and plentiful food expect to harvest a good and plentiful crop of corn?

IV

HIS CEREMONIES, FESTIVALS, PILGRIMAGES, FAIRS, MARKETS

The Year Bearer

PERHAPS the oldest of the many Indian ceremonial rites observed today is that of the Year Bearer (*Cargador del Año*) [1] held in Jacaltenango and other villages in the Department of Huehuetenango.

A day is something more than a period of time between sunset and sunset, according to precepts passed down from the ancient tribes. It is the personification of a deity; the name it bears is the name of the god it represents. And the deity of each day has, of course, his own power to dispense good or evil. Four of the days of the old Maya calendar of 18 months of 20 days each were considered so good that they were honored with the role of Year Bearers and are called *ik-um habil*—"Lords of the Year." For centuries one of them has been chosen annually to rule the coming year, and that deity's particular day opens the year.

In preparation for this event, the official Prayer Makers of Jacaltenango (where the ritual is best preserved) begin 20 days in advance to pray before the Christian cross of the village and the door of the church. Over little fires of *ocote* they burn incense and offerings of red flowers and evergreen tips; occasionally they burn black candles. These prayers increase in number, duration and potency as the day of the Year Bearer approaches.

First, however, the souls of small children must leave their bodies and go out into space to visit the Year Bearer. They return on the eve of the five extra days, known as the "five women," which fall between the end of the 360 days of one year and the

---

[1] *The Year Bearer's People*, a study by Oliver La Farge II and Douglas Byers; published, 1931, by Middle American Research Institute of Tulane University.

33

beginning of the next. To welcome them back, the Indians, particularly the parents of small children, pray before the village cross
and church with burning candles and incense. At this time, too,
home altars are decorated and lighted with candles, and where
there are children celebrations are held, and gifts, or at least some
special food, prepared for them.

Now the souls of the older people must go out to visit the Year
Bearer. As they are larger, they need all the "five women" days to
make the trip and return on the eve of the day before the Year
Bearer arrives. On this day, as soon as it is light, the Prayer
Makers and most devout villagers begin to pray in or around the
church. By evening the entire village is there, praying, burning
incense and candles.

The prayers finished by ten o'clock, they leave to burn candles
in their fruit trees and fields, homes and dooryards. Then they
can sleep, though many rise during the night to pray, and in some
homes one member of the family watches until dawn, burning
white candles.

Between two and three in the morning the Prayer Makers hold
the *cahampal* for the village, and many families hold private ones
in their homes. *Cahampal* is the name given to the most important rite of all the non-Christian ceremonies. Originally the word
is believed to have been derived from *cahan,* meaning sin, and the
rite, therefore, was one of atonement. Today that idea is lost and
the *cahampal* is made as a thank offering.

Private families who perform this rite are those who have—or
whose forbears have—initiated the custom in gratitude for recovery
from some disease or disaster. The obligation to carry it on descends from oldest son to oldest son. To fail to do so might result
in death or very serious illness.

Three days before making the *cahampal,* a family will "announce the candle," that is, declare they are going to make the
offering. Then every member of the family, even first cousins, and
the witch doctor who is to officiate, purify themselves by refraining
from sexual intercourse, quarrels, anger and drunkenness. And
the turkey or chicken to be sacrificed is solemnly tied to the leg of
the altar table.

On the night of the sacrifice the bird is hung upside down and spread-eagled. The shaman or witch doctor cuts off the head and catches the blood in a bowl. All pray to the body; then it is boiled with *pinol* (corn). The blood is burned on the altar and the bird eaten by the family and a few friends.

The *cahampal* performed by the Prayer Makers for the village is very similar. On very serious occasions all the shamans attend also. In these ceremonies the blood is caught in pieces of the inner husk of carefully selected corn and burned before the village cross and the small crosses that mark the boundaries of the village. Since the ceremony must be completed before dawn and the boundaries may be wide, marked with many crosses, the official charged with the delivery of the blood may entrust the shares for distant crosses to a wayside cross which will forward them in time.

During the Day of the Year Bearer, prayers continue in and around the church and village cross and in the evening all the Indians of the village and surrounding settlements gather there to pray. In the meantime the Prayer Makers of the village of Santa Eulalia enter a cave where they look into a pool of blood—probably the deep red droppings of bats—and make the prophecy for the new year for all the villages of the region.

Three days after the *cahampal,* during which the same continence and care must be observed, those who have carried out the sacrificial ceremony announce "the taking up of the three days"— that they have fulfilled their pledge. Then they call on the shaman to learn whether or not the rite has been successfully performed.

CEREMONY OF THE EIGHT MONKEY

The first day of the Tzolkin Calendar is an occasion of enormous significance to the Indians of Momostenango. This calendar has 260 days divided into thirteen months of 20 days each. Like the 360-day calendar, each day not only has its own power for good or evil and its own name, but each has in addition a number from one to thirteen. In the course of the Tzolkin year, each name day will come round thirteen times, each time taking a different number. When the entire cycle of 13 times 20 has been completed, the 260 days have passed and the 261st is the day of the New Year.

This ceremony has continued for centuries, the appointed day determined by calculations of Indian astronomers and seers, sometimes for long periods, as after the Conquest, without records to guide them. Yet through their remarkable understanding of astronomy, their calculations have been so exact that no mistake in naming the correct day has ever been made.

In Quiché idiom, the day of the new ritual year is known as *Guajxaquip Bats* [1]—the Ceremony of the Eight Monkey. Monkey is the name of the day; eight is its number. Some authorities call the day Eight Thread.

Between fifteen and twenty thousand Indians take part in this ritual, both those who live permanently in Momostenango and those who, born in the village, now live elsewhere. Not to be present, it is believed, may result in death or illness. Besides, prayers offered on this first day of the year are thought to be especially potent and to stand a better chance of being granted.

Originally, the purely pagan ceremony began at dawn of the New Year itself, but since the entrance of Christianity, a prelude in the form of a New Year's Eve service in the Catholic Church has been added. From late afternoon until nine at night, Indians kneel in the church in long parallel rows, facing each other. They burn candles and incense as they pray aloud in utter simplicity and sincerity.

At daybreak of Eight Monkey, they are on their way to Chuitmesabal (Little Broom), about half a mile west of the city where their altars are located. These are called *porobal* (the place where incense is burned).

Momostenango takes its name from these altars which are really mounds from three to ten feet high covered with broken pottery. The name means "place of the oratories." And since the town was so named long before the Conquest, it offers further proof of the antiquity of these rites. So does the fact that similar mounds are found in various parts of Guatemala indicate that their observance was general.

By nine o'clock, thousands of Indians are gathered about the

[1] *Guajxaquip Bats,* by Antonio Goubaud Carrera; Anales of the Sociedad de Geografía é Historia de Guatemala, 1935.

altars. Before each stands a priest or witch doctor (more than 200 in all, about one third of them women). Beside the altar of each one is a small bag, symbol that he or she is an authorized intermediary between man and the Dios Mundo.

Singly or by families, the Indians approach the altar and place beside it their offerings of broken pottery. The theory is that when a dish breaks, the god wills it, so they are returning to him the fragments. But it seems more logical, considering their use of symbolism and the fact that most of them are there to confess to sins, that the broken shards represent themselves as far from perfect human beings.

One or two at a time, never more, they turn to the witch doctor who is to intercede for them with the god. They tell him their names and the purpose of the prayer—to ask forgiveness for some sin, to give thanks for some request granted, to petition for some physical, spiritual or material benefit. In payment they give him a small coin, usually a penny.

The witch doctor takes a cornhusk packet containing twelve wafers of sacred incense—*kabawil*—and burns it on his altar in a pit made of potsherds and decorated with pine boughs. This offering, called *sipaj,* is expected to secure divine and favorable attention for the petitioner. Then the priest prays loud and long, including any details of the Indian's life, however intimate, that occur to him.

Sometimes the shaman offers the god a little *aguardiente,* not as a profane act but as a religious one, then drinks it himself. By certain signs, more clear to him when he is a little drunk, he can tell whether or not the god has accepted the drink. When an Indian accepts a glass of liquor offered by another, he indicates that they are men of one mind, spiritual comrades, and each drinks to the other. The priest, therefore, when he drinks the *aguardiente,* is paying the World God the courtesy due an equal.

Near these large altars are smaller, less popular ones, where recently initiated shamans officiate. And on the bank of a little stream are the altars for the exclusive use of the families of these pagan priests.

Rites continue until dusk, when everyone proceeds to the crest of the hill, Nim Mesabal (Big Broom), still further west. There during the entire night the shamans pray and burn incense before more altars. And for two days after Eight Monkey, they continue to pray to Dios Mundo and most Indians remain to pray with them. So great is the multitude that booths filled with food, candles, incense and beverages are set up there to serve them.

Fiesta de Santo Tomás

St. Thomas' own day on December 21 is the climax of a three- or four-day festival that attracts from five to ten thousand Indians annually to Chichicastenango. The majority, of course, are Quiché, descendants of the founders of the original village of Ziguan Tinamit, who live in the surrounding hills or valleys or return from all parts of the country to renew contact with their ancestors and their patron saint. But many come from villages of other highland tribes and some from other parts of Central America and Mexico.

The ceremonial costumes of the Indians of Chichicastenango are woven of pure black wool and elaborately and strikingly embroidered with the symbols of the Quiché. Scarlet sashes and headdresses of scarlet or white complement them. Dressed thus, the Indians move slowly and with great dignity in the innumerable processions, as they burn *pom,* the sacred incense, to their pagan gods on the altar built in the tiered steps of the Catholic Church, or as they kneel in the church beside rows of flickering candles embedded in pine needles and flower petals.

For three days the crowded streets about the plaza are a succession of parades as the saints of the surrounding settlements and from the fourteen *cofradias* of the village are carried by their devotees behind a corps of dancers to the church or to visit the headquarters of Indian officials and the other brotherhoods. For the final procession, St. Thomas, accompanied by St. Sebastian and St. Joseph, on red-canopied daises, leave the church and join the visiting saints in a tour of the village.

One of the most colorful groups represented in these festivities is that of the fireworkers, the manufacturers of the rockets used on countless ceremonial occasions throughout the country. Each fireworker carries a thick sheaf of rockets, their bombs wrapped in a ritual *tzut* or scarf embroidered with tribal symbols. Their sacred figure is a small horse and rider called *Tzijolach,* lavishly adorned with strings of coins that jingle incessantly.

The horse, of course, was adopted after the Conquest: the Indians who first saw the horse being certain—from its speed and the fire and roar from the conquerors' guns which they attributed to the animal—that it was a supernatural creation. Frequently it is said that horse and rider are the symbol of Santiago, the St. James of the Spaniards, but in reality Tzijolach represents the messenger who communicates between god and man. A rope is strung to the peak of the church and Tzijolach is raised and lowered on it during the fiesta to signify his purpose. During the processions a fireworker dances continuously with the horse on his shoulders and, between processions, on the steps of the church. Tzijolach, however, never enters the doors.

El Son, the secular dance of the Indians, is a prominent feature of the fiesta, numerous *cantinas* providing space and a *marimba* where Indians dance solemnly and alone for hours on end. In the street between church and chapel, the pole of the *palo volador* (dances, page 108) is erected, and about it one or more ritual dances are performed from morning until dark.

On the morning of St. Thomas' Day, all the babies born to Maxenos—Indians of Chichicastenango—living outside the community are taken to the church to be christened at the same time. Each receives Tomás as one of its names.

Because Chichicastenango is situated on a main traveled route, modern civilization is taking it over rapidly, and the Fair, once a supplement of the fiesta, is developing into the main feature. In the same way, modern dress is replacing the costume of the Indians. As they forsake the costume of the Quiché, they turn also from the *costumbres.* The Fiesta de Santo Tomás is another signpost, therefore, for those who are seeking to discover what road the Indian is following.

FIESTA DE LA CRUZ

Anciently during the summer solstice, when Indians everywhere were praying to the gods for rains and good crops, thousands visited the shores of Lake Amatitlán. There they bathed in the waters of the lake, said because of their volcanic origin and sulfurous content to have medicinal qualities, and exchanged products at a great fair.

Most important of all, they gathered at the famous Indian oratory hidden in the forests about the lake to pray to the Jefe Dios (Chief God) and carry out more or less elaborate fertility rites. During these rites children were thrown into the lake as sacrifices and the stone figures of lesser gods were brought from distant villages to do homage to the Jefe Dios and receive his blessing and counsel.

The Spanish priests were not slow to set up a strong counterattraction to these pagan ceremonies in the village of Amatitlán which they established across the lake. In the church they placed the figure of the Niño de Atocha, which soon won a reputation for its healing powers. In the years since then, thousands of pilgrims have crowded the church with petitions or to give thanks for prayers granted.

Because the cross was alike a symbol of Christianity and the Indian symbol for the four winds and the four directions, the priests adopted the old Christian ceremony of the Festival of the Cross held on May 3, a time when the Indians from near and far were arriving at the lake for their pagan rites.

Today the Fiesta—held on May 2 and 3—is a combination of pilgrimage, dances, music, water sports and fair, to which Indians and ladinos alike flock to pray and play and buy the gaily decorated boxes, *cajetas de Amatitlán,* filled with sweets of the season.

HOLY WEEK

Cathedral and churches in cities and towns celebrate Holy Week with all the pomp and pageantry of colonial days when the Church was the social and cultural as well as religious focus of life. In villages, in remote settlements, and on the fincas, however, the festival is a composite of Christian and pagan ceremonies and celebrations, all based on the same general idea but no two alike.

Coming as it does in March or April, Holy Week coincides in time with the fertility rites held anciently before the gods to win good crops and good rains. Because a period of abstinence from women, meat, anger and intemperance was required then, too, Lent is taken with doubled seriousness.

Anciently, too, some tribes observed the extra five-day period that terminates the calendar of 360 days as a ritual period and survivals of those elaborate rites have become identified with Holy Week. At that time the Dios Mam or Old God was believed to emerge from his subterranean cave and walk on earth. For the first day or two he was very strong and wrought great havoc, but rapidly he weakened until at the end of the fifth day he crawled back into his cave to store up strength for another year. To appease and divert him, all sorts of offerings and ceremonies were made for him.

In villages where the rites of Holy Week and pagan ceremonies are observed, shamans or witch doctors preside over all festivities. And in villages and on fincas where no Christian priest resides permanently, the festivities are in charge of chosen men who either through design or ignorance incorporate into the program of processions and services features that have no origin in Christianity.

The long period of preparation comes to a head in the Semana de Dolores (Week of Repentance), the week preceding Holy Week. Churches are cleaned and decorated with pine needles, flowers and streamers of silk or colored paper. New costumes are made for the images that in many cases symbolize both a Christian saint and some manifestation of a pagan god. Many of the saints are dressed in deep mourning, others in Indian costume. Final rehearsals are held for the dances and for the processions.

Some villages, after the manner of the Passion Play of Oberammergau, appoint different members to represent Christ, the Apostles, the Virgin, Mary Magdalene and one called Centurion. As a friend of Christ, Centurion dances before him continuously on Good Friday, making the sign of the cross with his sword. Until recent times, he also alternately sowed and gathered corn in Christ's path.

During this week of repentance, too, many villages erect arches of flowers, fruit and vegetables. Stuffed bodies of squirrels, raccoons, rabbits and other small animals of tribal significance are featured on them and often a live animal is used.

In Sololá, the flower known as Pie de Gallo (Cock's Foot) decorates the bower in which the Virgen de Dolores is carried in procession on Good Friday. This is the flower used traditionally on the bower of the pagan gods before whom the fertility rites were performed. Because of its crab-like shape, the flower symbolizes the Great Crab with glowing eyes of *eke* (a parasite of the forests) that once lured the gods of the Quiché through a saga of adventures before it was overcome and thrown into the waters of Lake Atitlán.

Considering the poverty and lack of resources of the majority of the villages, the completeness and variety of their Holy Week program are remarkable. Wednesday is the day of the Easter Market when not only supplies of food and flowers for the week must be purchased but also bread which is eaten by the Indians at no other time. Thursday and Friday are the important ceremonial days; Saturday is a time of buffoonery and horseplay. By Easter Sunday, when the Christian world is churchward bound, most of the Indians are in their *milpas* planting corn.

Ceremonial burlesque goes hand in hand with the most solemn dignity. In Chiantla, where all the roles of the Christian pageant except those of Mary, Mary Magdalene and St. John are taken by men, the apostles escape from the Good Friday procession to the Crucifixion and hide in the ravines. This affords the men and boys, dressed in purple robes and peaked headdresses, opportunity for a hunt; after strenuous hours all the apostles are dragged back to the procession. Meantime Christ is tied to a post in front of the church and the figure of St. John is rushed to tell Mary what has happened.

In villages like Santiago Atitlán, it is believed that Mary and John enjoyed a passionate interlude on the night before the Crucifixion. Therefore they are locked in separate cells in the village jail during Thursday night and released in the morning when some official or *cofradia* pays their fine.

The Quiché, Cakchiqueles and Tzutuhiles add another strange character to the cast of Holy Week. This is a scarecrow called

Maximón (The Great Lord Who Is Bound). He is variously identified as Judas, Alvarado, sometimes as the owner of the finca; in most villages he is an object of ridicule. In Atitlán he is worshiped seriously, and prayers, food, candles and incense are offered him. In certain villages the Maximón effigy is set up in a *cofradia* throughout Lent. Once he was observed sitting—cigar in mouth— behind a table on which were spread a deck of cards, a bottle and glass.

Most villages pretend at least that the scarecrow dressed in village cast-off clothing (or European dress if at all possible) is Judas. Throughout Holy Week he is mocked and jeered, and on Saturday his trial and death offer outlet in comic relief to the solemn and sorrowful services of Thursday and Friday. Haled before the mob, Judas is accused and condemned, and his last will, a collection of crude satires and lewd jokes, is read aloud to raucous applause. Then, at the heels of a mule, he is dragged about the streets, stoned, beaten, cursed and finally burned.

In contrast the simplicity and reality of the processions are startling. On Thursday evening, with muted drum, lighted candles and chanted prayers, the village escorts Christ to a nearby hill or cemetery to watch and pray during the night, and many remain to watch and pray with Him. Friday morning in solemn procession He is escorted to the Crucifixion, and Friday evening, heads covered and shoulders bowed in sorrow, the villagers bring a bleeding Christ back to the church, stopping before certain houses or the home of the master of the finca for showers of flower petals to be scattered over the body. Saturday morning the women carry Mary, dressed in deep mourning, and all the saints on a symbolic visit to the tomb.

Ceremonies of the Corn

The first four men created, according to the legend of the origin of the Quiché nation, were made of cornpaste into which the Heart of Heaven breathed life. Whether or not their ancestors were made of corn, it is certain that the Indians of today live by it. It is eaten at every meal in a score of different dishes; it is the

feature of every feast; it feeds their animals and chickens, thatches
their huts, is an important source of revenue.

Nothing is more important, therefore, than to insure by every
possible means that the harvest will be bountiful, for is it not reasonable to suppose that if man does everything in his power to
please the gods, the gods will respond with the proper proportions
of sun and rain and good growing weather?

Although some fields bear two or more crops a year, the main
corn-planting season extends from March into May. During these
months in some part of Guatemala Indians are not only burning
over and preparing fields for the sowing, but purifying themselves
for the event. Whether the Indian's patch of ground is large or
small, or, as is still the rule in many villages, the lands are communal property, each one must make peace with all his neighbors
before he sows a seed. For more than a week before the momentous day, men remain apart from their wives.

On a Sunday or two before the planting, a special mass is celebrated in the church where the seed is carried to be blessed. In
Chichicastenango each family selects its own spot on the floor,
places lighted candles, incense and flower petals about the seed,
then kneels in a circle round it to pray. Sometimes they make
mosaics of the red, white and yellow ears and embody the candles
in the design.

The night before the planting the men burn incense in the fields
and sprinkle the ground with *aguardiente*. The women watch
and pray at home before lighted candles. In the morning, carrying
candles and festive food for the sowers, they go to the fields and
place their candles at points representing the four winds or four
directions. After the sowing, they serve the feast.

At San Andrés Semetabaj on Lake Atitlán, three small pine
trees decorated with fruits are planted in the fields, and a picture
of San Isidro is hung from the central tree. Beneath them the
seed, graded according to size, is placed, and candles and incense
are burned while the villagers pray. In some remote districts,
ceremonies reminiscent of the old fertility rites of the Greeks take
place on mountain tops and volcano craters. There the witch
doctors preside and sacrifices are offered the gods.

The first seeds are sown by an Elder of the village. In Alta Verapaz this entitles him to first choice of the tortillas served at the feast afterwards.

When the corn is harvested (from October to December), another ritual season begins. Relatives and friends of each family help to gather the corn; festive music and food give them zest.

The selection of seed corn for the next planting is of prime importance and is determined in numerous ways. Sometimes the ears from the center of the field—*Corazon del Maíz,* Heart of the Corn—are chosen. Sometimes twin ears—*cuaches* or *gemelos*—are found. These are greeted with great rejoicing because in them is the spirit of the corn, assurance of a good crop next season. One ear is kept for seed, the other placed as a thank offering before the figure of the household saint. Such an ear must be carefully guarded, for many are eager to possess it, since with the ear goes the good luck of the family. Some bury twin ears in the mound of seed corn, believing it will inspire the seed with ambition to do likewise.

Not so long ago the corn was piled as harvested in a mound on the field, and the Indians gathered round to wait patiently for the ears that would jump out of the pile. These were chosen as seed, for they were surely moved by the spirit of the corn.

The largest ear is fastened to the end of a rocket in some localities and the rocket set off. If it reaches a great height, the family will sell the corn for an excellent price.

When the corn is gathered, it is carried in procession back to the village to the accompaniment of music and rockets. There a feast is held in which the principal dishes are turkey, *aguardiente* and fruits brought in for the occasion from other parts of Guatemala.

PILGRIMAGES

To the Black Christ of Esquipulas

This pilgrimage is not only the most famous in Guatemala but one of the most renowned in Central and South America. Until the government instituted passport regulations some years ago, as many as 100,000 people annually sought the shrine of the Black

Christ in the little town of Esquipulas on January 15. Now that fees bar poverty-ridden Indians, the number has fallen to 40,000.

Geographically, Esquipulas is located at the junction of three countries, Guatemala, El Salvador and Honduras. To this center, long before the Conquest, Indians came at certain times of the year to trade and perform rites on the spot where now stands the church that houses the sacred image.

The village is only a day's journey on foot from the ruins of the ancient city of Maya worship, Copán in Honduras, and there are indications that once the two sites were linked. Five large stone carvings, typical of the sculpture of Copán, for example, are set up on the bridge before the sanctuary. Two represent jaguars or pumas and probably symbolize Ek-Balam-Chac, the Black Rain Puma, venerated by the Maya. Nor can the persistent rumor be quieted that on the site of the church a strange stone idol is well hidden, the real source of the Indian's fervent belief that if he prays there his prayer will be granted.

The black, five-foot figure of the Christ itself offers significant testimony that the pilgrimage to Esquipulas is another survival of pre-Columbian rituals.[1] The Maya venerated Ek Ahau, The Black Lord, who was served by seven black retainers. He was the god who controlled death by violence in all forms, including sacrifice. Another black deity of the Maya was Ek-chuach, The Tall Black One, protector of all who traveled on the trails. The Pokomán nation worshiped an idol, "black, shining like jet," records Thomas Gage, a colonial chronicler. And today the Quiché Indians still perform the Dance of the Black Ones (Baile de los Negros) in which the chief character is Ek, The Black One.

The fact that for some reason the special privilege of dressing the Black Christ for the ceremony and of performing other minor offices falls to Quiché Indians of Chichicastenango and Nahualá is further evidence. No white man, even a priest, is allowed to live in Nahualá. In Chichicastenango, the whites, even the priests, are not allowed to interfere with pagan ceremonies. It seems unlikely, therefore, that Indians from these villages would travel long distances to take part in a Christian ceremony.

[1] See S. K. Lothrop, Bibliography.

The teachings of the Christian Church, too, have led many Indians to believe that something occult exists in the worship of a black Christ. Christ, according to the Church, was a Jew, they say; Jews are not black; therefore the rites at Esquipulas cannot be truly Christian. That the Indians accepted the Black Christ more avidly than any white one is in itself significant.

Chief Esquipulas was the ruler of the tribes in this fertile valley when the conquerors descended. Wisely, to avoid the slaughter of his people, he promised to make no resistance. The Spaniards named the village they promptly established there in his honor, and made it the trading center from which their goods, brought overland from ships anchored off the coast, were distributed to all parts of Central America.

There the priests established a religious center. They began the erection of El Calvario, and to secure a figure of the Saviour that would win the Indians, they offered 100 *tostones* (50 ounces) of silver to the famous colonial sculptor, Quirio Cataño, to make it. The money was raised by devout Indians who sowed and sold cotton for the purpose.

Because the Indians, terrified by the cruelty of the Spaniards, believed that all white men were evil and that Christ could not be a kind and charitable god if he were white, the priests commissioned Cataño to make the image of balsam whose dark color resembles the complexion of the Indian. Cataño did so, and time and smoke of generations of candles and burning incense turned it black. In 1595 it was installed in the chapel to realize all that the priests had hoped for it—and more. Soon it was credited with miraculous powers, but not until after 1737, when the newly elected Bishop of Guatemala, Pardo de Figueroa, was cured there of a severe chronic ailment, did its fame as a miracle-working shrine become widespread.

In gratitude the bishop ordered the imposing temple or Sanctuario that now dominates the valley to be built for the Black Christ. This temple was completed in 1758, and on the bishop's death his body was buried under the principal altar and his portrait hung in the church.

True pilgrims travel on foot to reach it, though today everything from mules to airplanes is available, and the little town has ladino-owned inns to serve the horde of visitors who now join the In-dians at the shrine. Many of the Indians have walked from two weeks to a month to pray and trade during the week of fiesta and view with scorn those who come by mule or car. Pilgrims can be recognized by their wide straw hats decorated with gray moss and yellow gourdlike fruit, commonly called *chiches* (breasts) because of their outline and texture.

The immense church is lighted by silver chandeliers, the gifts of wealthy pilgrims of long ago. Paintings by famous artists and crude sketches by grateful pilgrims adorn the walls. On one side hang hundreds of miniature replicas in gold, silver, wood and wax of heads, arms, legs or other parts of the body presented by the healed as thank offerings.

With its wealth of gold and silver decorations, the altar itself is unique. And the figure of the Black Christ, girdled in white satin embroidered with gold and laden with jewels, is striking against the light of the tall windows behind it.

All classes and conditions of people, from the simplest Indian to the most sophisticated members of Guatemala's aristocracy, kneel inside and outside the church, each with lighted candles, each pray-ing or singing while clouds of incense rise to lofty beams. Among them is represented surely every physical, mental and spiritual ill and enough faith to move mountains.

Naturally legends—most of them acutely pointed—have grown up around the Black Christ. One tells of the rich man, Señor don Juan Palomeque y Vargas, a leading merchant of Antigua in the early seventeenth century. Suddenly, because of prolonged ex-cesses, he became blind and no doctor could cure him. At last he made the pilgrimage to Esquipulas to promise a heavy gold chain if his sight were restored. After a brief prayer, he laid the chain at the feet of the Christ. Instantly his sight returned. Full of joy, he prepared for his journey home.

"What a joke," he laughed to his servant, "on the doctors who said that nothing could cure me."

"You are cured, thanks to our Saviour," the servant reminded him.

"Thanks to our Saviour? Thanks to the gold chain!"

As he scoffed, don Juan once more became blind, and in his hand appeared the chain.

Another legend concerns the man who also became ill after a sinful life, and who also vowed to visit Nuestro Señor de Esquipulas with offerings and gifts. But January after January passed, his vow postponed because of the tales of hardships returning pilgrims told; he finally died, his pledge unfulfilled.

An old woman was making the last stage of her pilgrimage to the Black Christ on her knees when, just as the church came in sight, she was horrified to find a grinning skull hopping along beside her. A man near by caught the skull, and together they carried it into the church and placed it on the altar. Immediately it disappeared.

When she and the man had finished their prayers and left the church, they were amazed to see the skull returning to the place where they had found it. As they watched, it started again toward the altar. Once there, it remained for hours, then vanished completely. And the priest told the congregation that it was the skull of the man who had failed to keep his vow: he could not rest in peace in his grave.

As one approaches the village, two boulders, one on top of the other, rise beside the road. Round them are strewn numerous stones. "The Rock of the Compadres" they are called, and point still a third moral. Godparents and parents of the same child are titled *compadres,* and among the rules of conduct laid down by colonial priests was one forbidding *compadres* to have more than a spiritual relationship with one another.

When therefore two *compadres* violated the law on this very spot, they were turned to stone and doomed to remain there forever. And every good pilgrim must bring small stones to throw at them and dance about them jeering and shouting to show his disapproval. Otherwise his prayers to the Black Christ will not be answered.

On the summits of ridges and hills overlooking the valley are cairns, built also of stones brought by pilgrims during the centuries. Before these altarlike structures, the Indians fall on their

knees to make their first prayer to the Black Christ as they arrive
and as they leave to make their last.

Each night on the return trail, they put up pictures or stone and
candy images of the Christ, bought in Esquipulas, and kneel before
them. When they reach their homes, they pause before entering
to fire off rockets as a signal that they are safely returned. Pilgrims from Quezaltenango stain their hands with the black juice
of a small lemonlike fruit called *guali*. They do this, they say,
"because it helps the Black Christ of Esquipulas to bear his burden
of suffering."

Pilgrimage to the Virgin of Candelaria

Once upon a time, long, long ago, a Spaniard named Almengor
owned a silver mine near the village of Chiantla, high in the towering mountains of the Department of Huehuetenango. In the
village was a church, originally built by the Dominican friars, later
placed under the jurisdiction of the Brothers of Mercy.

To this church Almengor presented a figure of the Virgin of
Candelaria made from the silver of his mine. Thereafter the veins
of his mine swelled so with ore that he became fabulously rich
and decided to return to Spain. Before he went he made a farewell visit to his mine and was far inside when suddenly a Negro
slave shouted to him to come out. When Almengor was safely
outside, the mine caved in. (See Huehuetenango, page 274.)

Clearly this was a miracle performed by the Virgin to save the
life of her benefactor and to make it forever impossible for anyone else to secure silver from that mine. Since then the fame of
the Virgin has spread until the annual pilgrimage each February 2
to her shrine is one of the three largest in the country. Pilgrims
also come from all parts of Central America and Mexico.

Pilgrimage to Jesús Sepultado

In 1670 the village of San Juan el Perdido was simultaneously
visited by a disastrous epidemic of smallpox and a plague of bats
before which the miracle-working image of the Entombed Christ
was apparently powerless. The survivors, therefore, moved to
another site, now San Felipe, a suburb of Antigua, and built a

little chapel for their figure. The chapel burned to the ground and they built another. The 1917 earthquake destroyed that and they built again, this time a church, said to be modeled on the Cathedral of Barcelona.

The fame of Jesús Sepultado has survived all vicissitudes, and on the first Friday of Lent each year its shrine is the goal of thousands of pilgrims. To this shrine the devout ladinos of the cities turn in heavy trouble, many from Guatemala City making the pilgrimage on foot.

Indian pilgrims usually wear huge hats decorated with moss. They carry candles in cases made from hollowed-out bamboo. As they approach the village in the evening, they sing chants, and these, accented by the patter of donkey feet and the tinkle of donkey bells, give a charming touch to the scene in spite of the cars and modern dress of the ladinos.

Pilgrimage to the Christ of Golgotha

Second in importance to Esquipulas, this pilgrimage to El Cristo del Golgota of Chajul on the second Friday of Lent is almost entirely an Indian event, because Chajul cannot be reached by motor. It is the favorite shrine of the Quiché Indians.

The figure of Christ stands on an altar brilliant with silver and gold vessels and ornaments. On either side is a life-sized figure dressed in a policeman's uniform. The uniforms were made and presented by a tailor who desired that the Christ who had restored his health should be well guarded.

Fairs and Markets

A market is a local affair held in each village on a definitely appointed day or days of the week. Its traders are primarily members of the municipality, and the products are local and perishable fruits, vegetables and flowers.

A fair is a glorified market that may continue for a week or more in connection with some fiesta, ceremony, pilgrimage or other religious or civic celebration. Not only the entire country may be represented among the traders but various parts of Central America and Mexico. Some markets, like those of Sololá and

Chichicastenango, are larger than some fairs, yet one always knows whether he has strayed into a market or a fair by the atmospheric difference. Never noisy or disorderly at any time, traders and customers at a fair always manage to convey the idea that this is a special and gala opportunity to buy.

One of the most impressive experiences for the foreigner in Guatemala is to watch the traders arrive. From trails and highways they pour into the main street, men, women and children in colorful and varied costumes, each with a burden on back or head. Some lead a mule or two, also but reasonably laden, or a cow or ox for sale. Some herd before them a brood of small, spotted pigs, goats, sheep or ducks. Chickens ride in baskets atop a woman's head, their quiet resignation startling in contrast to wildly bobbing Easter lilies sharing the same vehicle.

The traders advance steadily, with no sound save the patter of bare, sure feet on rough, irregular cobbles, the grunt of a staggering bearer or a guttural command to wife or beast. When an Indian is doing something, he is doing just that. Now he is going to the fair, scores and hundreds of him are going to the fair, and they go like some ancient migration or an inevitable and not-to-be-stemmed run of smelt or salmon.

At the site of fair or market all is ready for them. Men, arched beneath soaring loads of water jars from Chinautla or glazed ware from Antigua, turn automatically to the pottery section. Others, buried under baskets from Aguacatán or San Juan Sacatepéquez, settle down side by side though because of different languages they cannot communicate with each other. Whole streets are waiting for merchants of Salcajá and San Cristóbal and their assistants, laden with bolts of machine-woven cotton goods and brilliant *cortes* (skirt lengths) for women. Other lanes are set aside for the woolen goods from Momostenango. Bolts are piled high on benches and ground; temporary walls of wattled bamboo are hung with blankets and ponchos, stunningly striped or bewilderingly figured with man and beast and bird or stylized design.

Grains are here, leatherwork there, with shops to make sandals while one waits not far away. There are booths for straw hats, for straw mats, for rope and horsegear, for bags of cotton and fiber. Chile, bright and pungent, from Jutiapa. Raw cotton, carded cotton, spun and skeined cotton, dyed and undyed. Tables of silk skeins in every shade of every color. Wool in all stages. And dye materials, in packets, in plant and bark. Grinding stones for corn from Nahualá. Gourds, plain and decorated, from Rabinal. Onions and garlic, their tails neatly braided, from Sololá. Pine chairs, boxes and little wooden trunks, set on four legs and painted and varnished like Noah's Ark from Totonicapán.

A new street added in recent years is growing longer and longer. This houses the booths and cheap imported articles from Germany and Japan—soaps and combs, thread on spools, scissors, beads and store shirts, buttons and flashlights. Soft-drink stands, glasses already filled with liquids dyed every color of the rainbow. In out-of-the-way corners, sly games of chance are other contributions of modern civilization.

Most popular is the street lined on both sides with food shops from which savory odors rise over open charcoal fires and small ovens and the soft pitty-pat of tortilla-shaping hands. About the edges squat women behind baskets of mangoes and avocados, a score of succulent tropical fruits and every known and some unfamiliar vegetables. If a foreign woman passes, they pull her skirt and whisper that they have a blouse or scarf to sell.

Round the corner is the cattle fair where scores of small horses and mules, sheep, goats, pigs, cows, calves and oxen, even ducks, turkeys and chickens, gaze as stolidly as their owners at prospective buyers.

By ten o'clock at the latest the fair is in full swing, with many customers and few purchasers, for each must first feel and compare everything. Only foreign visitors and itinerant venders buy, the first because they know no better, the second because they buy to sell again in the markets of distant villages and must be on their way. The rest know that the last day, the last hour, is the time to close a bargain.

Although they are called traders, the Indians do not trade; they buy and sell for cash. The fixed price is unknown. Life would be dull indeed if one knew in advance just what a trader would sell for, just what a customer would pay. Instead each must bargain and the best customer is the one who bargains most expertly. Sometimes it appears that the trader is taking a severe beating or that only a fiend would offer him less than the pittance he asks, but most of them have a minimum price below which they will not sell.

For his space the trader pays a fee or tax based on the value of his wares; this runs from two or three centavos a day up. As an Indian never considers the cost of his time or labor, he counts that day well spent that rewards him with a profit of 25 to 50 centavos. For it has given him in addition an opportunity to burn a candle in the church and, in the evening when his wares are folded away, the pleasure of dancing or watching the dancers, of sampling the food shops and possibly the wares of a cantina.

V

HIS LIFE

The Indian Village

THE same Indians who have developed such a myriad variety
of designs, symbols, and *costumbres* that no one can say anything about one village with any certainty that it will apply to the
next, live in villages very much alike. The explanation is that the
village is of Spanish manufacture. Alonso Lopez Cerrato, a lawyer of Antigua during the second quarter of the sixteenth century,
initiated the idea. Through the village plan he hoped to protect
the Indians from abuse and exploitation; the priests saw in it a
medium for bringing their pagan flocks under direct control of the
Church.

To persuade the Indians to leave their scattered, independently
located huts and fields, they used a most convincing argument.
Selecting a strategic site for a village, the priests planted corn
about it, built huts and started the foundation for a church. When
the corn was ripe, the Indians were invited to see it and to dance
and feast. Shortly each hut would have its occupants, more would
be under construction, and the village was a fact accomplished.

Each village was projected about a small park or central square.
At the head of this plaza, the church, an enormous structure entirely out of proportion to the village and intended for that reason
to overawe the Indian, was erected. About the other three sides
were built the Commandancia, military headquarters and barracks,
and the Alcaldia, headquarters of the civil offices of the government. To this original plan, modern times have added a telegraph office, a school, a jail, and sometimes a small hospital or
dispensary.

In villages distinguished as capitals of Departments, a long, low
building of small rooms was also given place beside the plaza.

These rooms served, and still serve occasionally, as committee rooms to which the heads of surrounding municipalities could come to discuss their local problems with the authorities of the capital and, if necessary, with the governor.

The original plaza contained two features which in early days served as the village newspaper. One was the *pila,* a flowing well, to which the women came daily to fill their water jars, wash the family clothes, and exchange gossip. The other was a towering amatle tree or a ceiba ("The Tree of Counsel") under which the men gathered. Under this tree, too, on specified days, the market was held.

From this central square, the streets of homes were allowed to wander off at will, resulting in the labyrinthine thoroughfares found in the older villages today.

Recent invasion of these villages by ladinos has resulted in the *pila* being transformed into a fountain; the open square laid out to more or less precise walks and gardens, and the ceiba being supplanted or supplemented by a wooden bandstand, equipped in some places with a bellowing radio amplifier.

Any village will impress the visitor with its cleanliness and order, and those where the ladino and his radio have not penetrated, with their quiet. The streets are swept and sprinkled daily; the earthen yards about the homes swept as clean as a floor, and usually they are bright with flowers and vines. Modern sanitary inspection has placed screens on the doors of food shops and white caps on the heads of those who sell food.

And the new liquor law of 1938, forbidding the sale of liquor except by the bottle, is restoring peace and self-respect to the villagers. Until this law was passed, drink threatened to be the Indian's undoing, both as an individual and as a people. Before the advent of the white man, ceremonial drinking and drunkenness were as much a part of every ritual as the costume and *costumbres*. But Indian liquors were mild and mellowing concoctions made from cornpaste and fruit juices to induce a happy and devout frame of mind.

The hard, distilled liquors of the whites excite the Indian to disorder and irreverence, and ladinos, exploiting his age-old habit

Eichenberger

SAN PABLO LA LAGUNA, LAKE ATITLÁN

Biener

ADOBE AND THATCH HOME, SANTIAGO ATITLÁN

VILLAGE TYPES

Biener CHICHICASTENANGO

Eichenberger SANTA LUCIA UTATLÁN

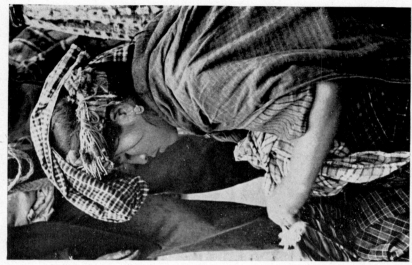

Eichenberger   MOMOSTENANGO

Eichenberger   COTZAL

VILLAGE TYPES

Biener

PALÍN

Eichenberger

SAN CRISTÓBAL TOTONICAPÁN

VILLAGE TYPES

Eichenberger

TODOS SANTOS

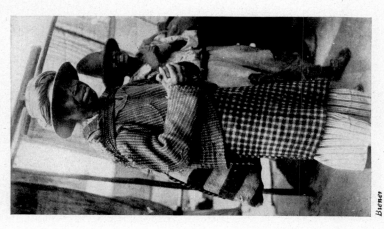

Buen

SOLOLA

MARKET BOUND

Biener

ON FOOT: TRADERS FROM SANTIAGO ATITLAN

Eichenberger

BY OX CART: NOTE THE LICENSE ON EACH CART

MARKET-BOUND

Elsie Weil

BY BOAT: TRADERS EMBARKING AT SAN PEDRO LA LAGUNA

Eichenberger

MARKET DAY, SAN FRANCISCO EL ALTO

FILLING THE WATER JARS

Eichenberger

AT THE VILLAGE WELL
Before the ruins of the Colonial Church at San Pablo La Laguna

Biener

IN THE LAKE
In the shallows of Lake Atitlán, Santiago Atitlán

of drinking, made them available to him at every turn, cheaply and by the glass. Finding them a quick road to escape from drudgery and poverty, the Indians, both men and women, sought them avidly with results so profitable to the ladinos though degenerating for the Indian that not until the present administration has it been possible to have restrictive laws passed.

It is not strictly accurate to say that the Indians live in these villages. The village is rather the headquarters of the municipality. If the village is large, the Indians live in *barrios* or *cantones* (wards) located about it. If it is small, little more than the village center is there. The Indians live in the ravines or hills. This explains why, when the population of a village is given as several thousand, the village itself appears to contain but a few hundred.

The Indian Home

Indian homes are of two general types. One is built of adobe, mud or tile bricks, roofed with tile, and fitted with both doors and windows. The other is windowless, with walls of mud or stone, wattles or reeds, and thatched with straw, palm leaves, corn husks or grass. In the hot lowlands, the houses are frequently built on stilts, walled on only three sides and thatched.

Some huts have very high peaked roofs, with eaves extending almost to the ground as a protection against burning sun and pounding rain. Others have a ridgepole roof, and a third variety is tepee-shaped, with an inverted clay dish capping the tip.

Adobe homes have two or more rooms, and may be built quadrangle-fashion about a patio. A corridor may run across one side or encircle the entire house. These are the homes of the well-to-do. They are comfortably furnished and frequently, if they are located on a main street, contain a small store.

Thatched huts may have one or two rooms, and may stand alone or in compounds where several huts outline a central square, their doors opening to the square, never to the street. In these live the grandparents, the parents and married sons of the family. And if grandparent or parent is head of a *cofradia,* one hut will be set aside as its headquarters.

Furnishings are simple: mats or a crudely made bed, a chair and benches, a table. Hanging from beams or stored above the rafters are the looms and other implements of their crafts, fishpoles and nets, oars and baskets, extra garments, and the seed corn.

Every house has its open-fire stove, built on the floor or on a raised platform. Each may have its own outdoor beehive oven in which to bake ceremonial bread, or there may be a communal oven. And each household has, of course, its own *metate* for grinding corn.

Every house will have its altar, simple or elaborate according to the means of the family. In general, this consists of a table on which stands a small image or picture of the patron saint of the family, of the *cofradia* to which they belong, or of the village. Flowers and pine needles, bright trinkets—bits of tinsel and looking-glasses—candles, an incense burner and possibly a small stone figure dug up in the fields, are spread about it.

The homes of certain villages also have their *temaxcals* or sweat baths. These are miniature houses about four feet high, walled with stone and roofed with wood, then covered with clay. Inside is a pile of stones which are heated in a fire, then drenched with water. Some villages have one large *temaxcal* for communal use. This fashion of bathing may have come down from the Maya, as excavators have found similar buildings in Maya ruins.

THE INDIAN AND HIS LAND

During the administration of President Barrillas, the government took large areas of land from the Indian and gave them to ladinos for coffee raising. One day hundreds of Indians from Nahualá, in full tribal costume, arrived before the Palace in Guatemala City. Alarmed, the President ordered that only the Alcalde and Municipal Secretary be permitted to enter. The Indians refused; they had come as one man; they would be admitted as one.

Admitted they were. When they entered the reception hall, they fell on their knees in rows, foreheads to the floor. One remained erect, "a tall, well-dressed Indian of severe yet serene countenance." And when the President commanded that the others rise, this spokesman said, "I will not order my companions to rise, señor President, until you have given us justice, for it is justice

we have come to ask." Without giving the President opportunity
to reply, he went on:

"You have ordered us to leave our lands so that coffee can be
sown there. You have done us an injustice. In exchange you
have offered us 600 *caballerias* of land on the coast. What do we
want of land on the coast? Our brothers, our women, our children will die there. . . . You ask us to leave the land where our
grandfathers and fathers were born, where we were born, where
our sons were born. . . . Why have you committed this injustice?
Is it because we do not know how to grow coffee? You know
very well we know how to grow coffee, señor President. Are we
not the ones who sow the coffee on the fincas, wash it, harvest
it? . . .

"But we do not wish to grow coffee on our lands. We want
them only for our corn, our animals, our wood. And we want
these lands where our grandfathers and fathers worked. Why
should we leave them?

"These lands have always been ours and furthermore we have
paid for them three times. . . . We paid for them in the time of
President Carrera; here are our titles to them. We bought them
the second time from President Cerna. . . . And we bought them
for the third time from President Barrios."

With each statement, he opened his bag and drew out the proper
titles, placing them before the President.

"And now, do you wish that we buy them from you also? Very
well. We have brought the money. How much do you want for
our own lands, señor President? I ask, how much do you want
for them!"

President Barrillas had no reply except to order in the presence
of the Indians that not an inch of Nahualá lands should ever be
taken from them.

This is only one illustration of the tenacity, the resourcefulness
and sacrifice the Indian employs to hold his land. He not only has
for it a strong sense of property rights but he feels for the soil a
deep mystical relationship. In the soil are the roots of his race, of
his family, his children and their children to be.

Even when the land is taken from him, he still considers it his.

In the long dissertations pronounced by elders of a village over a bride and groom, they are urged to remember and to teach their children to remember that the land taken from them by the conquerors will one day be theirs again. In some villages whose people have been forced by earthquake or government order to move, a bit of soil from the original site will be secured each year before the corn planting and carried from door to door for all to kiss and bless. Then it is placed in the ground with the first seed.

After the Conquest, the villages were located in the center of large land grants awarded to be cultivated communally for the benefit of all. Many villages still have these communal lands. In others, as the local government needed funds, the communal lands were divided into small parcels and sold to Indians who had some wealth. In this way a small capitalist class rose.

Today each Indian in a village, either by purchase or by original grants, has sufficient land for a home for himself and his oldest sons when they marry, and either his own land or his share in the communal lands for the cultivation of his corn and vegetables. If there are too many sons for the land to support, the younger must leave the parental roof and start for themselves elsewhere. To keep the property intact, inheritance is usually made to the eldest.

LABOR LAWS AND CONDITIONS

Except on the weekly market or feast days, visitors to a village may find but a handful of people there. The men will be in the fields or gathering wood or traveling with their wares to another village market. And during certain seasons the village will be deserted by all but the old and infirm. Families and household goods, chickens, mule and cow will have departed to the coast to work on the coffee fincas.

Traditionally highlanders, the Indians have made this trek since centuries before the Conquest when they went to cultivate their own cotton and cacao in the lowlands. They may be gone from two to four or more months. Perhaps a few families will find permanent work and settle down on a finca as *colonos*.

This freedom of movement and choice of labor is a modern innovation, too new to appraise as yet. Its possibilities for the development of the Indian as a citizen of Guatemala, if not as a member of his own tribe, are vast.

Following the Conquest the Indians were divided into two main classes. Those assigned to *Encomiendas* were called *tributarios* because they were allowed to work communal lands. They were forced to pay so high a tribute, however, that the title was merely a polite word for slavery. Indians assigned to *Repartimientos* were subdivided into *ladinos,* artisans who worked in the cities, *nahorias,* domestic slaves, and *laborios* or *jornaleros,* laborers. Whatever the name, the fact was slavery, not so horrible perhaps as in Cuba, where seventy out of each 100 slaves died each year, but so cruel as to have bred the sense of freedom and pride out of the Indian and secretiveness and distrust of the white man and all his works into him. Thousands died of overwork and ill treatment, but death and abuse meant little to them in comparison with the two great tyrannies—the seizure of their lands and of their women.

In 1824, slavery was abolished, and for more than 50 years the labor situation in Guatemala was in chaos. Content and able to exist on little, the Indians refused to work. With the development of coffee and banana cultivation, however, labor was needed, and in 1879 a law for the regulation of labor, *Reglamento de Jornaleros,* was passed to supply it.

This was a new form of slavery. Owners of fincas and plantations were permitted to advance money to the Indians which they were forced to repay with work. As wages were low, allowing only for the most meager necessities, the Indian was in debt for life. If he died, his children inherited his debt, and, working it off and at the same time acquiring debts of their own, were involved in lifelong slavery themselves.

In 1936 this system was abolished. The indebtedness of all Indians was canceled and they were started fresh as their own masters. Thousands remained with their old employers; other thousands left to try new masters or to enter the developing industries.

Four centuries of exploitation and oppression could not be thrown off as quickly as a law can be written. The Indian today has a dependent, childlike attitude toward his employer, still regarding him as lord and master, "father and mother." Or, under no pressure to work, he is content to remain idle.

To force him to become self-supporting and independent and at the same time to stabilize the labor supply, a Vagrancy Law operated until recently. Under this law, each Indian was required to cultivate his own lands for 100 days of each year or, if he had no land of his own, to work 150 days annually for others. Members of the second group carried *libretos,* issued by the Department of Agriculture, in which each employer recorded, over his own signature, the length of time the Indian had worked for him. These books were available at all times for government inspection, and any Indian whose book could not show that he was complying with the law, had work found for him.

Today the *libreto* has been abandoned in favor of a *Codigo del Trabaljo* or Worker's Code, and a national labor office, *Oficina del Trabaljo,* set up to apply it. By this new system, *mozos colonos* or laborers, during the height of the coffee picking season can now earn as much as sixty cents a day. In addition, workers are provided with a ration of black beans, maize, salt and lime, a place to live, medical attention and, for their children, a school where they are taught reading, writing, arithmetic and some geography.

By North American standards wages are fantastically low, but in proportion to the cost of living and the few demands the Indian makes on life, they are sufficient for the time being. They range from ten or fifteen cents a day, plus corn, house, patch of land on which to raise vegetables and keep a cow and chickens for the *colono* or man living on finca or plantation, to a flat rate of ten dollars a month, more or less, if the Indian supplies his own food and shelter. In the cities, the minimum wage per day for the unskilled laborer averages around 25 cents when he provides his own food and shelter.

Taxes for the Indians are as low: a few cents for the *cedula de vecindad,* the document that identifies him as a citizen; a small municipal tax, and two dollars a year for road tax, *vialidad.* This last the Indian seldom pays, preferring to work it out with one week's labor on the roads every six months.

VILLAGE GOVERNMENT

Each village is well and variously governed. First is the military authority, the *comandante,* usually a ladino, appointed by the Minister of War. Second, the *intendente,* formerly called *alcalde,* or mayor, appointed every two years by the President. He may or may not be a ladino, and in purely Indian villages he may or may not be a member of that village, though, if not, he must speak its language. The *intendente* is assisted by *regidores* (aldermen) whose number depends upon the size of the population, and a *Fiscal* or *Sindico,* a ladino versed in national and Indian law.

Next comes the Church with the priests and *fiscal de iglesia* (church lawyer). Associated with them are the *cofradias* or brotherhoods whose officers are drawn from the upper classes and exert great influence on community affairs. Then there are the Elders (*Principales*), the wise old men, who may or may not hold office but whose judgment is respected above all others. The Indians will not act against their decisions, and knowing this, ladino officials depend on them for advice. Finally there are the witch doctors, whose point of view must always be included in matters affecting the entire group.

If extraordinary circumstances arise, however, the Indians will set aside all local and religious authority and with their Elders go straight to Guatemala City to the highest authority in the land. The President they will see and no one else.

Religious and civil governments of a village are so closely allied that, with the exception always of the military authority, it is difficult to tell where one authority ends and the other begins. Each borrows ideas from the other for the general good. A notable example was the practice of the *cofradias* in one highland village of lending money to their members.

When each new set of officers was installed and the amount in the treasury checked, they lent from one to three dollars at three per cent interest to their members. With this capital the member purchased wool or dyes for his weaving, sold his textiles, invested the profits in more materials, until by the end of the year he had at least a fingerhold on a livelihood. Just before election of new *cofrades*—and, it should be said, without any pressure—he returned principal and interest to the *cofradia*. The *cofradias* profited so largely by the plan that the municipal government adopted it and also within a few years was showing a profit.

INDIAN CASTES

The political organization of the Indian tribe before the Conquest (and, with slight variations, all tribes had the same) determined their social organization. In government an absolute monarchy, the hereditary and governing class, made up of the heads of the principal families who sat in council and acted in an advisory capacity, formed the nobility and aristocracy. Next were the priests and military castes, then the general population engaged in trade and agriculture, and last, the slaves.

Members of uncontaminated Indian villages today are as rigorously divided—and by the Indians themselves—into three social classes. The upper class or aristocracy is made up of descendants of the nobility, the high ranking dignitaries and pagan priests who survived the Conquest. Today, that modern phenomenon, the aristocracy of wealth, is also rising. *Medianos,* the merchants and traders, form the second or middle class; and last and lowest are the masses, the plebeians or *el populacho,* made up of the burden bearers and day laborers who work on the roads, till the fields.

In the older villages, where caste is strictly observed, there is no beggar-to-banker tradition. Each Indian knows his rank and keeps it. In villages of large ladino populations or when an Indian himself turns ladino, however, there are no limits to his ability to rise. And many Indians have thus risen to wealth, position, political power.

To the Indian who has become ladino, life is not too simple or happy, particularly for the first generation of the family. He is neither red man nor white. He has lost the respect of his tribe and most of his own; he still has to earn the respect of the ladinos.

LANGUAGES

In the *Popul-Vuh*—Sacred Book of the Quiché—it is written that the descendants of three of the first four men who walked on earth—the fourth was sterile—formed many different tribes, each speaking its own language. They could not understand one another and all were at odds. This was true of the Guatemala the Spaniards found. Even groups that had drifted just over a mountain from their clan had so changed and corrupted their tongue as to make it an independent language.

The situation is much the same today, though it may not be tomorrow. The Spaniards' policy was to keep the Indian in ignorance and slavery, so they made no effort to teach him Spanish, preferring to learn the Indian dialect themselves. The priests, in order to travel about, learned several. A few priests compiled Indian grammars and dictionaries for their own use, volumes that today are of invaluable assistance to historians and scientists, but they did little to enlighten the Indians.

The present administration has made the same curriculum compulsory for all schools in the country and Spanish the language in which it must be taught. Eventually this policy must contribute to the transformation of Indian into ladino, but to prevent the Indian languages from disappearing entirely, plans are now being made to include some of them in school or university curricula.

At various times attempts have been made to classify the Indian languages, and the Carnegie Institution of Washington is now engaged in making an exhaustive study of them. Here it is sufficient to say that the majority of Indians speak one of the sixteen or seventeen varieties of the Maya-Quiché or Mayence languages, whose roots, of course, are Maya. Some tribes speak one or another of the Mexican languages known as Pipil or Nahuatl, introduced by Mexican immigrants to Guatemala before and after the Conquest. A third and little-known tongue, spoken by tribes along the Pacific Coast, is Sinca. This is said to be the only autochthonous language in the country.

The language of the hands, so well developed and understood by Latin Americans generally, is almost unknown to the Indian. He stands or sits quietly and speaks in subdued, guttural tones.

EDUCATION

The same curriculum is followed by all schools of the country, and the same organization—segregation of boys and girls in separate schools—is maintained for Indian children living in villages. They are required to enter school at the age of seven and to continue through the six grades of grammar school. Rural schools are supplied on fincas and plantations. Evening classes in Spanish for adults are available in all villages.

Although high school and university training is optional, an increasing number of Indian students are going on to one and sometimes both. To do this they must leave their communities for the larger towns and cities and, while attending classes, wear ladino clothes. When they are graduated or leave these upper schools and return to their villages to practise law or medicine or teach, they usually return also to the costume of their tribe.

Only one concession is made in regard to Indian schools. The teacher, whether Indian or ladino, must speak both Spanish (*Castilla,* the Indians call it) and the Indian tongue of the village. One of the regulations laid down for teachers is that they must "combat the use of vulgar phrases, epithets and coarse jokes in the Indian idiom and in the Spanish."

The year of military service required of every male eighteen years old or over is proving one of the most impressive factors in the education of the Indian. Each man in addition to his military training is taught to read and write and the value of physical fitness. Many become so interested that they voluntarily return for a year or more. Such soldiers are called Volunteers and given higher military—and incidentally, social—rating than the regular forces. In the large Indian centers Volunteer Battalions—each in its own tribal costume—are stationed and do much toward inspiring the small Indian to study and live healthily.

VI

HIS CRAFTS

INDIAN CRAFTS

SINCE the days of the first nomad tribes, the Indian has taken from nature the materials and implements for his crafts. Trees and vines provided gourds for household needs and religious ceremonies, and when the use of sand and clay was realized, the gourds gave him models for his pottery. Rushes and reeds supplied him with materials for mats and baskets, and later, other plants gave him fibers and cotton to spin and weave and wear.

From the stones of rivers and the wood of hard trees he fashioned crude implements for modeling and weaving, from plants and insects made his dyes, and from trees and flowers, birds and animals, mountains and seas he took his designs. The Indian had only to supply a method, and the primitive methods he evolved centuries ago are the methods he uses today.

In different regions of the country—because of sand or clay deposits here, reeds or gourds there—particular crafts developed. And in time certain localities within each region became known for a particular type of pottery or basket, gourd or mat, or for special colors and designs. As the Indian traders traveled the old trails or broke new ones, carrying pots to the lowlands or straw mats to the highlands, the fame of these centers spread. To have a water jar from Chinautla, a gourd from Rabinal, a basket from Parramos was to have the best of its kind. Indians would wait long or travel far to possess them. Long before Columbus made history's greatest mistake, the Indians were expert in specialization.

Only within the past ten years have the ladinos seen possibilities for profit in these Indian crafts and introduced modern ideas and machinery to secure mass production. They have started potteries, textile factories, mat and basket industries.

To these factories, simple too as yet, the Indians are turning from their handcrafts and fields to become once more Guatemala's pioneers. Unaware that the same machine which can make cotton cloth from cotton fiber can also make an Indian into a ladino, they are the first to be absorbed. One day the machines will still be spinning but the Indian and his *costumbres* and crafts will be no more.

GOURDS

Primitive tribes ranging Central America found on the morro tree round gourds useful as bowls and dippers, and smaller, oblong gourds good for cups and jugs. (The first are called by the Indians today *guacales;* the second, *jicaras.*) And from the cucurbitaceous vines they took gourds which we call calabashes.

As these gourds came more and more into general use, thriving centers developed where the morro and the vines flourished. And the nobility and aristocracy of the different tribes, demanding always different and better utensils than those used by the plebeians, stimulated Indian artists and craftsmen in these centers to etch, paint, stain and design.

The calabashes, used principally for utilitarian purposes, are never decorated. Free for the picking or cheaply purchased, they are thrown away when stained or cracked. Cut in half they are used as containers and measures in the markets, for dippers and bowls. Uncut they are the water jugs the laborers carry with them. In the highlands a very large *jicara* (*tol*) is used to hold the snakes featured in snake dances.

Very popular and sought after are the etched and stained *guacales* and *jicaras,* particularly old ones from colonial times with their silver brims and legs. Of these decorated gourds, those on which white designs in high or low relief stand out against black backgrounds are most in demand.

To make these, the surface of the gourd is first rubbed clean and smoothed with oak leaves, then stained black with a mixture made from grease and lampblack secured from the smoke of pitch pine. When this has set, the artist, with a crude knife he calls *burín,* draws or etches his patterns into the black surface. Last, to give a high and permanent gloss, he applies a greasy substance (*nij*) made from boiling louselike insects. Until recently these designs in their intricacy and accuracy were beautiful examples of craftsmanship, but frequently now under the pressure for production they are merely flamboyant.

More attractive though less popular are the brown or yellow painted gourds. Some of these in use by market women are very old, having descended through several generations. They bear quaint and dim designs of animal and human figures from pre-Columbian legends. These *pintados*—painted gourds—are prepared in the same way as the black, but their designs are more typical of the Indian's art. When painted both inside and out, they are used in the celebration of tribal rituals.

Decorated gourds are essential to most Indian ceremonies whether Christian or pagan. In them the ceremonial food for the dead is placed at the head of graves and from them the festive food for christening, betrothal, and funeral feasts is served. Specialists, like the witch doctors, have their own *guacales,* known as *de brujo,* in which they mix the various articles of the person on whom they are to bring good fortune or bad. Out of these gourds, too, the grotesque or stylized masks for the ceremonial dances are frequently made.

Until recently, the decorated gourds served the high-caste Indian of the Quiché as a medium for borrowing and repaying loans. The borrower would send his servant with an empty gourd and a series of polite messages to a friend or *compadre.* According to whether the messages asked that the gourd be returned level or overflowing, the *compadre* would fill it with silver or gold. When the borrower repaid the loan, he returned the gourd filled to the same level. At no time did either borrower or lender count the money; that would have been a serious breach of faith. Since the coming of the white man, this custom has disappeared, the Indian having learned to be neither so trustworthy nor so trusting.

As far back as colonial times, ladino artists experimented with the decoration of the gourd. Excellent examples of their skill are still found today in old homes and antique shops.

BASKETS

If a Guatemala basket is more or less shallow and has no handle, it is a he; his name is *canasto*. If, no matter what its shape, size or decoration, it has a handle, it is a she; her name is *canasta*.

Intended to be carried on the head, the *canasto* is the true Indian basket. Each variety, in addition to sex, has its own name, style and purpose. *Canastas* with their handles are Indian-made for ladinos and foreigners who, of course, would consider anything on their heads beneath them.

Canastos differ principally in size; their shape remains almost the same. *Canasto panadero,* very large and wide with strong sides, is a bread basket. The *cajero* will hold up to 25 pounds of fruit or vegetables; the *cuartillero* up to six pounds of either corn or black beans. The *cafetero* and its small step-brother, the *medio canasto* (half a basket), are for the use of coffee pickers; the first for steady picking, the second for the berries of one small tree.

Smaller and more closely woven than any of these is the *colero* which sieves cooked corn so thoroughly that only the eye remains in the basket. The aristocrats of the sex are the *coles,* a nest of baskets ranging from two to eighteen inches square, each with its own lid, useful for innumerable purposes. Finally are *Las Petacas* which in spite of their feminine ending are *canastos,* oblong in shape and lidded, varying in size from less than a foot long and six inches deep to a yard and a half long and a half a yard in depth.

Canastas may be of any size and shape and highly colored and decorated. In comparison with the beauty *canastos* frequently achieve, they are merely pretty and, in a self-conscious way, useful. Recently they have become a special feature of the fair held in connection with the pilgrimage to Esquipulas. Devout pilgrims returning to all parts of Central America and Mexico purchase them to insure a warm welcome at home.

Whatever the type of basket, the technique is much the same. Six or ten splints of wicker, rush, or reed are moistened until pliable, then crossed until they ray out from a central hub like the spokes of a wheel. In and out of the main splints, warp splints are woven to make the basket *fino* (fine) or *ordinario* (common). In the fine baskets the main splints are woven back into the warp splints to give finish and strength; in the common baskets they are simply doubled back and fastened. Handles are made by crossing main splints from one side to the other and wrapping them with splints of the same material.

Although many villages specialize in basket weaving, the two basket markets are Guatemala City and Antigua. At Antigua baskets from the near-by villages of Parramos, Itzapa and San Martin Jilotepéque are especially prized for their workmanship.

Recently ladinos have started the manufacture of baskets modern in shape and style, decorated with primitive Indian symbols and colored with aniline dyes. Baskets of whatever make are an essential of housekeeping in Guatemala, serving as everything from market bags to baby cribs.

MATS

When expeditions excavating Maya cities came upon patterns imprinted in the soil they did not have to study long to understand what had made them. For the patterns were identical with those of the mats used today by the Indians to cover the walls of their huts, to wrap the dead, to serve as beds and tables.

Rushes and reeds growing wild in the marshes of the lowlands gave origin to this Indian craft. When the marshes dried and the rushes died, the weavers moved to a new source of supply. Later, they thought to stabilize their craft by sowing and reaping rushes and reeds as they did their corn.

As with the corn, a ritual associated with the moon developed. Rushes must be planted when the moon is young and cut when it is full. Otherwise the plants will not take root and the matured ones will not attain the quality necessary to insure long life to the mats and to the reputation of the mat makers.

Until 1917 the Indians of El Salvador had a profitable market among the rich homes of Guatemala City for their large thick mats were in demand to cover the red brick floors. These mats, wet and stretched and nailed down, were a mixed blessing, as fleas found happy homes in the dust that collected beneath them. After the 1917 earthquake, tiles were substituted for bricks in the new homes and Guatemala society was left with time on its hands.

Rabinal is famous for its mats, *petate chiapaneco,* so called because they are woven from the leaves of the palm—*palma chiapaneca.* They are prized for their thickness, endurance and distinctive color designs. The *petate tule* is made chiefly in San Antonio Aguas Calientes. Usually two yards square, this mat has a simple under-and-over pattern finished with a cordlike twist. Another and more common variety is made on the shores of Lakes Atitlán and Amatitlán. Ladinos and foreign residents find them attractive substitutes for lawn and beach umbrellas and useful for many purposes.

Many villages situated near swamps and rivers that leave good soil deposits for reeds weave the mats known as *petate ordinario.* Woven from the *cyperus canus* reed, they are used by the Indians.

ROPE

Less ornamental but infinitely useful are the products of the fiber-weaving craft. From the fibers of henequen, agave, maguey, pita pitón, pita floja and other plants native to Guatemala, everything from the finest string or cord to rope and cables is made, and from the string and rope, bags, hammocks and all sorts of horsegear are woven or knit.

To secure the fiber, the leaves of the plant are beaten to a pulp by a heavy-headed stick or *pilón.* The pulp is then scraped away with a forklike tool and the fibers remaining washed in a convenient river or lake. When dry, they are combed until each filament is separated, then skeined for use or sale.

String is made by the men, frequently on the way to market or waiting endlessly to interview some official. Casually rolling two strands of fiber up and down on bare thighs, they intertwine them in a firm and well-made cord.

Women and children usually make the rope. One holds a two-piece gadget (*taravilla*), a length of wood with a nicked throat about which one end of coarse string is fixed. While she twists the handle of the *taravilla* rapidly round its axle, her assistant feeds her another coarse strand which, winding round the first strand, forms the rope.

Hammocks, saddlebags, large-meshed bags are made by attaching the end of one fiber to the branch of a tree, then twisting and braiding into it other fibers. Saddlebags and other pack-animal accessories are woven of untwisted fibers on primitive upright looms.

Bags of fine and coarse texture worn by the men (Costumes, page 94) are finger-woven or knit with steel or wooden needles. San Pablo la Laguna is known for a special variety of bag made of colored strands. The cords are first stretched between sticks and painted at definite intervals so that when woven the effect is of a tie-and-dye textile.

Several centers are popular markets for this rope craft—San Cristóbal in Alta Verapaz, San Miguel and San Sebastián in Huehuetenango, and lowland villages where maguey and henequen grow plentifully.[1]

CERAMICS

Comparing the beautifully moulded and decorated pottery of the Maya with the simple pots made by the Indians today, it is easy to conclude that this ancient craft has degenerated in Guatemala. One must remember, however, that the first effort of the conquerors was to destroy Indian culture, and that until very recently the ladinos of the country found neither use, interest nor beauty in anything Indian.

Given neither opportunity nor incentive to develop or continue this craft, the Indians made only the simple pots and dishes necessary for their use. The ability to duplicate the workmanship of their ancestors is latent, perhaps, but to achieve it they would have to be taught again the art of the Maya and given incentive to emulate it.

Two classes of ceramics are made today—the old hand product, made by women and children in their villages, and the products of the potters' wheel and kiln made by Indian men in ladino-owned potteries in villages and towns where there is a large ladino population.

[1] Note 10D.

The hand-made pottery is achieved by incredibly simple methods. A new pot is moulded over an old one, or inside straw shaped as a model, or free-hand. Sometimes a gourd still serves as a mould. Lacking kilns, they bake the pots in open fires, then polish and clean then with stones, broken bits of pottery, a piece of bamboo or perhaps a fragment of some historic implement or weapon dug up in their fields.

In the highland villages pots are cured by pouring into and over them a mixture of water and cornpaste. When this dries, it is brushed off and the pot is ready for market. In the lowlands, the pot is rubbed on the outside with a black, native soap and inside filled with soapy water. Both methods make the pots waterproof. To cure the water jars, a banana or platano skin, lard or a mixture of lime and water is spread over the outside and the jars are sub-merged in water for some time.

For decoration, a few geometric lines, human, animal or flower figures are added according to the skill and fancy of the potter. Most of these hand products are devoid of decoration and do not need it.

Utensils to be used over or near fire are made of white clay mix-tures; those to contain liquids, of red clay. In Huehuetenango, where black pots are made, the clay is first dyed in the smoke of *ocote* pine or with pitch (*brea*).

Chinautla is famous for its water jars; Momostenango and San Pedro Carchá for red clay vessels used to distil native liquors; San Raimundo for well-glazed pots for cooking tamales. Sololá and Antigua potters specialize in incense burners, those of Antigua adorned with more or less recognizable ducks. Totonicapán has a wide market for its highly glazed toys, candlesticks, and all kinds of pitchers and jugs.

Pottery moulded on the potters' wheel is a more finished product with an excellent glaze and polish. Made for trade purposes, an increasing variety of shapes, sizes and decoration is being offered in all shades of color. Ten years ago it was impossible to secure a kitchen utensil in Guatemala; everything was imported. Today every sort of utensil is available. As these factories improve their kilns and introduce modern equipment, they are able to reproduce the old models and duplicate modern designs with increasing skill. Totonicapán and Antigua are the chief centers of this industry.

TEXTILES

By the time Columbus arrived on the shores of Central America, Indian textiles had reached a high degree of art in craftsmanship and design. One of the first things Alvarado reported was that textiles, intricate and valuable, were among the gifts brought him by the natives.

When the Indians of Guatemala evolved methods of spinning and weaving textiles is another of the questions still unanswered. That they developed them early is evident from the costumes and adornments of infinite detail and precision of chiefs and priests carved on monuments and walls of ancient Maya temples and public buildings. Quiché mythology gives the time when the first four men walked on earth as their date of the origin, which is the same as saying "in the beginning was" the textile.

The earliest tribes found everywhere fibrous plants. Under King Hunapuh of the Quiché cotton was cultivated on the Pacific lowlands long before the Conquest. Wool was introduced by the Spanish colonists when they brought herds of sheep and goats to help them settle the New World. They also imported *seda floja*—untwisted silk—still imported by the Indians for their finest textiles. Modern times have contributed rayon and cheap silks, with the result that many varieties of textiles which once boasted a few prized silken threads are now made entirely of sleazy silks for trade.

Today fibers are only occasionally found, and in the smaller textiles. Cotton textiles are made from homegrown cotton and, as the supply does not equal the demand, from cotton thread imported ready for dyeing. Of the native cotton there are two kinds: the ordinary white and the *ixcaco* or *cuyuscate,* a natural tawny shade which eliminates the need for dyeing textiles brown. Of the herds of sheep and goats that roam the country a large percentage is black. From their undyed wool the heavy garments worn by the men of the cool and cold highlands are made.

With these materials and the most primitive tools, the Indians developed a wide range of textures—a very thick, padded cloth, a combination of thick and thin, of ribbed, of open work, and of crepe. To these they added various methods of embroidering and decoration. Some work the decorative threads into the textile during the weaving with the fingers. In this manner the cross-stitch, shadow work, embossed designs and open work were developed as distinctive features of the art of one tribe or another.

Later applied designs found their way into the textiles. One village devised the plan of drawing the design on the finished textile with a quill dipped in the blue juice of the *sacatinta* plant. Others used chain stitch, outline or appliqué. One village even acquired a technique that resembles filet.

The ancient use of feathers, silver and gold thread and an intricate netted technique employed on ceremonial textiles were abandoned eventually for the tassels, plain and knotted fringes, coins, buttons, even snaps of our more realistic day.

Whatever the texture, technique or design, they created in their textiles an art that now commands interest and appreciation in a world market. Museums, universities and individuals in the United States and Europe have made collections of representative costumes and textiles of the different tribes. In Guatemala City, the National Museum of Archeology and Ethnology is making a collection of Indian costumes and textiles.

Originally each village wove its own textiles for costumes and ceremonial uses according to strictly traditional styles and colors. And each took pride in preserving intact designs developed out of the symbolism and rituals of its race. Isolated as these settlements were one from the other, each developed, too, its own technique of weaving and its own equipment.

The Spaniards naturally were the first great influence to effect changes in the textiles. Delighted with their beauty and color, they demanded quantities for European export. And as the tourists of today ask for cocktail napkins and spreads for twin beds to be woven on the old hand looms, the Spaniards insisted that designs significant to them be substituted for the ancient tribal symbols. Forced to submit, the Indian still found ways of duping his masters. He introduced the new designs, but designs that were at the same time of both Spanish and tribal significance.

Also the Spanish policy of almost annihilating the nobility, priests and artists of the different tribes resulted in destroying the demand for the gorgeous textiles used for rituals or worn by the upper classes. The few masters of the craft who escaped the slaughter took refuge in small, outlying regions. There they continued to spin and weave and teach others, unaware that they were laying foundations for the textile centers of today or that they were bequeathing to certain sections fame for making more beautiful textiles than others.

Finally, the Spanish introduced the foot loom. Though primitive, too, it has had far-reaching effects. It simplified the weaving of the larger textiles, the skirts of the women, blankets, and all wool materials. It made possible exact duplication of textiles that formerly, made on the hand loom, always bore some stamp of the individual weaver. Most important, it made mass-production materials cheap in comparison with materials of the hand product.

Next came roads and more roads and now bus lines to open up communication between the markets and peoples of villages and cities. Textiles and designs were exchanged and new combinations discovered for them. Today women frequently appear in the skirt of one tribe, the blouse of another, with perhaps a scarf or head ribbon of a third. To these they are now adding shoes and stockings. Men indiscriminately mix their tribal costume with store-bought shirts of bright shades, hats and shoes. As no record of the authentic textiles of each people and the meaning of their symbols has ever been made, knowledge of the true costume and ceremonial textiles is almost lost.

Though quantities of beautiful textiles still are woven on hand and foot looms, modern Guatemala is in that confusing transition stage before the tribal costumes disappear altogether. Because of the climate and the fact that textiles were and are made for use, long, hard use, no ancient or even comparatively old textiles exist.

Tourists and buyers ranging over the country to purchase blouses from women's backs, napkins from their baskets, and bonnets from their babies' heads, leave round dollars in startled hands. These dollars are seldom used to buy thread and dyes to weave a new blouse or bonnet. Instead they will purchase cheap cotton yard goods and leave something over for dishes and umbrellas, bus trips and the movies.

Long ago a textile was begun with prayer. It would require months to weave and would be worn or used for years with all the pride of ownership and craftsmanship. Something of the owner's own spirit was thought to be woven into it. Even today personal pieces are parted with reluctantly, kissed and fondled in farewell, and sometimes the man, if the textile is a part of his woman's costume, will beat it to make sure that no part of her spirit remains to go with the purchaser.

A long-used textile also develops a personality of its own for its wearer. In the market in Guatemala City sits an old woman on whose blouse gay chickens and rabbits such as a child would enjoy are embroidered over the otherwise true tribal design. They are there "so that the *huipil* can have something to cheer it up."

Spinning

Long before reaching a village or isolated hut one may hear a high rhythmic hum as if a swarm of bees were gathering. The sound is made by two sticks with which a woman is beating a deer or goatskin pillow filled with corn husks, or rather, the mass of raw cotton that lies on the pillow. She is carding it in preparation for spinning the thread for a new blouse or some other textile for personal or household use.

When the cotton is clean and fluffy, she turns to other simple equipment to spin the thread. Her spindle is a pointed stick about eighteen inches long. Four or five inches from the point is a whorl made of clay or wood. Placing the point in a clay dish or gourd, even on the bare ground—though this is slower—she twists the whorl with the fingers of her right hand while in her left she holds a tuft of carded cotton. Miraculously the cotton draws itself out to wind about the spindle in a continuous fuzzy line.

In the highland villages where the textiles largely are made of wool, the men do the carding and spinning. For the first, they use a dry, thistlelike flower or a primitive carder made of wood set with spikes. Much of the thread is spun onto spindles by lonely shepherds tending their flocks.

From the spindle the thread is transferred to a reel. This may be anything from a cagelike wheel, made of split bamboo topping another short stick, to a spool. The woman holds the spindle in her left hand, turns the reel with her right, and again the cotton or wool extends itself obediently from one to the other, thinning out in thick places, thickening in thin ones as it goes to make a strong even thread.

If the thread is not to be dyed, it is now ready for the winding frame on which the warp lines are stretched in the traditional length and width necessary for the textile to be made. These winding frames vary in different villages, but in general they are nothing more than a perforated board or very low table. Pegs are placed in holes at either end and the warp lines stretched between them. For large textiles woven by men on foot looms, the warp is stretched between pegs set into the outside of the house or, if a telegraph line runs conveniently near, between two poles.

WEAVING

The hand loom is made of two sticks, 17 to 20 inches wide, cut from a spruce tree, some lengths of rope, and the woman herself. The warp lines are transferred from the winding frame and stretched between two sticks. To the ends of one stick, ropes are fastened to tie the loom when in use to tree or post. To the ends of the other, a tumpline of hide, rope or decorated leather is fixed. This tumpline, passing round the woman's waist or hips as she sits on the ground to weave, holds the loom taut and at the proper angle between her and the tree.

Beside her are her various threads wound on bits of sticks for shuttles and a handful of longer sticks of different lengths and sizes. One of these is very precious. It is the batten, carefully shaped of cedar or oak, with which she will pound back the woof lines as the weaving progresses. With the other sticks, sometimes as many as ten or twelve, plus her fingers, she will adjust threads as the intricacy of the technique requires. With these sticks and her fingers she amazes experts with the variety of techniques she can employ in one textile.

Her heddle may be a round heavy stick; usually it is of bamboo or reed in which dried seeds or pebbles are sealed. Gossip says that their rattle as the heddle moves back and forth informs the husband where his wife is and what she is doing, but the truth is that her simple soul enjoys the soothing rhythm. As she weaves, she rolls the completed textile on a stick before her and wraps it in a protecting cloth.

Easily made as these looms are, they are valued possessions. Many are old, the heritage of one generation to another. As children early are taught to weave, there are usually small looms in the house and sometimes also special looms for making belts and head ribbons.

Hand looms are used today chiefly for blouses, scarfs, basket napkins and other small textiles made of cotton or cotton with silk or wool. In a few isolated villages they are still used to weave the skirts and shawls and even the all-wool textiles. A hand-woven textile may take six months to complete, but it will last years in spite of hard wear and frequent beatings on the stones and soaking in icy waters.

The foot looms on which the large textiles and those of wool are made are almost as primitive as the hand looms. Bulky and awkward, they occupy most of the space in an Indian hut. Special foot looms are used for the intricate head ribbons which require special techniques and for the new cotton textiles now woven for trade. Foot looms are always operated by men, the women being reduced to bobbin threaders.

DYEING

Perhaps it is no accident that the colors used most frequently in the Indian textiles of Guatemala are yellow, red, white and black. These are the colors of the corn.

Though they evolved no rigid and comprehensive psychology of color as have other peoples, color has always played an essential and important role in Indian life. The old chroniclers picture the pageants of color when an Indian army marched out for battle with plumes and banners flying and the brilliance of costumes and textiles brought together for religious ceremonies. Today the Indian finds in color almost his only means of expression in an otherwise drab world.

Red, the color of fire, they associate with warmth, life. Blue, the color of their skies, suggests nobility. Yellow to ancient tribes was the color of sorrow and green signified eternal life. Purple was always a favorite, and after the Conquest, when the Indians saw it used for robes of the priests, they adopted it for their own ceremonial textiles. But chiefly because they saw a god in every manifestation of nature, they reproduced in the weaving the colors of nature, of gorgeous-hued birds, of flowers and fruits, of the skies at noon and midnight, sunrise and sunset.

Nature not only gave the Indian the colors for his dyes but took a hand in producing them. It is the action of strong sunlight and air, the frequent washings in rivers and lakes, that give beauty and richness to softly blended tones, that make in time the vivid red skirts of the women of Tactic, for example, the subtle and soft rose that rouses foreign visitors to wonder.

Certain colors and combinations of colors like certain designs were peculiar to each tribe. Even when more than 60 per cent of the skirts of the women were of blue, each village had its own blue and its own arrangement of broad or narrow, perpendicular or horizontal stripes or checks to distinguish it. Now colors are becoming increasingly interchanged and varied.

As in every other craft, the Indians turned to nature for dye materials, using plants and tree bark, insects and molluscs. They developed secret formulas both for the dyes and for the setting liquids used to hold colors fast as long as the hardy threads held together.

Two methods of dyeing are used. By one, the cotton thread is dipped into the liquid dye to obtain a uniform color. The other is the tie-and-dye or resist-dye method, employed to color the cotton thread at different intervals, producing the highly esteemed *jaspes*.

For these, strands of white cotton are carefully and firmly tied where required, so that when the strands are dipped, the knotted sections resist the dye. As the best *jaspe* effects are achieved according to the number of threads tied at one time, villages like Salcajá and San Cristóbal Totonicapán, where every few threads are counted, produce extraordinarily effective results with this method.

To give a complete list of Indian dyes is impossible, of course, but the following may indicate the range of dye materials and the ingenuity which produces them. (Ordinary aniline dyes are used in trade textiles and all silk thread is dyed in the countries from which the thread is imported.)

Cotton Dyes [1]

Purple. The best dye is derived from a mollusc found on the coasts of Nicaragua. This creature lives but seven years, and to attain the best color must be gathered during the tropical spring when the moon is full. The dye, *purpura patula,* is secured by rubbing two molluscs together until they release a saliva secreted in the gland in the gills. Threads dyed with this liquid have a seaweed odor and a salty taste. To make sure they are buying the genuine dye, Indians will first chew a thread. A mulberry-toned purple is secured from the mora del campo or nance morado tree.

Blue. Almost any shade desired can be secured from the sacatinta plant, one variety of which grows in all altitudes, one only in the highlands. The dye is made by mashing the leaves on a dried oxhide and to the liquid adding the proper amount of water. The jiquilite plant or anil (indigo) is used also. An almost black blue is derived from the fruit of the nacascolo or dividivi plant.

Black. A small snail called *jute,* found in the streams of southwest Guatemala, contributes a liquid, *jugo de jute,* for this dye.

Brown. Light brown is made from the skin of the nance, a yellow, cherry-like fruit; dark brown from the bark of the aliso tree, a member of the alder family.

Yellow. Orange yellow is made from the camotillo: reddish yellow from the seeds of the achiote tree; bright yellow from bird excrement.

Red. From cochineal, grown chiefly on the cactus-dotted deserts around Zacapa, Salamá and Amatitlán.

[1] For botanical names of plants, see note 10F.

Green. A yellow liquid extracted from curcuma, a tumeric root resembling ginger, is mixed with indigo or campeche or Brazilwood to give the green desired.

To the dyes used for cotton materials, a solution made from the leaves of the tempate tree is added to insure fast colors.

Wool Dyes [1]

Blue. The wool is first washed in a solution of bichromate of potash, then immersed in a solution made from the boiled pulp of the campeche tree.

Black. From sulfate of iron.

Brown. The wool is boiled slowly in a strong lime-water solution, then dipped in an extract made from the bark of the aliso tree.

Yellow. This color—also khaki color—is obtained by boiling the pulverized heart of the palo de mora tree.

Red. For every pound of wool, 30 lemons are boiled over a slow fire and to the liquid cochineal is added. When a very bright red is required, a plant which the Indians call chinchinegrito (five little niggers) is added to the solution. Red shades are also secured from various trees of the palo brasil or campeche family; one variety gives a colorless liquid that turns red when exposed to the air.

Green. The macerated wood of the palo de mora or palo amarillo is combined with bichromate of potash.

Designs and Symbols

The Indians of Guatemala have never had to wait for trees to be turned into paper, or paper into books. Their textiles were their books and each one wrote his own. A journey must have been an exciting and crowded experience when true tribal costumes were worn by man, woman and child.

In the designs and symbols and in the way the garments were worn, one could read the biography of the wearer—from what people he came; his social and official—civil, military or religious—rank; his profession; his approximate age; whether he was married and happily, or unmarried; whether he was at the height of his generative powers, approaching or past it; whether he was sterile. And one could tell at a glance whether the textile-covered basket

[1] For botanical names of plants, see note 10F.

or bundle contained food for household or market or offerings to the gods and what gods.

Each figure of the design had its own particular significance and position on the textile, and if it was part of a costume, on the body, according to laws of usage and dress laid down by chiefs and priests. Nobility and aristocracy were entitled to and insistent upon having exclusive and elaborate designs on whatever they wore or used.

Designs became simpler in meaning and pattern as they were adapted for the middle class or the plebeians, but always on each textile appeared the chief symbol of the clan in some form. Sometimes the same symbol used on the textiles of two or more tribes, though different in design, revealed that in some past era the two peoples were one.

Long ago, though symbols and designs were the same, each took on some individuality from the character and craftsmanship of its weaver. Usually it was enough to look at a textile to know who had made it, but some weavers in addition incorporated a tiny figure as a signature.

Because of the nature of the hand looms, designs woven into the textiles, even though they appeared curved, were always made of straight lines. This was true also of applied embroideries, the small stitches being so well and carefully placed that they appeared curved.

No piece, however great the pride of the artist, was ever made completely perfect. Even in the finest textiles to be worn by the highest dignitaries or used in the most sacred rituals, one small patch would be left undecorated or made with different-colored threads. Only the gods and their works are perfect. What Indian would dare to equal them?

All this is true today of the pure tribal textiles, but more and more villages are turning over to the foot looms the spinning, weaving and embroidering of their textiles. They supply the patterns for their designs and colors to a near-by weaving center and turn their efforts to other things.

Originally each weaver was taught as a child the designs of his clan and class, but since it has been proved simple to work from patterns, patterns are in use now even in the villages that weave their own textiles. And as it is as simple to work from one pattern as another, weavers of one village now incorporate in their own designs features of the designs of other villages that please them.

The result in many cases is a flamboyance of color and design that to the older Indian must be as confusing to decipher as a page printed in a mixture of Spanish, Chinese and Sanscrit. Flamboyance, of course, signals decadence, and it is true that as far as tribal textiles of authentic design are concerned, they are approaching the road down which the Maya and their arts vanished.

This is the trend. In the meantime many villages continue to make and use traditional textiles, while others little by little are changing designs and even dimensions of their textiles to supply modern demands.

The bewildered visitor, seeing hundreds of different Indian costumes, need feel no embarrassment in simply enjoying them. Few Indians know the significance of the symbols of any costumes but their own now, and many do not know their own. The proportion of ladinos and foreign residents who after years of observation can distinguish them is almost invisible to the naked eye.

A symbol—like that of the horse or the small human figure—may be realistic or, like the Plumed Serpent, be so stylized and various-formed that only a hairline distinguishes it from the undulating symbol of mountains or waves. Or, as in the symbol of the double-headed eagle, the figure may be half realistic, half abstract.

The Plumed Serpent, as the symbol of Kukulcán or Gucumátz, the god of the Maya-Quiché (*Quetzalcoatl* to the Aztecs) who created the world out of silence and darkness, is found on textiles, stone, wood and metal in many sections of Guatemala and particularly on the textiles of Quezaltenango and on the belts of San José Nacahuil.

Belief in the supernatural powers of the snake is not peculiar to Guatemala's Indians, though by the time they finished embellishing its symbol it was a very different reptile from the rattlesnake Dr. Herbert J. Spinden believes served as their model. Scrolls and other sinuous details, he says, were attached to its body, also the plumes of the quetzal and ornaments of man such as ear and nose plugs and headdresses; even the head of a man was placed within its distended jaws. So adorned it became the motif that controlled the character of Maya art. As used by the post-Maya and post-Conquest Indians, however, it appears as a nice clear S lying on its side or as two intertwined undulations suggestive of the Yin and Yang of the Chinese.

The double-headed eagle is an example of the double-meaning symbol. To the Spaniards who ordered it incorporated in the designs, it signified the reigning house of Charles V; to the Indians, the duality of the gods. One head looks forward, they say, one back; one looks for the good men do, the other for the evil. To the Quiché, this eagle symbolizes one of the first four men created by the gods.

A post-Conquest symbol adopted by the Indians of their own accord is the horse. Because of the fire from the guns of the Spanish cavalry, the horse, according to one explanation, became to them a manifestation of the god of fire. Another viewpoint holds that because the horse was so swift and powerful, they substituted it for the monkey who had previously served as messenger between gods and men.

The sun, creator of life on earth, and the moon, subject to the sun's influence, are easily recognized symbols on the textiles of Chichicastenango and San Mateo Ixtatán. The sun is the symbol of man, as he too is the creator of life; the moon, of woman, whose physical life is regulated by the moon and who is dominated by the sun or man.

Various small figures in series or rows are found on the textiles of many tribes. Those of men always symbolize in some degree the *chacs,* various manifestations of god in nature which contribute to the fertility of the soil—rain, sun, wind, etc. Bees, wasps, tigers, eaglets, birds of all kinds in realistic or stylized symbols represent the legendary origin of the race.

Other symbols prominently displayed on textiles of various villages are those of ancient ruling houses. So in Sololá, the bat of

the Cakchiqueles—erroneously called a butterfly—is a distinctive
feature, and on the textiles of the various Tzutuhil villages about
Lake Atitlán appears the single-headed eagle, symbol of the House
of the Eagle of the Tzutuhil nation.

VII

HIS COSTUMES

CONSIDERING the fate of the indigenous costume in other parts of the world, that the dress of the Indians of Guatemala has survived with only relatively minor changes is further testimony to its tribal significance. Even now, whatever they may wear on ordinary days, Indians of mountain and highland villages retain intact the ceremonial costume for social or religious occasions.

On the coasts, both because of the heat and the mixture of Negro, Mexican and other foreign elements brought into the country to work on coffee and banana fincas and in the ports, few vestiges of any native costume remain. And in the towns and cities where there is a large ladino population, the Indian costume may range from the true dress to one so completely false that it acquires a special flavor of its own.

Neither those who claim that the Indians were naked when the Spanish arrived or those that believe they had developed the final character of their tribal costumes are justified in those opinions. Pre-Conquest legends, sculpture and painting and first-hand observation of colonial chroniclers all testify that the Indians of Guatemala wore costumes, though costumes very different from those of today.

Nobility, dignitaries and priests wore richly embroidered cloaks, broad sashes with embroidered apronlike panels ending in fringe or net, front and back, anklets and armlets, and gorgeous headdresses. Women of the upper classes were wrapped from waist to thigh, knee, calf or ankle in the tight skirts seen today, wore scarfs or *tzutes* about their throats, quantities of jewelry and head ornaments. For ceremonial occasions they all wore long straight garments decorated in brilliant colors, with a hole for the head cut in the center.

Men of the lower classes wore a loin cloth and a square textile or *tzut* knotted like a scarf at the neck to protect their backs from the sun. Their women wore a brief apron front and back.

On this foundation, ideas from the dress of the conquerors and their ladies and from the early Spanish priests' conceptions of what constituted a modest dress, particularly for plebeian women, developed the tribal dress of each Indian nation. The short red coats of Cotzal and other villages are adaptations of the red coats of Spanish officers. The long full skirts worn by some women are imitations of the skirts of the Spanish ladies of the sixteenth and seventeenth centuries.

Among the Indians who wear these tribal costumes today, clothes are not considered as everyday and best, but mundane and ceremonial. Ceremonial costumes include those worn for social gatherings and fiestas as well as for rituals, since originally all were held for religious purposes. The wealthier, upper-class Indian may have several costumes, but the average Indian is satisfied with one complete outfit.

Special costumes are the privilege of those who hold either civil or religious office in a community. Civil authorities carry a staff or cane and wear either distinct styles of costume or insignia of rank or an extra cloak thrown round the shoulders and a larger headdress than the lay citizen.

Dignitaries of the various brotherhoods connected with the Catholic Church—and subterraneously with their own pagan worship— wear even more elaborate costumes and accessories. Witch doctors are set off by an extra amount of decoration on headdress and sash, by a distinctive hat, perched on top of the headdress, and a small bulging bag.

The richness of an Indian costume is in the textiles and embroideries, not in the style. Except for the trousers worn by the men of some tribes, each garment is practically made when it leaves the loom. A hole is cut in a straight length for the head, a few stitches taken at the sides to make a woman's blouse. Skirts are wrapped tightly about the hips or laid in pleats about the waist. Another blouse made on the same lines, thrown over the shoulders when the air chills, serves as cloak or cape. Everything else is a straight or square piece folded or tied to fit.

Costumes of the Men

Coats—Cotones, Sacos

Modern adaptations of the coats of the ladinos, plus any ideas the Indian himself may have as to what is vogue, add up to coats that are usually short and very stiff. They are worn with or without a shirt. In the highlands and mountains they are made of thick, closely woven wool and in warmer areas of cotton. Small figures of animals either woven into the material or embroidered on it in bright silks or cotton, braid, tape, buttons, fringes and pockets adorn it. Pockets are particularly good, though not for use; the more pockets, the better and more expensive the garment.

Shirts—Camisas

These are an innovation of the past 20 years and duplicate those worn by men everywhere. They are bought in bright colors in the markets. Homespun and made shirts are embellished with many buttons for use and ornament. Colored glass buttons are especially favored, and animals and flowers embroidered in bright silks. The neckband of these shirts, always too small to fit any human throat, is finished with a binding of the material or ribbon and well twisted threads, and worn open. Cuffs are finished the same way so that the sleeves may be rolled back to or above the elbows.

Trousers—Pantalones

Of the two main styles, the increasingly popular one is that of the foreign trouser of machine-made or homespun cotton (or sometimes flour bags on which the red and blue trademarks are valued as decoration), or of black, blue or brown wool. The second or *pantalon rajado,* more typical, has many varieties. Whether long or short, it is slit up the outside of the legs to the thigh in an effect reminiscent of the primitive loin cloths.

Of the short variety, those of the men of Chichicastenango are most interesting both for their cut and their elaborate embroidered symbols. They are adorned with a panel or finlike wing on each side, richly embroidered or simply, according to age, physical powers and rank of the wearer. Other villages wear a short trouser profusely embroidered with silk, but over this they wrap from waist to knee a short apron or rug of wool, usually in black and white, so that the men appear to wear a skirt. These *ponchitos* are also worn in some villages over long trousers.

Long trousers are generally worn over pantaloons of white cotton edged with ruffles, store-bought lace or embroidery. Some tribes wear a trouser that is long in style but short when worn. It has as much material above the seat as in the legs. The trouser, therefore, ends at the knees and the surplus above the waist is twisted and rolled round the body. Men of other villages wear long, white cotton pantaloons, over them a second pair of wool which, as they have no outside leg seams, appear like a long loin cloth. Others wear trousers with seams neither inside the leg nor outside, so that they fly freely in the breeze.

In villages where wool is used, trousers and coats for ceremonial wear are decorated with tribal symbols, tassels, ball fringe, buttons, preferably of bright red; sometimes also the costumes are lined with red.

Belts and Sashes—Cinchos or Bandas

These range from the humble liana (*bejuco*) torn from a tree in the forest to lavishly decorated and varicolored sashes. For mundane wear, sashes are plain. For ceremonial wear, they are not only embroidered with tribal designs but must be worn so that the designs are exactly placed on the body. They may be either wrapped round the waist and the ends with their fringe or lace allowed to hang to the knees or the ends may be twisted into the girdle. Leather belts, homemade or store-bought, are coming into use, though frequently the Indian adds a few stitches of colored silk or cotton to brighten their drabness. Small leather belts are also worn about the crowns of hats.

Headdresses—Tzutes—and Hats—Sombreros

The *tzut,* a square cotton textile embroidered with animals and stylized symbols, was the original headdress of the man and in most sections is still worn for ceremonial occasions. Since the introduction of the hat, some villages, willing to compromise, approve of wearing the straw hat on top of the *tzut.*

Tzutes in various sizes are also used by both men and women as handy accessories—handkerchiefs to wrap incense and offerings to the gods, decorative hat bands, neck scarfs; or as wrappers for staffs of office when not in use or to drape over the staff supporting an ikon carried in a religious procession. Women sometimes use them as a sling for babies, to cover the contents of their baskets, or to cover their heads when they enter a church. The textile itself is always rich in color; but for ceremonial use it is decorated in proportion to the importance and solemnity of the purpose it serves.

A variation of the *tzut* is the *servilleta,* used by both men and women to wrap fruit for a journey, to cover market baskets, or to serve on festive occasions as napkins and tablecloths.

The hat may be made of straw, palm leaf, rushes, cowhide, felted wool. Homemade hats are usually decorated with ribbons or designs of the tribe, or, if worn by dignitaries on ceremonial days, dyed black. Many villages distinguish their hats with a special feature—a very wide or rolled brim, a peaked or square crown, ribbons gaily embroidered with animals or flowers. The hat of felted wool is stretched over forms of black beeswax to attain peculiar shapes for ritual wear. If the wearer can afford more than one, he sometimes wears two or three, one on top of the other. In Santa Maria de Jesús, this felt resembles the top hat. Manufactured felt hats are increasingly supplanting the homemade varieties.

Cloaks—Capixajes

This *capa y saya* or cape and skirt is made of white cotton or of wool either natural black-brown or dyed blue or black. It is woven in one long piece with a hole in the center for the head and has fringed ends. It may be short, stopping at the waist, or fall to the knees or ground. If long, it is bound about the waist with a colored sash. Some varieties have a sort of seamless sleeve which flies free; some with these sleeves have cuffs that fasten at the wrist. Obviously an adaptation of the long vestment of the early Spanish priest, it is frequently worn as a ceremonial garment or as a sign of rank.

Footwear—Caites or Zapatos

Whether mundane or ceremonial, the footwear of the Indian is a sandal. The *caite* or common sandal is nothing more than a leather sole with thongs to fasten it to the ankle. In the mountain regions, this has a heel cup and heel. The *sandalia* or ceremonial sandal today provides almost complete covering for the foot, the uppers being of leather, frequently dyed and decorated and fastened with shiny tin buckles. Many Indians either through necessity or preference go barefoot.

Raincoats and Umbrellas—Zuyacales

Palm leaves sewed together to form a long rectangle provide these combination garments. They are thrown round the shoulders like a cape or placed over the head so that the rain streams off front and back. On the cape style, the strips of palm hang free like a fringe. Every Indian on the trail carries a *zuyacal* from May to November. When not in use, it is tightly rolled and tied to his carry-all.

Canes and Staffs—Palos or Varas

Staffs are carried by every Indian trader and burden bearer on the road. As a sign of office, each official wears a short cane, stained black or brown, highly polished and tipped with silver and long black silk tassels. When one official enters the presence of another of higher rank, he places his *vara* on the table between them. There it remains until the interview ends as a sign that in the presence of higher authority, he himself has none.

Bags and Pocketbooks—Matates, Redes, Bolsas, Morrales

Every Indian must have his bag to carry his provisions on the trail, his money, his various papers of identification and vouchers proving that he has complied with all military and civil obligations.

These bags are woven of wool, sisal or henequen, hemp or jute fiber in a tight or loose mesh in all shapes and sizes. Witch doctors' bags are small and particularly fine in texture. Bags for general use are the natural color of the fiber; for dress wear some are black and white, strikingly patterned with small black figures or with colored strands.

Large bags or *redes* are loose netlike weaves that can be drawn together with a cord. They are worn on the back by man and beast to carry coal, charcoal, fruit and vegetables, any loose bulk, to market. Large ones are slung from the tumpline about the Indian's forehead. It is not uncommon to see an Indian bearing two or three of these *redes* filled with charcoal while his little mule carries but one or two; the reason is that the mule is a valuable animal, worth eight dollars or more and must not be abused.

Originally the purse that held the Indian's valuables was a tube of bamboo or cane, hollowed out and polished. Later a tin cylinder of the same shape and size was substituted. Today an Indian drawing his *bolsa* from his bag is apt to display a modern purse of leather.

Tumplines—Mecapales

These must be considered both an article of dress and the laboring Indian's most valued possession. They are made of oxhide, cut to the width and height of the forehead and worn with the hairy side next the skin. In time the hair wears off and both sides are alike, but by that time the tumpline has become moulded to the shape of the head. To this band are fastened the ropes to support whatever burden is to be carried. The Indian man never thinks of carrying anything on his head.

Carry-alls—Cacastes

Ordinarily a carry-all is not a part of costume, but those worn on the backs of Indian traders and bearers during most of their waking hours must be considered articles of dress in Guatemala. A wooden crate set on short legs, a *cacaste* is between three and four feet high. It contains a vender's merchandise, sometimes serves as a chair on which to transport people. Usually it is enveloped in a large string bag (*red*) to which is tied a small bundle of *ocote* (resinous firewood), small onions and garlic, a coffee pot, a box of matches, raincoat and extra poncho.

COSTUMES OF THE WOMEN

Blouse—Huipil

The name comes from the Aztec and means *mi tapado,* "my covering." The *huipil* is always the most striking and prized feature of a woman's dress. It may be short, extending only part way to the waistline; tucked into the waist; long, extending under the skirt to form a sort of petticoat, or outside, hanging loose almost to the knees.

Some are very wide and loose, made of two or three widths of the loom, with the sections joined together by a heavy *randa* or satin stitch in brilliant contrasting colors or embroidered together with a flowered design. Some are finished round the neck with embroidery, others with a ribbon binding, a ruffle of net or of the material.

The women of Cobán wear an all-white *huipil* of soft and lacy shadow work, but the majority of blouses are entirely covered with woven or embroidered designs in color or have a large area of design on back or shoulders or about the neck. Extra *huipiles* serve as coats, as lingerie, as a covering for the head when entering church, or if need be, as a shopping bag.

When working in the fields or at home, women frequently wear the *huipil* inside out to protect it from sun and dirt, and women in the markets do likewise to preserve it from foreign buyers.

Skirts—Refajos

Although there appear to be almost as many ways of wearing a skirt as there are women, in reality all fall into one of two classes: the tightly wrapped skirt (*envuelto*) and the pleated (*plegado*). The first is from five to five and a half yards in length, the second, eight yards.

Skirt lengths, called *cortes* usually but *morgas* if the material is very heavy and closely woven, are made and sold in exactly these dimensions, neither more nor less. Worn, some extend from waist to ground, some stop short of the knee, others extend halfway to the ankle. To save wear, the pleated skirts are hemmed on both sides so that either one can serve as top or bottom. Either wrapped or pleated, they are fastened about the waist with a sash or dexterous twist impervious to the laws of gravity.

Sashes—Fajas

If stiff and narrow, the sash is wound many times about the woman's waist. If wide—and frequently when made of wool—it is looped round from two to five times to form a firm girdle. In addition, the sash serves as purse or cache for candles to be burned in the village church. An extra one may be extended round a baby to hold him to his mother's back.

Sashes may be woven of almost any color, but the generally preferred style is of black and white stripes. Some are decorated from one end to the other; some only in the center. Fringes, straight or intricately knotted, or tassels of many colors complete them.

White cotton, decorated with tribal designs in colors, is used for the wide maternity belts worn under the costume. Into this, the women of San Juan Sacatepéquez sew two obsidian points so that if one pregnant woman meets another, each will retain her own baby.

Shawls—Perrajes

Shawls are gradually replacing the extra *huipil* as a wrap. Woven for the most part on foot looms, they are made of cotton or a cotton-and-wool mixture, though recently the all-rayon creation has appeared on the market. Some are made of two lengths of material, sewed together and fringeless; others are three yards long, tie-dyed and finished with wide, knotted fringes or tassels.

In use they are worn over the head and shoulders or looped round the baby and tied over the chest. When not in use they are folded over one arm or worn with a casual air on the head. The women of Mixco, famous as wet nurses, wear large white cotton squares as shawls. These are folded so that the point almost reaches the hem of the skirt in the back.

Headdresses—Cintas or Tocoyales

Really ribbons, cords or narrow strips of cloth from two to twenty yards in length, the *cintas* are combined with the hair to achieve spectacular, beautiful or grotesque effects. They are worn instead of hats and to enhance the attraction of the hair in which the women—and their men—take great pride. Recently an epidemic at San Juan Sacatepéquez brought down a government order that the women's long hair should be cut short. At once, all the Indian officials of the village donned their ceremonial costumes and descended on Guatemala City to interview the President and have the order canceled. It was.

Cintas are of plain colors, of elaborately striped or embroidered design, sometimes finished with tassels.

Tocoyales are perhaps the most commonly worn headdress. Strands of colored wool—ribbon is a modern vogue—twisted first by hand are woven into the two long black braids which may then be wrapped round the head so that strands of the wool stand up in all directions, or may be allowed to hang down the back. In this case the *tocoyales* may extend below the braids to the hem of the skirt, where, if they are of ribbon, they end in a large waggling bow.

The women of Santa Maria Chiquimula achieve a striking effect with black cord and large tassels, winding the hair about their heads in such a way that the tassels hang down at the sides. Into this mound they put any hair that falls out, as it is bad luck to lose even one hair; also any money they may earn at the market.

The headdress of Cobán, called *tupui* or Coral Serpent, is very distinctive. The ceremonial *tupui,* a complicated strand of yellow and red wools three yards and a half long, is wound into two braids that fall down the back to end in enormous tassels. For the mundane *tupui,* the cord is wound like a tight casing around one braid.

In Tamahú and Tucurú, red cloth cut into narrow strips is wound round and round two braids until they resemble small red tires. These are crossed above the forehead to form a huge crownless turban. Some villages, like Santiago, are known for their halo headdresses. Yards of narrow, closely woven ribbon are first bound round the braid, then the braid bound round the head and then round that yards and yards of ribbon are wound until the completed headdress represents a halo several inches wide—an effect very becoming to most women. Totonicapán women have created one of the most beautiful effects: wide silk ribbons are tied round the head bandanna fashion and crowned with enormous balls of brilliant colors, tipped with silver.

Footwear—Zapatos

In their own villages women seldom wear anything on their feet. Occasionally for a long journey they don a simple sandal—*caite*—consisting of a leather sole and thongs to tie it about the ankles. In towns and cities they acquire a taste for shoes and stockings.

Jewelry—Alhajas

Rings (*anillos*), earrings (*arretes*), and necklaces (*chachales*) are worn by every woman who can possess them. In some villages unmarried girls wear quantities of ornaments but discard all except one necklace when they marry. In others it is the married women, particularly the matrons of the *cofradias,* who gleam and tinkle.

Several rings, usually broad silver bands bearing a dove, two clasped hands or a cheap stone, will be worn on one hand. Earrings of gold or silver may be worn as flat ornaments against the lobes of the ear or dangle from ear to shoulder. The women of Chajul pierce their ears in several places through which they slip thin woolen strands and knot them in small tassels.

Necklaces are the crowning adornment, however, some women wearing dozens of strings of beads and coins to form a nest out of which their heads rise oddly. Once these necklaces were of jade and silver coins; now they are of cheap glass, tinsel or pearl.

COSTUMES OF CHILDREN

In the lowlands children run nude until they are six or seven years of age. In the cool and cold sections, a child, almost as soon as it can wear anything, is dressed as a small duplicate of father or mother. The only strictly "baby" feature is a cap called *mon-*

tera or *gorra,* beautifully decorated with tribal symbols. This must be worn—preferably down over the eyes—for at least three months to preserve the child from the glance of anyone with the Evil Eye.

Among the older, purer tribes, such as the Quiché, the symbols on the boys' trousers and the length of the girls' skirts indicate their age and whether they are married or unmarried.

The law of costume even applies to the dolls the children play with. These are crudely carved of wood in one piece or with movable limbs and dressed as duplicates of their small owners.

VIII

HIS ARTS

LITERATURE

LONG before the Christian Era, the Maya had achieved a rich literary tradition. Hieroglyphs and symbolic figures painted and carved on ceramics of all kinds, on buildings and temples, formed their first recorded writing. These describe in detail the events of their daily lives, their religious rituals, customs, achievements.

Next came books or *codices* to reveal through human and animal figures and innumerable hieroglyphs their complex life. These were made on deerskin, *amatle* bark, or prepared lime-coated paper folded accordion-fashion and painted in several colors. Only three of these Codices are extant; owned by museums in Dresden, Paris and Madrid, they, like the Maya, are lost to Guatemala.

On this Maya foundation, post-Maya tribes built their own literature, both written and spoken. The Spaniards destroyed the books but they could not seal the tongues and to Indians blessed with "the gift of the word" fell the task of transmitting history and legend by word of mouth. This literature is still heard, debased and changed perhaps, on the lips of the village storytellers. And as each tells the tales that were taught to him, he trains a successor to tell the tales in turn to the next generation.

Even after the Conquest the Indians continued to write of their traditions and customs in their own tongue, but this literature, like everything else, took on a post-Conquest flavor and features of the Christian teachings became inextricably blended with the teachings of the ancestors. The Maya-Quiché Bible, the *Popul-Vuh,* for example, not only repeats the story of Adam and Eve as the explanation of the origin of that nation, but makes it four times better. Four Adams were created from cornpaste by the gods; four Adams went to sleep and woke to find four beautiful Eves sleeping at their sides. And the chronicle of the Cakchiquel nation tells of the time when, on coming to a great body of water, their ancestors struck it with their redwood staffs and the waters, rolling back, allowed them to cross on dry land to the other side.

From the Indian writers of the Colonial period come the books called *Chilam-Balam—Chilam Balam de Chumayel, Chilam Balam Mani, Chilam Balam de Nabula* and others. Though each took its name from the village on the Yucatan peninsula where it was written, they must all be included here because they concern the intensive Maya civilization developed on Guatemala soil. In them is traced the history of the Maya from 160 A.D. for 1400 consecutive years.

In the latter part of the seventeenth century a mouldering manuscript was found in the wall of the convent of the church in Chichicastenango by the Spanish priest, Francisco Ximenez. It turned out to be the *Popul-Vuh* or "Manuscript of Chichicastenango" as it is called today. Authorship was ascribed to the devout Indian convert, Diego Reinoso, but its true writer is unknown. In it are related the history of the Maya-Quiché nation and traditions concerning their mythology and symbols.

Another invaluable record is the "Annals of the Cakchiqueles" or "Records of Tecpán-Atitlán." This traces the chronology of the ruling dynasties of the Cakchiquel nation both before and after the Conquest and also includes many of their legends. Its author was the Indian convert, Francisco Hernandes Arana Xajilá of Sololá, a descendant of the ruling House of the Bats.

Several extant records of territorial grants of this period also contain significant historical data. The most interesting perhaps is the "Territorial Titles of the Nobles of Totonicapán."

Of their creative literature and drama, the outstanding example is the famous dance pageant of the Rabinal nation, the *Rabinal Achi*. This is based on a legend and, as transcribed by Brasseur de Bourbourg and published in France in 1862, reveals both intellectual content and scope.

Rabinal Achi, brave and handsome prince of the ruling house of the Rabinaleros, was finally successful in defeating Queché

Achi, brave and handsome prince of the Cunen and Chahul peoples, in a long and bitter battle. Queché Achi was taken captive and condemned to be sacrificed alive to the gods of the Rabinaleros. The long drama describes the honor in which the king of the Rabinal nation held his royal prisoner, granting him every privilege but one—that he be allowed to return to his home to bid farewell to his mountains and valleys. On the eve of his sacrifice, he first dances before the throne with the priests, the Twelve Eagles and Twelve Tigers who formed the royal bodyguard, then after gazing in farewell at his distant homeland, he ascends the high altar for the sacrifice.

For four centuries the *naturales,* as the Indians prefer to be called, were enslaved body and soul and their arts with them. Although many could read and write in their own language, as many can today, they had neither opportunity nor heart for creative literature. Today a few, rising above the multitude, have begun to interpret their people, their customs and tribal symbols. Today, too, the new generations are being taught to read and write in the language of their forefathers' conquerors. Tomorrow in this tongue they may not only continue the interrupted record of their people but create a literature of their own.

INDIAN DANCES

When the Conquerors had time to observe the new people they had conquered, they found that one *costumbre* the Indians stressed was the dance. Whether it concerned the gods, victories in battle, or the planting and harvesting of the corn, each dance was a solemn ritual, presented only on most important religious occasions.

Spanish priests, simultaneously horrified at the symbolism of the fertility dances and eager to make use of this new medium for proselyting, suppressed some, adapted others, and substituted new ones. The Indians as promptly gave to the new or adapted dances their original significances with the result that pagan rituals of utmost sanctity were performed under Christian guise. Some of these dances continue to be performed at the present day in their modified form.

Although in significance and importance many of these dances equal or excel those of the Southwest Indians in the United States, little is known of them and less written. Anciently they were taught by word of mouth and still are, but after the Conquest they were written down in both the Indian tongue and Spanish. Copies now are either owned by a village or rented with the costumes for the use of the village elder or maestro who trains the dancers.

Gaudy costumes, grinning masks and grotesque antics may suggest that dancers and spectators are engaged in an amusing entertainment. Actually all are taking the dance and themselves very seriously. The score or more of dancers are leading men in their communities, chosen as an honor or permitted to take part in order to fulfil a sacred vow.

They must be men of great physical strength and endurance to undergo the long months of preparation as well as the fiesta itself when for three or four days they must dance almost continuously. And they must be men of means, able to contribute financially and to give long hours daily to rehearsals. Several days before the fiesta begins they must purify themselves and refrain from women until the close of the ceremonies. Women are never permitted to take part in ritual dances; their roles are danced by men.

Steps are simple but exact and a man loses considerable prestige who fails to perform perfectly in public. In general, the dancers are divided into two lines as in a Virginia Reel, and as in a reel, each man goes through the same steps in turn. As few can read, they are taught their lines by rote and one should be impressed when listening to speeches from several minutes to an hour long, delivered in a high plaintive voice without a slip. That the dancers of today have only a vague conception of the significance of steps or words is evident. To them it is sufficient to perform according to tradition.

Costumes range from skins of deer, sheep, tigers, squirrels, monkeys and other animals to the elaborate regalia used indiscriminately to symbolize Spanish conquerors, bull fighters or any important human characters. Incredibly gaudy, made of cheap velvets and silks in a clamor of clashing colors, ruffled and fringed and ribboned, they are further embellished with gold braid, tinsel, imitation jewels, coins and mirrors.

Hats are of velvet or silk, plumed and rosetted. High boots of red or black leather are worn by the chief characters, shoes and stockings by the rest. As a final touch the leading dancers can always be distinguished by the large, black cotton umbrella hooked over one arm and sometimes by a folded bathtowel. Other accessories include gourds filled with dried seeds and small bells which rattle and tinkle constantly.

Wigs of sisal fiber are stylized affairs with long blond or red curls falling over the shoulders. Masks originally were of beautifully carved wood, but papier maché or decorated gourds now serve equally well. For the Conquerors, the faces are a bright smooth pink, the lips drawn back in an empty, vicious smirk that in time fills the onlooker with something of the horror the Indians must have felt for the Spaniards. As these masks are usually smaller than the face, the neck and exposed parts are tightly wrapped in cloth. These wrappings are frequently not removed during the three or four days of dancing, many of the dancers suffering the discomfort as part of their vow.

As the costumes and accessories are rented and the community pays the fees, on the ability of the community to rent simple or elaborate costumes depends the choice of dances to be given. Two principal costume houses serve the entire country. One, in the city of Totonicapán, is famous throughout Central America. Miguel Chuj, who inherited it from his father as his father inherited it from his, does a fabulous business annually.

Some time before the fiesta, two or three Indians from a village will set out on the long trek—frequently traveling days—to secure the costumes. In their heads or bags are the measurements and requirements of each dancer. When the costumes arrive in the village, they are cared for like crown jewels. A guard stands over them day and night. Daily they are brushed and cleaned, sunned and if necessary mended.

Music for the dances is almost the least factor considered. For all but two, which now require a special post-Conquest instrument (music, page 116), a *marimba,* drums and fifes, anything that will pound out the rhythm is satisfactory. As whatever the melody, the rhythm is the same, no special music is necessary for any dance except the secular *El Son*.

The great day arrives. The dancers, perfected in their roles and endurance, begin the long ordeal. They must dance before the church, before the different *cofradias*—sometimes as many as fifteen in one town—and in the daily or twice daily processions which circle the cobbled streets for miles. If there are any interludes, they must return to the church and continue dancing.

Of the wide variety of pre-Columbian and post-Columbian dances and the innumerable variations developed on each one, even named by each village, usually only one or two can be given during a fiesta. Of pre-Columbian survivals, the Deer Dance (*Baile del Venado*); the Dance of the Jesters (*Baile de los Gracejos*), and the Dance of the Snake (*Baile de la Culebra*) are most popular.

The Deer Dance symbolizes the struggle between Mankind and Animals. In its original form it is a long and involved ritual. For forty days before it can be presented the dancers must abstain from women. And some time before the dance, the men of the village, to the accompaniment of music and fireworks, proceed to the forest to select a tree that is straight as a rod for at least 75 feet. When this is stripped, it is carried back with more music and rockets to the village plaza and placed under guard. If by chance, contracting, it should emit strange sounds at night, the days of labor must be repeated and a new tree secured, for the sound is the voice of the spirit of the tree saying that this one is not ready to take part in the dance.

The pole is laid beside the large hole excavated to support it and here the shaman presides over a ceremony of tribal significance. Various characters dressed as animals assist him. Candles, pine needles and *pom,* the sacred incense, are placed around the hole, and on the pole nine clay containers filled with *pom*.

When candles and incense are burning and fireworks have been set off, long prayers are offered. Then the animals embrace the pole and flagellate it nine times in the form of the Maya cross, symbol of the four directions. The pole is then fitted into the hole, and when securely based, incense and prayers are offered it by the witch doctor.

Now a rope is passed from the top of the pole to the peak of the church. If anyone should pass beneath this rope, superstition says that the dancers performing on it will fall. Frequently when this happens, a new pole has to be secured and a new ceremony gone through. To prevent this, guards, armed with whips, stand watch to beat off anyone who approaches.

On the day of the fiesta, the witch doctor, a dancer dressed as a monkey, and others in the skins and masks of puma, tiger, tapir, lion and other wild animals, gather in one line beside the pole. In the opposite line are the dancers representing Mankind, one of them dressed as a jester, others as Old Man and Old Woman, personifications of the ancestors. The monkey embraces the witch doctor with the sign of the cross, then climbs to the peak of the church. The shaman climbs to the top of the pole.

There he waits with open arms while the monkey, performing gymnastic feats and ludicrous antics en route, crosses on the rope to him. Once more they embrace, then the monkey descends the pole, rousing the crowd to cheers as he hangs by hands or feet performing all manner of foolery. On the ground, dancers, dressed as dogs, howl dismally.

When the monkey touches the ground, the dance begins, animals and mankind dancing solemnly round and round him in a very simple step. That's all; there isn't any more. But sometimes these dancers have been known to dance—with only very brief rests— for fifteen days before the animals finally yield to the domination of man.

A village that can afford to present this Dance of the Deer is pleased and proud, believing that it must surely have won favor with the gods. When the dance at last is over, the pole is lowered and chopped into small pieces so that each villager may have a bit as an amulet of good luck. Most villages can afford to present only a simple variation, dispensing with the pole and allowing man to win victory in from one to four days.

The Dance of the Jesters reveals clear title to the claim that it is descended from the old fertility rites. Both performance and costumes, as a result of improvements imposed by Spanish priests, are farcical. The men are dressed as laborers or in the skins of sheep and deer. Each carries a whip and a gourd rattle. Woman is represented by a man in a costume derived from the Mother Hubbard and coyly flaunts a large colored handkerchief.

The theme is revealed as rivalry for her favor between Man and Animal. One dancer at a time from one line or the other dances before her with gestures ranging from the suggestive to the obscene, inviting her to go with him. During and between these dances, the jester performs hilarious antics. At length a stranger enters the dance and, as strangers often do, proves successful where the home-town rivals fail.

Before the Snake Dance, a number of men of the village, accompanied by the witch doctor, go into the forests to find a snake. They burn copal and candles until the snake is located, then extract its fangs or sew up its mouth. Placing it in a clay jar or gourd, they carry it back to make its entrance to the dance.

These dancers also are dressed as laborers, wearing large hats and carrying whips. Some are burlesque figures: one is dressed as a woman, another as a European. Their masks are of unpainted or dull-painted wood.

In some versions the bewildered snake, representing Evil, is danced with by each man in turn, his steps and gestures symbolizing the struggle between good and evil. Good finally conquers and the snake is thrust down the neck of the dancer's blouse or jacket to be greeted by howls of applause when it slips out of a trouser leg. There it is seized by another dancer and the steps repeated.

Of the post-Columbian dances adapted by the Spanish priests are the Dance of the Devils, in which saints struggle to victory over the evil ones; the Dance of St. George and the Dragon, and the Jewel Dance in honor of the Virgin Mary. More popular, however, are those based on historical Spanish themes.

The Dance of the Conquest (*Baile de la Conquista*),[1] written by a Spanish priest in 1542, is oddly enough the most popular. It

[1] Recently in Chichicastenango a minor version of the Conquista, the Ajitz (Witch Doctor), has been revived for the entertainment of tourists. The leading dancer is the Ajitz who foretold the coming of the white man and the conquest of the Indians.

celebrates the victory of Spanish arms over the Indians, but the Indian descendants today dance the roles of either conquerors or conquered with equal zest, seemingly unaware of the significance the theme has for them. Similarly, the Dance of the Volcano (*Baile del Volcán*) commemorates the famous victory of the Spanish and their Mexican allies over the Indian insurrection in 1526 in the shadow of the volcano Agua. Another favorite is the *Baile de los Moros,* in which the Spaniards conquer the Moors.

For some reason, Indians living in colonies on the coffee fincas prefer the Dance of the Bull Fighters above all others. In this the dancers form two opposing lines; each in turn performs a solo dance, challenges a bull, dances a symbolic dance of combat with him, invites a toreador from the other side to try his luck, dances a minuet with him, then, still dancing, retires to his own side. Last, the leader, identified variously as Alvarado, as the chief of the colony or the owner of the finca, challenges the bull to the death. The leader is gored, and, dying, bequeaths his possessions and counsels to family and friends.

Of the ritual dances, the two most famous are the dance pageants or spectacles, *Palo Volador* and the *Rabinal Achi.*

Palo Volador (The Flying Pole) is another pre-Columbian ritual, possibly of Mexican origin. It is performed before the planting or harvesting of the corn, depending on the time when the village holds its chief fiesta. In Chichicastenango and the Quiché region, it is given in honor simultaneously of the god of nature, whose manifestations are found in the sun, rain and wind—the essentials for the corn—and St. Thomas, patron saint of the village.

Whether the crop has been good or bad, the dance is performed just the same during the three days preceding December 21—the Saint's Day—and with more fervor perhaps after a poor crop in order that the god of nature will pardon whatever sin of theirs brought on such a punishment and also to prevent his being offended and prejudiced against the next crop.

Practically the same ritual is gone through to secure the pole as in the case of the Dance of the Deer, with one addition—that no women may approach the pole.

When on December 16 the pole is being set up before the church,

a young man masked and costumed as a monkey rises with it, cling-
ing to a small frame lashed to the top. From there he hauls up
and fixes four or five ladders, each 20 feet long, to the length of
the pole.

Then with much difficulty a swinging rectangular frame is sus-
pended from a socket at the top of the pole and fixed in place.
Two ropes long enough to reach to the ground are wound tightly
about the top of the mast and passed over the sides of the frame,
their ends knotted in loops. Performers climb the pole by twos,
seat themselves in the loops, and swing out over space. As the
wheel or frame turns, the rope unwinds and the pull of gravity
carries the fliers in widening circles to the ground, where dancers
in brilliant costumes are performing patiently.

Originally four fliers in vivid bird costumes and four assistants
swung down at the same time, while the monkey (*El Mico*), symbol of the messenger between the gods and man, performed antics
of ceremonial burlesque. Because of deaths and accidents, many
communities banned the *Palo Volador;* others limited it to two
fliers.

From a solemn ceremony it is rapidly degenerating today into
something like a carnival merry-go-round or Ferris wheel on which
any man may ride for a small sum.

The *Rabinal Achi* (page 101), even more famous, has not been
performed since 1856. Its elaborate ceremony and expensive costumes are beyond the capacity of any village at present. This must
be the fate eventually of all ceremonial dances. Changing economic and social conditions, the time, labor and money involved
have already debased and simplified old rituals until their original
significances are lost.

The one secular dance, on the other hand, is becoming increasingly popular, as the ladinos have now taken to it enthusiastically.
El Son (The Sound or Tune) has three variations—exhibition,
comedy, and social.

El Son San Juanero (St. John), the exhibition dance, permits
both men and women to occupy the floor at the same time. The
men carry handkerchiefs which they wave to the rhythm of the
marimba. The women dance coyly, lifting their skirts a bit with

the tips of their fingers and keeping their eyes on the ground. Each dances alone until, at the conclusion, the men kneel before the women and place their handkerchiefs at their feet.

The comedy dance, *El Son del Borracho* (Dance of the Drunkard), is usually performed either by men or by two couples. The men, holding bottles under their arms, stagger about as they dance in simulated or real intoxication.

For all forms of *El Son* the step is the same, a simple jiglike movement. Until recently in the social dance men and women danced independently, but the Indians, quick to copy ladino styles, now permit a man and woman to dance face to face. To this variation the ladinos have added an accenting stamp of the foot.

INDIAN MUSIC

[*For the technical information on this subject we are indebted to Professor Jesús Castillo of Quezaltenango, who has made the only scientific study of Indian music in Guatemala, a study extended over forty years. Composer and teacher of music, he is recognized both in Central America and abroad as the authority on Indian music and instruments.*]

If the Tolteca Indians of Mexico, believed to have been the common ancestor of Aztec and Maya, came originally from Asia, as some contend, then the East must be allowed some influence on Indian music. After the Conquest Spanish music influenced Indian as Indian in turn influenced Spanish. No evidence indicates, however, that the Indian was incapable of creating his own music, and much proves that he had his own musical forms and instruments long before the Conquerors arrived with guitars and banjos in their kits.

Modern excavation of Maya cities has revealed a design depicting two Indians en route to meet their king. Preceding them is a musician playing an enormous *caracol* or shell. The *caracol* itself is significant of the antiquity of music in Guatemala as it is decorated in the same technique as that used on Maya jewelry. Also, a small picture in relief has been found in which Indians dance, surrounded by musicians playing various instruments. And in the *Popul-Vuh*—Bible of the Quiché—several references are made to singing and playing and to different types of flutes brought from legendary Tulan on the great migration to the lands of Guatemala.

To discover the most potent influence, if not the source, of Indian music in Central America, one need only listen to the choral of a luxuriant tropical nature, particularly to the birds who find the cornfields a happy hunting ground. Of these, two varieties, the *cenzontle de agua* or *primavera* and the *cenzontle de huatal,* have a song containing a perfect natural scale. The Indians call the *cenzontle* "the bird of 400 voices." [1]

In its abundance of arpeggios, tonal range, elements of modulation, syncopation, pauses, rests, transitions from dominant to tonic, are all the constructive musical elements on which the foundation of the theory of harmonics is based today. More, the song of the *cenzontle* contains only the intervals from second through sixth. These are identical with the intervals employed in his music by the Indian of Guatemala. He uses no more, no less.

There is also the song of the *guarda barranca* which consists of a succession of intervals and notes, produced so rapidly that they appear simultaneous. Analysed, it proves to be composed of quarter tones and other tonal fractions, some so minute that there is as yet no universal method of recording them.

Songs of native birds are only one of a myriad sources provided the Indian by nature for his music. He listened also to the wind in the trees, the rain, the sound of falling water, the waves on the shores of lake and sea. It is because his music follows so closely on Guatemala's own natural sources that Professor Castillo and European musical authorities consider it so incontrovertibly original in character.

The Indians did not write down their music but transmitted it from father to son by word of mouth and ear from generation to generation. That they once had their own composers is evident in the fragments of musical ideas surviving. Professor Castillo has five complete Indian compositions and numerous fragments. The ballet music for the dance-pageant, *Rabinal Achi,* has been preserved in its integrity, and in 1856 when Brasseur de Bourbourg wrote down words, stage directions, details of costumes and prop-

[1] Note 8.

erties, he also secured a transcription of the music which was published in France. Samples of Indian music are extant whose scale phrasing cannot be found in Spanish-Moorish rhythms.

True Indian music, in general, is of three types, all characterized by a profound feeling for nature and a complete lack of sensuality, a lack in perfect accord with the chastity and high moral standards of the race before the advent of the white man. Another characteristic, more apparent to foreign ears, is the strain of melancholy that pervades every composition no matter for what purpose it is performed.

The effect is symphonic rather than harmonious or melodious. But when, during the annual military review, an Indian corps of drums and trumpets announces the arrival of the President, it is strikingly impressive, reducing the martial strains of a hundred-piece military band to a pallid second.

Ritual or ceremonial music, intended to please and curry favor with the gods, is the oldest form. Its structure is very archaic with the second major as its basic interval. Prolonged notes alternate with fragments of rapidly played scales to produce an effect extremely melancholy and of scant esthetic significance. When carefully observed, the resemblance of this ritual music to the songs of *cenzontles, guardas barrancas* and other native birds is clear.

Rabinalero music is seldom heard now. It contains more melodic ideas than ritual compositions and is of a distinct warlike flavor. Early examples extant employ major and minor thirds most frequently; later music uses also major and minor seconds.

Finally there is the *Tzijolaj,* the music of the ancient shepherds. This has greater resources, employing a major truncated scale of which only the fifth and seventh tones are missing and using all the intervals except the sixth.

Six Varieties of Mayan Music and the Scales on Which They Are Based

Interpreted by Jesús Castillo

1st EXAMPLE:

(Protracted into the C Key)

This example illustrates an autochthonous tetraphonic type of intonation heard in the Quiché region. It lacks half tones and its scale is protracted into the key of C.

2nd EXAMPLE:

(Tetraphonic Scale in C)

Although of the same type as No. 1, this is somewhat different in character.

3rd EXAMPLE:

This, from a tune of the Mam Indians, reveals a striking resemblance to the songs of native birds, particularly the *pito real,* or "royal whistler," of the linnet family.

4th EXAMPLE:

Full of poetry and mystery, this music can be linked to no definite region or tribe in Guatemala. If compared with the European scale, its scales appear somewhat anomalous.

5th EXAMPLE:·

A rare type of music. Note the irregularity in its descending scale.

6th EXAMPLE:

Here we have an example of the type of intonation known as *son* (tune). It is distinguished by a strange melodic rhythm.

INSTRUMENTS

No study has been made of the instruments of the various Indian nations of Guatemala, but those of the Quiché, studied by Professor Castillo, may be taken as typical; others may differ in form or use while retaining the same general characteristics.

Their melodic instruments are *el caracol, la ocarina* and *el tzijolaj.*

The *caracol* is a large shell blown upon like a horn to give sounds somewhat similar to those of a bagpipe, though the range of tones is less and limited to the middle register. Only Indian players can extract the full range, those of Cobán achieving complete melodies. Its original purpose was to summon warriors for battle.

The *ocarina* is of very ancient origin and for centuries was made of stone or baked clay in the form of idols, strange animals and beings. Although a flute, it bore no resemblance to the obligatory cylindrical form of European flutes and must be considered a truly original Indian instrument. Today ocarinas are made of reeds, cane or bone.

The *tzijolaj,* the Indian piccolo, is made of cane or reed, usually with three, sometimes four, perforations. It was used by the Maya Quiché for ritual music as well as by the shepherds.

Percussion or noise-making instruments are more numerous than the melodic, and though original in form, are of course not original instruments with the Indians of Guatemala, as every primitive people has evolved its own.

El tun is a drum made of a section of hollowed log, its ends sealed. Two rectangular slits are cut in one side of the cylinder, and these, when played upon by rubber-tipped sticks, produce sonorous tones. This was an all-important instrument for Maya Quiché rituals and was also used by the Rabinal people with two trumpets to accompany the *Rabinal Achi* ballet.

El tambor is another drum of ancient origin still in use today. It comes in three sizes, large, small and medium, and as a rule is covered with the traditional deerskin. In the *Popul-Vuh,* it is called *el atabal* (kettle drum) and in the *Rabinal Achi,* the war drum.

Los chinchines are rattles made out of gourds of the morro tree or calabash vines. Filled with seeds or grains of corn, beans, etc., they are almost identical with the *maracas* of Cuba.

El ayotl or *la tortuga* is made out of an empty turtle shell. Tapped with bits of bone or hardwood, it sounds like a small drum.

Another sonorous instrument whose Indian name is lost resem-

bles the *guira* of Cuba. This is a large hollowed bone, grooved
transversely on one side for its entire length. Sound is produced
by rubbing a shell forcefully and in rhythm up and down the
grooves.

To these indigenous Indian instruments many others modeled
on those imported by Spaniards and other foreigners have been
added. One is the *chirimia,* a species of oboe, crudely made and
used to guide the steps for the Dance of the Conquest. Another is
the *zu,* a simple imitation of the European flute, made of cane and
used to guide the steps for the Dance of the Moors and Christians.

The Indians were also quick to make their own adaptations of
violins, guitars, trumpets and other European instruments. During the annual fair in Guatemala City or for special fiestas in the
villages, orchestras of violins and guitars or combinations of Indian
and foreign instruments are frequently one of the most popular
features. They also furnish further proof that the Indian knew
music before the white man taught him. If not, he would not
have been able to adopt and adapt so promptly foreign music and
instruments to his own rhythms and purposes.

The *marimba* is still the subject of controversy and as yet cannot
be classified as truly Indian or truly foreign. Though its origin
is said to be African, it is known that the Indians had a form of
marimba long before the arrival of either black or white man.
This consisted of a string of gourds tied about the waist of the
musician; on them he played with two sticks tipped with rubber.

The simple marimba, a sounding board whose tympanum is
composed of various-sized gourds, can still be seen and heard even
in Guatemala City, but the modern instrument with sounding
tubes of *hormigo* wood and a double or chromatic keyboard is supplanting the gourds and single, natural-scale keyboard.

IX

TWO PEOPLES SET APART

THE CARIBS

THIS unique and little-known people, neither pure Indian nor pure Negro, live along Guatemala's Caribbean seaboard. Their origin, like that of their matriarchal regime, is ancient and involved.

Centuries before the Conquest, fierce and warlike Indian cannibals left their homes about the mouth of the Orinoco River in South America and made their way to the islands now known as the Lesser Antilles. They conquered the tribes there, seized the women of the vanquished, and settled down to continue their own cannibal life and culture. Later some of them emigrated to the mainland of Central America in the neighborhood of the town of Trujillo, Honduras, which the Spanish founded in 1502.

Columbus (in his letters) and early Spanish chroniclers speak of them as Caribs, though, strangely, no mention is made of them in accounts of the Conquest or the years following. John L. Stephens, arriving in Guatemala in 1839 to begin his Odyssey over Central America, visited thriving villages in different regions occupied by what he calls "Carib Indians."

In 1796 the British began importing Negro slaves from the Leeward Islands to settle Roatan and other small islands they had seized off the northern coast of Honduras. Many of these slaves escaped and fled south to hide in the marshes of the coast that surround the tributaries of the Rio Dulce in Guatemala. There they found the Caribs, and from the inevitable intermingling of bloods developed the people known today as Caribs or Morenos.

They should not be confused with descendants of the Negroes brought from Jamaica and its neighboring Caribbean islands in the nineteenth century to work on the banana plantations. In appearance and way of life the Caribs are entirely different. They have their own culture, *costumbres,* dialect, though now they also speak Spanish. Peaceful and orderly, cheerful and healthy, usually found with a smile, a song or both on their lips, they keep to themselves. Well-to-do Caribs live in Livingston in much the same style as well-to-do ladinos; they even have their own club there.

Legend says that the Caribs founded Livingston; in fact, that Marcos Sanchez Diaz, specifically, was its founder. He was a witch doctor who, arriving in this marshy, mosquito-ridden region, disposed of the insects in short order by his magic. Then he sent to Honduras for his people, and with them established a settlement at the mouth of the Rio Dulce which they named Labuga (Mouth of the River). Later, when a port was established there and the Virgin of the Rosary named as its patron saint, Labuga was changed to Livingston to honor the Louisiana jurist whose code of laws had been adopted for Guatemala.

In Carib settlements, women are the dominant sex. They even have a language of their own, unintelligible to the men, in which they talk with one another. They keep the straw-thatched huts meticulously clean, rear the children, cultivate the small cassava patches attached to each house, and run the community in general.

The men hunt and fish and sometimes work on banana plantations. Groups of them go together to work on one plantation. Among them is a head man, known only to themselves, who looks after them and whose orders they obey. If some dispute arises concerning wages or treatment of a member, the owner or manager of the plantation is apt to find himself without the services of the entire group. The head man will have gathered them together and taken them quietly away.

Although Caribs intermarry occasionally with Indians or Negroes, they prefer to marry Caribs "to preserve our descent," of which they are very proud. They celebrate it annually on St. Vincent's Day in May with a Fiesta de Recuerdo de Nuestra Descendencia ("Feast to Commemorate Our Descent").

Their principal food is not the corn of the Indian but the *manioc* root—cassava or mandioca. The root is first mashed or grated till very fine, then the powder is placed in a basket about

twelve feet long, woven from the bayal vine, which grows plentifully along the coast. This basket, called *culebra* (snake), is hung
like a hammock from the rafters of the hut, and the family in turn
or together sit on it until the poisonous juice has been pressed out.
Water is then sluiced over the *culebra* again and again and allowed
to drain. When the powder once more is dry, the family has flour
sufficient to supply round, tortilla-like cakes for some time.

Family life is complicated but very satisfactory. When a man
marries, his family and the bride's join to build them a house.
After the wedding ceremony—performed by a priest if one is
available—the groom goes into the forest to fell trees. These the
bride cuts into firewood lengths, some of which she sells; the rest
she keeps for her own use. This done, she turns to planting and
tending the cassava patch already cleared for her by the provident
groom, and he returns to his hunting and fishing.

Each man marries several wives, and for each wife a separate
house is built and new ground cleared for her cassava patch. The
first wife is the matriarch, ruling the group of wives and having as
her special privilege and responsibility the making, washing and
mending of the clothes of their mutual husband.

When a Carib dies, friends and family gather, the men sitting
in one room, the women in another. For nine days, the oldest
man of the group relates in a monotonous voice—repeating, if
necessary—all that is known both of the public and private life of
the departed. The women in the meantime tell one another
legends and stories. While each speaks, she holds a smooth stone
in her hand. When she finishes, she passes it to another, who carries on.

The Caribs have their own repertoire of dances and songs and
occasions for dancing. Chief of these is the *Yanganu,* which lasts
from Christmas until the Day of the Kings on January 6. On
December 23 the head men of the Caribs go out to search the forests for "Guarinee," the great chief of the festivities. This ceremony may have come down through the centuries from those first
ancestors who left South America, probably members of the
Guarani nation of Brazil and Paraguay.

Guarinee is, of course, a previously chosen member of the com-

munity. He arrives dressed in leaves and acting like a savage.
His first command is that the *Yanganu* must be danced continuously until he is civilized. By January 6 he has gone through several stages of civilization, emerging at last, dressed and in his right
mind, as a Carib.

As in the dances of the Indians of Guatemala, only men take
part, some of them dressed as women. These wear a short skirt
instead of short trousers; otherwise, all wear plumed headdresses,
masks made of window screens, long stockings and low shoes, and
flaunt a large colored handkerchief. Bright ribbons hang from
various parts of the costumes; anklets and bracelets made of rows
and rows of shells clink to the rhythms of the dance.

Music is provided by two drums, the larger one covered with
pelican skin, the smaller with deerskin. Women and other spectators clap their hands and sing to the beat of the drums while the
dancers perform varied and intricate steps.

A special feature of this dance is the *Pio Manati* (probably a corruption of Tio Manatee or "Uncle Sea Cow"), named for the
manatees once plentiful in Lake Izabal. Because it is believed that
the constantly dancing men need doctors, another group (some
also dressed as women) simulate hunchbacks and, clothed in rags,
go through the motions of performing miraculous acts of healing.

Gubito, another dance of ancient origin, is performed only on
rare occasions. A man who becomes ill is thought to be possessed
by the Spirit of Evil. To rid him of the demon, the men of his
family, with a witch doctor or *bulle* as master of ceremonies,
gather in one house. There a hole is dug in the center of the
earthen floor and in it a jar filled with *jiu,* made from cassava
flour, is placed.

While one man dances and leaps back and forth over the *jiu,*
the others dance round and round it, moving no part of their
bodies except the feet, and these they hold tight together.
Throughout the dance they sing festive songs in their own dialect.
At midnight the witch doctor, by his magic, produces a strange
and loud noise on the roof. This is a signal that the Evil Spirit
has departed.

The *jiu* is then served to dancers and sick man. He must eat no

IN CEREMONIAL REGALIA

Officers of a *cofradia* in Quezaltenango in official dress

FIREWORKS MAKERS IN PROCESSION

Scene in Chichicastenango, each man carrying rockets
wrapped in ceremonial textile

Dr. J. J. Dozy

WITCH DOCTORS' CROSSES

On the shore of Lake Chicabal, important center for shaman rituals

Biener

PAGAN RITES

Prayers and incense rising to pagan god from steps of church

Buener   INDIAN BOYS AS COFFEE PICKERS

Osborne   SOLOLA BIRD VENDER

Biener

RELIGIOUS CEREMONIAL PROCESSION
Scene at Patzún: Note the masked dancers in background

Eichenberger

BOUND FOR FIESTA AND FAIR
Indian traders resting on the shore of Lake Atitlán

Biener

GETTING READY TO WEAVE A NEW SKIRT

Santiago Atitlán woman stretching thread on winding frame,
preparatory to weaving: thread colored by resist-dye method

Eichenberger

WEAVING HER OWN COSTUME

San Antonio Aguas Calientes weaver at work on her hand loom

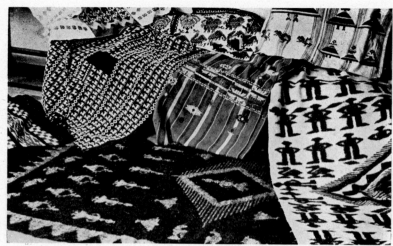

Dr. J. J. Dozy

COTTON AND WOOLEN TEXTILES FROM
INDIAN HAND AND FOOT LOOMS

Biener

MODELING AND DECORATING POTS FOR MARKET

INDIAN DANCE

James McElroy

DANCE OF THE BULL-FIGHTERS
Special performance on the lawns of Finca
el Pacayal in celebration of Holy Week

James McElroy

FINAL SCENE OF THE BULL-FIGHT
The gored leader of the matadors, dying, bequeaths his goods and counsel to his comrades

Eichenberger

INDIAN MUSICIAN FROM SAN MARTÍN SACATEPEQUEZ

Biener

FLUTE AND MARIMBA PLAYERS OF CHICHICASTENANGO
Note the tympanum of the marimba, composed of graded gourds

other food but *jiu* for three days. Whatever remains is placed in
another room for the Evil One to eat if he returns. The immediate family of the invalid finances the expenses of witch doctor and
food.

Like the Indians of Central America, the Caribs were early taken
in charge by the Spanish priests. Today they consider themselves
devout Catholics and have a priest come over once a month from
Puerto Barrios to hold mass, to marry, and to baptise.

A century ago visits by a padre were few and far between.
Stephens, arriving in one settlement with a young Irish priest,
found everyone gathered to welcome them. In his *Incidents of
Travel in Central America* he describes the occasion, a description
that with but few changes could be duplicated today:

> "There was little to be done in the way of marrying, there being a
> scarcity of men for that purpose, as most of them were away fishing
> or at work in the forest; but a long file of women presented them-
> selves, each with a child in her arms, for baptism. Of the first he
> asked a question which in some places it would be considered im-
> pertinent to ask a mother who offered her child for initiation into
> the Church, viz., whether she was married. She hesitated, smiled,
> laughed, and answered No. The padre told her that this was very
> wrong and unbecoming a good Christian, and advised her to take
> advantage of the present opportunity to marry the child's father. She
> answered that she would like to do so, but that he was away cutting
> mahogany; and here, as his questions and her answers had all to pass
> through an interpreter, the affair began to be complicated; indeed,
> so many women interposed, all speaking at once, that the padre be-
> came aware he had touched on delicate ground and so passed on to
> the next."

THE LACANDONES

Today in the isolated area of the Department of Petén that includes the River Ixcán, a tributary of a tributary of the Usumacinta
and in that section of Mexico ceded by Guatemala in 1882, lives
the dwindling remainder of a wild and almost unknown people.
When the Conquerors arrived, however, the Lacandones were so
savage that no outside tribe ventured within their territory.

And from the first Spanish expedition against them in 1555 until 1695 they were victorious too in repulsing every effort of the white man to subdue them. Then Padre Pedro de la Concepción made a peaceful conquest, established the village of Nuestra Señora de los Dolores de Lacandones within their boundaries, and brought them to accept at least a semblance of the forms of Catholicism.

The Lacandones are still wild, primitive and superstitious, antagonistic to outsiders of whatever color and to intercourse with the outside world. Though some of the men now work in the *monterias* or chicle camps and speak a mixture of Maya and Spanish, as late as the memories of living inhabitants in neighboring regions they had no direct and visible contact with Indians of other tribes with whom they traded.

In the dark of the night they brought the peppers they cultivated to their boundary lines and left them there. In the morning Indian traders would remove the peppers and leave dogs in payment. Whether the Lacandones used the animals for food or pets is still unknown.

In appearance they are distinctly savage and give evidence of mixed blood. Some have curly hair and reddish, with sharp features; others, straight black hair, thick lips and flat noses. The men dress in long, loose cotton or fiber tunics, stained in splashes with the red juice of wild berries; they let their hair hang free and unkempt. The women, shorter than the men, wear a long loose *huipil* of unadorned cotton over a tightly wrapped skirt.

Their language is a form of the old Maya tongue. Divided into clans, they live a semi-nomadic life, setting up crude huts in *caribales* or encampments near their cornfields, hunting and fishing grounds. Each clan reveres some animal as the Head or Parent of the group, and all the male members bear its name, transmitting it from father to son. Each clan has its own laws which are strictly enforced.

Polygamy is practised among them, but no intermarriage within the clan is permitted. As the groups are widely scattered and frequently not on good terms, it is often a matter of life and death for an offer of marriage to be carried from one clan to another.

When a woman marries, she must join the clan of her husband, never to see her own again. For this reason, only men can inherit. The woman, in fact, loses all identity, as she not only takes the surname of her husband's clan but must surrender the given name by which all the women of her own clan are called and answer to the name given all women of the husband's clan.

As a feature of the annual fair in November, 1938, a family of Lacandones was secured for the Indian Village. Contact with civilization affected them badly, as they all became ill and were thoroughly miserable until allowed to return to their home.

COLONIAL GUATEMALA

X

THE CONQUEST AND ITS UNKNOWN SOLDIER

ON December 6, 1523, Pedro de Alvarado, 34-year-old Captain of Hernando Cortes, left his commanding officer still deep in the Conquest of Mexico and set forth with an "army" to subjugate the cities of Uclacán (Utatlán) and Guatemala (Iximché or Tecpán-Guatemala) seventy leagues to the south. His army consisted of 120 horsemen and 173 horses, 300 soldiers (including 130 musketeers and crossbowmen), four pieces of artillery, plenty of ammunition, and 200 Mexican Indian warriors.

Cortes' instructions were that Alvarado should "endeavor with the greatest care to bring the people to peace without war and to preach matters concerning our Holy Faith." Alvarado, however, was neither peacemaker nor preacher; one commentator credits him with "almost a lust for murder." From his entrance to Guatemala until the end of 1526, his expedition was a series of massacres.

In spite of his reports that

". . . appeared three or four thousand Indians there; we defeated them. . . . I saw more than 30,000 men coming towards us . . . we attacked them . . ."

the struggle continued month after month with desperate bitterness, the Indians preferring death to submission.

"The country there is very broken," Cortes wrote in excuse to the King,

"and the population very dense and the people so warlike and brave and at the same time so trained in all kinds of warfare, offensive as well as defensive, that they have invented pits and other engines to kill the horses; and though the said Pedro de Alvarado has continued to make war with upwards of 200 horsemen and 500 foot, all Spaniards, besides 5,000 and sometimes even 10,000 Indians, he has been unable to reduce them under Your Majesty's rule, but on the contrary they become stronger every day."

The unknown and savage land was indeed more difficult to conquer than the innumerable Indian foes. Themselves and their horses weighted with armor, the Spaniards had to battle intemperate and variable climates, wild beasts, and venomous insects in clouds so thick they darkened the air; cross treacherous malarial swamps, deserts where neither food nor water was available, virgin forests that no human foot had trod before, rivers that appeared to them like arms of the sea; and climb slopes of the Cordilleras as steep and rugged as those of any mountains in the world. Most of all they had to fight the fear of the unknown in this land where mountains tossed fire and stone into the sky and streams of boiling water ran into others icy cold.

What they lacked in numbers and equipment, they made up in superlative courage, born of fear. There was no turning back; they had to conquer or die. Fanatic religious zeal and love of homeland and King inflamed them—and greed. As one of them wrote, he endured such hardship for Cross and Crown "that I might receive both mundane and heavenly favors." Their greatest strength was their leader, Pedro de Alvarado. Handsome and brave to a fault, avaricious and cruel, he was unconquerable.

In the Municipal Building in Guatemala City there hangs a full-length portrait of Alvarado, restored in 1808, two centuries after his death, by Delfina Luna de Herrera. Strangely, no portrait or sketch seems ever to have been made during the life of this unknown soldier whose Conquest of Guatemala ranks in importance with those of Mexico and Peru.

"Of good size," as Bernal Diaz describes him, "he was well proportioned, with a very cheerful countenance and winning smile. Because he was so handsome (and because his hair and beard were red), the Indians called him *Tonatiuh,* The Sun. He was very active and a good horseman and, above all, frank-hearted and a good talker, and he was very neat in his attitude but with rich and costly clothes. He wore a small gold chain about his neck with a jewel and a ring with a good diamond."

Alvarado was twenty-five when, as just one more obscure young adventurer, he left Badajoz, Spain, to join Diego Velasquez in the Conquest of Cuba, and, in 1519, to serve as Captain under Cortes in the Conquest of Mexico. Inordinately ambitious for wealth and power, he had hardly established his first headquarters ("capital," he called it) in Guatemala in 1524 when, on the ground that some-one else was to be named governor over the land he had not yet conquered, he began bombarding Cortes to publicize him to the King,

> ". . . as he has had no notice of me and for this nobody is to blame but Your Grace for not having given an account to his Majesty of how I have served him . . . in these parts, and where I am, and what I have conquered recently, and the will I have to serve him and will have in future, and how in this service I am lamed in one leg and of how little return I and these hidalgos in my company have received up to the present."

Perhaps he had some reason for his complaint. It is significant that at the same time that Cortes was preparing for an expedition to Guatemala, via Honduras, because, he wrote the King, "the unsettled state of affairs under the administration of Alvarado re-quires my presence," Alvarado, swallowing a rumor that Cortes was dead, prepared to dash for Mexico.

Cortes, after his historic 1000-mile march to Honduras, received word to hurry back to Mexico and mend his own fences, and Al-varado, arriving in Honduras to meet him, learned that he had sailed. Returning unexpectedly to Guatemala, Alvarado found that the tyranny of his brother Gonzalo had roused a general rebellion. The Indians were on the verge of triumph, and three bitter battles, one against 30,000 rebels, were necessary before comparative peace was restored.

Leaving his brother Jorge in charge, Alvarado hurried to Spain to speak for himself. He did very well, receiving from Charles V appointment as governor over the territory he had conquered, and from the Duke of Albuquerque, head of one of the noblest and most powerful families, his young niece, Francesca de la Cueva, in marriage.

In Mexico on his way to Guatemala, Alvarado's glory tarnished. His wife died of fever and, Cortes being absent, his enemies and rivals tossed him in prison. Released on Cortes' return, he did not reach his new capital at Almolonga until 1530.

To a man of his caliber, governing a conquered people offered little satisfaction, particularly when reports of the wealth Pizarro was reaping in Peru reached him. Against the wishes of King and advisers, he equipped an expedition and set sail. Pizarro and Almagro, however, desiring no rivals in Peru, bought him off for 100,000 castellanos and sent him back to Guatemala.

There, learning that the King's Visitador was en route from Madrid to take him prisoner, he slipped out of the country on pretext of quelling rebellion in Honduras and got to Spain. Again he not only made peace with Charles V but was appointed Captain General and Governor of the Kingdom of Guatemala, given the additional titles of *don,* Adelantado and Comendador of the Order of St. James, and authorized to make an expedition of discovery to the Spice Islands (California) and from there to China. More; this time the Duke of Albuquerque gave him Beatriz de la Cueva, sister of the dead Francesca, as bride.

This was the apex of his career. Sailing for the Spice Islands after three more years in Guatemala, he stopped at Jalisco, Mexico, where he was entreated to go to the aid of Diego Lopez de Zuñiga, a Spaniard fighting a losing battle against Indian rebels in the mountains near by.

The Indians were entrenched on the crest of a steep hill. As Alvarado stormed up it, a riderless horse above him stumbled and fell and, rolling down the slope, struck the Governor-General, injuring him fatally. Undaunted, he commanded another soldier to don his uniform so that the Indians should not discover his absence, then was carried away to Guadalajara, where on July 4, 1541, he died.

Alvarado is still the unknown soldier. "About 1485" is given as the date of his birth; until recently, June 29 as the date of his death. His parents were Gomez de Alvarado and Leonor de Contreras, but until recently, too, Diego de Alvarado and Sara de Contreras were also named. His expedition to the Spice Islands has also been

destined for the South Seas and the "Seven Cities of Cibola" in
northern Mexico. The dates of his comings and goings are hope-
lessly confused.

The final irony is that in spite of his request to be buried in
Mexico City where all might do him honor, his daughter, Leonor,
brought his body back to Guatemala to be buried in the Cathedral
in the capital. Falling walls made his tomb inaccessible; today
no one knows exactly where he lies.

XI

ALMOLONGA, FIRST "PERMANENT" CAPITAL

INDIAN hostility having made the first capital at Iximché untenable, Jorge de Alvarado, as acting governor, selected a new site in the peaceful valley between the volcanoes Agua and Fuego, called, because of the many streams flowing down the mountainsides, Almolonga or *Bulbuxya,* "Where the Water Gushes." There on St. Cecilia's Day, November 22, 1527, the first Spanish city in Guatemala was founded.

That the old name, Santiago de los Caballeros, was retained is not strange. Both Spaniards and Indians credited St. James with the Spanish victories, the early chroniclers recording solemnly that Santiago killed more Indians than all their armies. The Indians, judging Catholicism by their own polytheistic cult, believed this saint to be but one of the Conquerors' many gods. His symbol was a warrior mounted on a white steed, they said, and the sword he brandished, the weapon that saved Cortes in Mexico and Alvarado in a hundred battles.

In 1532 Charles V awarded the new capital the picturesque coat of arms seen frequently today about the country. This presents Santiago galloping across blue skies, waving his sword as he goes; beneath him a row of three precise volcanoes, the central one in full eruption.

Streets of the capital were laid out according to Spain's excellent plan of city building about a central square or plaza, and the first crude huts, thatched with grass and walled with cane and mud, erected. Ten years later, thanks to the endless supply of Indian slaves, a Cathedral was rising at the head of the plaza, and beside it the Palace of the Captain General and, as the seat of local government, a Cabildo or Ayuntamiento. Streets of new and comfortable homes, two hermitages, three convents—Franciscan, Dominican, Mercedarian—a hospital and school were completed or nearing completion.

Areas on the outskirts were awarded the Tlascala and Cholula Indians from Mexico who had aided Alvarado in the Conquest. By royal decree they were forever exempt from paying tribute or taxes. Surrounding slopes and valleys were under cultivation, and so were the first seeds of the political, social and religious intrigues that were to blossom later.

Such was the capital when Alvarado returned with his second bride, the beautiful and imperious Beatriz, and twenty young noblewomen for whom he was to find husbands before sailing for the Spice Islands.

In August, 1541, when word reached the city that Alvarado was dead in Mexico, the capital was plunged into prolonged mourning, and the young widow went into action. Only twenty-two, she had two ruling passions, love for her husband and ambition.

To satisfy the first she stained the palace inside and out with black clay and substituted black for the crimson and gold draperies and upholsterings. A cry of horror rose from the populace. Such grief was impious in the sight of God; some dreadful disaster would befall them.

Truly, as soon as their leader was dead, disaster did strike again and again. Dogs imported from Spain to hunt the Indians destroyed herds of sheep and swine. Fire devoured parts of the city. Thieving, gambling, drinking increased to scandal, and as one chronicler puts it, "the honor of the knights and the virtue of the ladies palled." Cattle destroyed the sown seed, and to add to the growing apprehension, "a doctor had arrived who alone buried more Spaniards in one year than had died in the ten wars of New Spain." In this unhappy August, the Cabildo forbade the practice of medicine.

Disaster did not baffle Beatriz. Various factions intrigued secretly to place their candidate in Alvarado's offices, but nothing, they felt, could be done until the ceremonies for their dead chief ended. The last solemn mass was celebrated September 6; the Cabildo began its sessions. And when the vote was counted, Beatriz, Alvarado's widow, was named to succeed him!

A three-day thunderstorm had crashed over the city as the Cabildo debated and voted. It continued to crash when, on September 9, Beatriz signed the decree making her Gobernadora of Guatemala, the first and, to date, only woman to head a government on the American continent.

Her signature was another impiety in the sight of God. Firmly she wrote, *La Sin Ventura, doña Beatriz,* then, with one stroke, crossed out her name, leaving only "The Hapless One."

The storm increased in violence. Lightning struck buildings and trees, and the rushing waters swept them away. At midnight on September 10, earthquake added its horrors. It released waters dammed back high on the slopes of Agua, and the racing torrent, carrying trees and boulders with it, hurled itself over the city.

More than 700 Spaniards and 600 Indians perished. In the Palace that in the livid light of the catastrophe "loomed like an immense coffin," Doña Beatriz left her bedroom, the one safe place in the entire building, and, with her ladies in waiting and the five-year-old natural daughter of Alvarado, mounted to her little chapel on the roof. Its unsolid walls collapsed; the roof fell in. When the waters dropped, she was found dead, still gripping the cross, the child and her eleven attendants dead around her. Terrified and credulous, the survivors saw in the disaster God's punishment on the Gobernadora. Only at great cost and effort was the Bishop able to persuade them to bury her.

The earth was still shaking when conferences began to select a new site. Of the scant 100 knights and ecclesiastics surviving, many held their King in such blind idolatry that they urged securing his consent before abandoning the collection of ruins, fouled water, mud and fevers that was now Santiago.

Two sites were considered: one at Tianquesillo ("Little Market") on the plains of Chimaltenango; the other in the beautiful valley of Panchoy ("On the Lake"), so called because of evidence that the land had been long submerged. Juan B. Antonelli, an engineer sent out by the King to build roads, decided for the second. Far enough from Agua to escape its disasters, near enough to be sheltered from unseasonable heat and cold, it was surrounded by fertile soil, watered by good streams.

Fourteen years to the day after the founding the first "permanent" capital, the survivors founded their second. For a league and a half the little procession marched to the Indian Hermitage of Santa Lucia, Bishop Marroquin and the figure of the Virgen del Socorro [page 167] at their head. After a solemn mass, they stretched the cords to mark the streets.

Today the first Spanish city of Guatemala is known as Ciudad Vieja (Old Town) though authorization was granted in 1927 to use the original name of Santiago de los Caballeros. In the Cathedral, the figure of the Virgen de la Concepción—affectionately called La Chapetona ("A European lady recently arrived in America")—before which Beatriz and her ladies knelt in prayer, still stands.

And in the *cofradia* of La Chapetona is a chest which contains the three priceless jewels presented to the figure by Bishop Marroquin—a gold arrow, a Castilian cross of rubies, and a reptile of emeralds. These the *cofradia* guarded safely for more than three centuries, until in 1902 the Archbishop transferred them to Guatemala City for even safer keeping. The membership of the *cofradia* marched in a body to the capital, demanded the return of the jewels, and won it. Now the chest has seven keys, each entrusted to a *cofrade*. To open the chest seven officials with seven keys must be present.

On March 10, 1543, authorities officially transferred the capital to the new site.

XII

SANTIAGO DE LOS CABALLEROS

FROM that day in 1541 when the Virgen del Socorro presided over the mass, the new Santiago was destined for splendor. With abundant unskilled labor as well as skilled masons, stone-cutters and other craftsmen from neighboring Indian villages, with architects, artists and master artisans from Europe, the colonists built solidly and well. Their troubles were over. "Build to last" was their motto.

All trade routes led to the capital. Over them were carried the fantastic luxuries arriving on every ship from Spain. Gold, silver, and other metals from colonial mines; hardwoods and dye plants, cotton, cacao, tobacco, and other products from forests and fields; turquoise from Mexico, emeralds from Colombia, coral and pearls from the coasts. Worn by the feet of men and beasts to narrow channels that in time sank between walls head-high and in rainy seasons became beds for mountain torrents, these trade routes were doubly hazardous with hostile Indians, wild beasts, and insects—and bandits, whose numbers swelled alarmingly as more and more riches to and from Spain toiled over the trails while the colonists' own fortunes shrank proportionately.

In the grandeur of its public buildings, churches and homes of the nobility, in the flamboyance of its religious, social, political and artistic life, the new capital shortly ranked with Mexico City and Lima as one of the three great centers of Spanish culture in the western hemisphere. In 1566, as if to perpetuate and give additional weight to its glory, it was officially named *Muy Noble y Muy Leal Ciudad de Santiago de los Caballeros de Goathemala,* "Most Noble and Loyal City of St. James of the Knights of Guatemala."

Although it was to know intervals as tranquil as its gardens, its history is a compilation of disasters, natural and man-made. Between 1541 and the final catastrophe of 1773, flood swept it four times; four times Fuego erupted rivers of boiling lava and rains of ashes; four times pestilence decimated the city, and once drouth brought it to the verge of famine.

Innumerable earthquakes rocked it. In fourteen different years these were prolonged, violent and destructive; in 1717 more than 3000 buildings and homes were razed and others so undermined that pressure rose to find a new site. As if nature's efforts were insufficient, riots, crime, religious and political conflicts, scandals, the terror of the Inquisition and economic crises rode the people. And when word of the wealth Spain was garnering from America reached England and France, threats of piratical invasions led by such experts as Francis Drake were added to the trials of the colonists.

One of these pirates, Wallace by name, laid the foundation for the cause that agitates modern Guatemala and makes the territory known as Belize (corruption of Wallace) Guatemala's Irredenta. Wallace established headquarters on one of the islands off the Petén and defended it so successfully against the Spanish that he raised the English flag and claimed the soil for England.

Thus the situation remained until 1859, when the Republic of Guatemala, in a treaty with Great Britain, agreed that in return for a highway to be built with English money and by English engineers from Guatemala City through the Petén to the Caribbean, the now substantial area known as Belize should continue under the British flag. The highway was never built; the British flag still flies, and Guatemala now claims the territory as her own under the unfulfilled agreement.

The same courage that carried the Conquistadores to victory carried the colonists through building and rebuilding physically and psychologically their capital. By 1773, although many public buildings, patched and repatched after quakes and floods, were unsafe, they were still in use by a population grown to 80,000 in the city itself and thousands more in the surrounding valleys.

Early in 1773 tremors began to shake the city. Apprehension increased until, by June, shakings and rumblings continuing, the people were in terror. Many moved out into the fields or slept in their coaches in the plaza. Indians refused to enter the capital and food supplies ran low.

Finally on St. Marta's Day, July 29, by "divine mercy as a warning of the ruin to come," occurred a shock so violent that everyone, even the sick and permanent invalids, fled into the streets. Ten minutes later followed a shock so terrific that within two minutes the city was strewn with crashing walls. But for the warning, thousands instead of less than 200 would have been killed.

Years before, a mad nun, Juana Ocaña, had prophesied the end of the world. On the day foretold, citizens of Santiago massed about the church of San Francisco to await judgment, but when their worst fears were unfulfilled, they tarred and feathered their prophet and thereafter ignored all similar prophets of doom. Deafened by the uproar, blinded and choked with dust, with bells of churches ringing of their own accord, frenzied horses, dogs and other animals running wild with horrible screams and cries, bricks and stones leaping crazily from pavements and walls, the conscience-stricken populace now believed the prophecies were coming to pass.

Kneeling in the shambles of the streets, they shrieked repentance and prayed frantically for mercy. Queues formed before priests sitting among the ruins hearing confession. Men left women with whom they were living unlawfully; some became reconciled with wives; some married. Lifelong enemies forgave one another; proud Spanish dons embraced and asked forgiveness of Indian slaves they had abused for years. Thieves returned stolen property and honest men aided 400 convicts to escape their chains.

Instead of the end of the world came rains to destroy archives and treasure the quakes had spared, epidemics of disease heightened in horror by lack of water, food and medicine, and on September 7 and December 13, two more destructive quakes. Catastrophic as the earthquake had been for Santiago, it was merely the source of an even greater to follow.

Resentment against the Church was then at fever heat (page 145). The Captain General, the Real Audiencia and Officiales Reales saw immediately that in a change of site lay opportunity to free the country from ecclesiastical tyranny. The Archbishop and the Orders, aware of their danger, were equally determined that Santiago de los Caballeros should remain the capital.

Lines of battle were clearly drawn. Captain General don Martín de Mayorga led the state party or Traslacionistas; the Archbishop, Dr. Pedro Cortes y Larras, the Church party or Terronistas. For seven years, while to the north thirteen little colonies were fighting with bullets for political freedom, an epic struggle for religious freedom was fought with words in Guatemala.

Four days after the earthquake, reports from both factions were on their way to the King and conferences were begun to decide what was to be done. Even official records of these conferences differ. Some maintain that the Captain General was authorized to move temporarily all government offices across the mountains to the Valley of La Ermita; others that his departure on September 9, 1773, with the Real Audiencia, government staffs and equipment was a cowardly abandonment of his people.

In January, 1775, from La Ermita, Mayorga and the Real Audiencia issued formal orders to abandon Santiago. A commission to study the ruined capital had reported the impracticability of reconstructing it. Others, after studying three possible sites—the plains near modern Chimaltenango, the rich area near the Rio de los Esclavos (River of the Slaves), and La Ermita—had decided on the last. Although the ingenuity of ambitious individuals rather than the superiority of its natural advantages won the choice of La Ermita, the arguments for the people were that it was healthful, that earthquakes could never affect it because the deep surrounding ravines would absorb the shocks, and that rich mines existed in the neighborhood.

The Terronistas countered by swearing that Santiago was not fatally damaged and that much of the destruction was done at Mayorga's orders to secure building materials for La Ermita. Even when the King's Edict of June 16, 1775, supported the Captain General and ordered the transfer of the capital, the Archbishop and Orders refused to obey. Reconstruction of Santiago continued.

Mayorga banned all public spectacles in Santiago (a blow to the great church processions and fiestas), ordered all government buildings evacuated, closed all industries and shops, stopped delivery of

food supplies, and ruled that anyone opposing the transfer by written or spoken word would be guilty of treason. Four years after
the earthquake, the Terronistas were still rebuilding and the Real
Audiencia's command that all loyal vassals of the King and those
of *splendor y conveniences* (the Orders and University) should
move to La Ermita within one year, was ignored.

Then came the King's acceptance of the resignation of the Archbishop tendered eight years before and refused at that time! The
Archbishop now refused to acknowledge it and excommunicated
Mayorga, members of the Real Audiencia and other officials. In
turn he was threatened with excommunication unless he left for
Spain at once. At last in 1780 arrived the Papal Bull commanding
his departure, and the long struggle ended.

Citizens of Santiago, those in favor and those opposed to the
transfer, alike reluctant to abandon their beautiful valley, moved
to La Ermita a few at a time as pressure and necessity became
overwhelming. Dramatic accounts of 60,000 people crossing the
mountains in one great trek are pure fiction.

Remained finally among the ruins almost 10,000 people, half of
them Spanish and creoles, the rest, mestizos and Indians. Except
for a small company of soldiers, a few priests and one or two
families of means, this residue was composed of the poor and unskilled for whom the new capital had neither place nor need.

With a huge abandoned city at their disposal, they made themselves at home in the least damaged buildings. In some they set
up small shops, potteries, looms; in others, kept their pigs and
chickens. The vast enclosures of convents and monasteries where
grass soon grew luxuriantly made excellent pasture lands for cows
and mules. Indians once more ventured in with their wares and,
finding the ruins of the Jesuit convent more ample and sheltered
than the plaza, established the market that exists there today.

Life went on, tranquil if not prosperous. Spaniards and Indians
intermarried, developing in time a people taller than the Indians,
a little darker than the Spaniards, of a serene and happy tempera-
ment, accustomed to nothing and satisfied with little.

In time too some houses were restored, and ruins once forlorn
took on beauty as trees and vines grew in and over them and rain

and sun softened jagged lines and gave a rich patina to raw walls. In 1850 José Maria Palomo y Montufar, as mayor, restored the Palace of the Captains General, the church of La Merced, made the property of the former leper hospital into a cemetery, and brought about other changes and improvements.

In the latter half of the nineteenth century, when coffee cultivation was undertaken on a large scale, men from the new capital hastened to take over great areas of the Panchoy Valley and plant coffee trees in and around the ruins. Visiting these coffee fincas today, one can realize the extent of the boundaries of the once glamorous Santiago now known as Antigua.

So until yesterday Antigua remained, a serene colonial city in a modern world. Today the modern world is discovering it. Tourists and scholars and artists find its ruins among the most significant and grand on the American continent, rivaling those of the Old World in beauty and interest. Its pottery, textiles, iron work and wood carving command a ready market; so do its fruits and vegetables, coffee and cotton. And its equable climate and beautiful setting, with the volcanoes Agua, Fuego and Acatenango striking against indigo skies, are attracting others to live there in new or restored homes.

XIII

THE KINGDOM OF GUATEMALA

WHILE the second "permanent" capital was rising toward magnificence, the Kingdom of Guatemala was taking form and direction. Six provinces made it up—Guatemala, San Salvador, Honduras, Nicaragua, Costa Rica, and Chiapas. In theory the Captain General ruled them all in the name of the King, and in each province ruled a governor in the name of the Captain General. In practice, owing to lack of transportation and communication, each functioned as an independent kingdom, their jealousy of one another only surpassed by their unanimous jealousy and hatred of Santiago.

Perhaps those weeks of travel over heartbreaking trails provided provincial governors and officials summoned by the Captain General and merchants time and material for the cultivation of the hatreds that later were to determine the fate of Central America. The capital came in time to represent to the provinces the same evils of exploitation, tyranny, injustice and waste that Madrid represented to it.

Differences in the caliber and policies of the conquerors and officials who subdued and ruled the different sections made for some differences in structure, viewpoint, and treatment of the Indians. In the main, however, the provinces took their pattern from Santiago and imitated everything from architecture to skirt widths as rigidly as circumstances allowed. As Santiago lived, so, in greater or less degree, lived the Kingdom.

RELIGIOUS GUATEMALA

The Franciscan Brothers who arrived with Alvarado's army, and Juan Godines, army chaplain, for a time bore the entire burden of serving the spiritual needs of the soldiers and attempting to

plant Christian hope and humility in the hearts of the terrorized
Indians. By 1532 the Dominicans, Mercedarians and Father Fran-
cisco Marroquin, who two years later became the first Bishop of
Guatemala, had arrived.

To reward these first Orders, and primarily to avoid trouble,
the wise and liberal Bishop granted to each one or more of the six
provinces as its domain, with huge *repartimientos* (concessions) of
Indian slaves. The Orders, viewing their grants as private king-
doms, labored mightily to develop agriculture, commerce, the arts
and crafts within them.

From enormous incomes derived from wheat and sugar cane,
cattle, sheep, mills and mines; from fabulous gifts made by the
devout in gratitude for wealth and position won in the New World,
and from diverse substantial fees, the brotherhoods became increasingly rich. Further, they were exempt from the tithe or tax of ten
per cent on their incomes, which every lay citizen was required to
send the King.

Other Orders, including the Company of Jesus, hastened to
establish themselves. The three pioneers and the Jesuits in acute
rivalry founded chapter after chapter over the country. Convents,
monasteries, churches and hermitages rose at an incredible rate.
By the middle of the seventeenth century, Spanish America—which,
all told, did not possess a million people of European origin—was
supporting 840 convents and more than 7000 churches. By the end
of the century the numbers were still greater, particularly in Mexico,
Peru and Guatemala. In Santiago alone were 80 churches, most
of them with their own convents or monasteries and hermitages.

Increase in their ranks was not due entirely to religious vocation.
Spanish immigrants fleeing from the tyranny of the mother country brought with them an absurd illusion of grandeur—that work
was beneath a Spaniard, fit only for Indian slaves. With little or
no income, they hastened to enroll in a religious Order where they
could live in comfort, shoulder to shoulder with those of high
degree.

Although it was a tradition that the second son of each family
should enter an Order, the family was rare that did not include
at least two more friars or nuns. "The flower of the whites," one

historian declared, buried themselves in the cloisters. Converted Indians were assigned convents of their own.

Of all the Orders, the Company of Jesus became richest and most powerful throughout Spanish America. In Paraguay it ruled supreme and in other colonies nearly so. Arrogant in their isolation, the Jesuits were practically independent of both Rome and Madrid.

The result of this concentration of wealth and population in the Orders was power—religious, economic, political. Between the Church and the Inquisition, whose eyes and ears were everywhere, the colonists literally could not call their souls their own. Eventually and inevitably in Guatemala, the colonists became so impoverished that church and government authorities appealed to the King for an early and effective solution.

Although the Holy Office of the Inquisition functioned in Guatemala from 1572 to 1820 with both religious and temporal authority, little is known of it. Few documents were left behind when the Office was abolished and the House of the Inquisition, facing the Jesuit College, was so completely rebuilt that no suggestion of its purpose remains.

That its ferocity never reached the peak charged in other countries is evident in the denunciations of laxity hurled at Guatemala from the Holy Office in Mexico. Finally, infuriated by the stubbornness with which the Indians clung to their pagan faith, the Mexican Tribunal prepared and published widely a curse on the whole Kingdom which "fell like a rain of fire on the already unhappy people."

> "May the wrath and curse of Almighty God fall on them and each one of them. . . . May the plagues of Egypt and the curses which afflicted Pharaoh and his people afflict them. . . . May they be cursed in their eating and drinking . . . in their waking and sleeping . . . in life and in death . . . May they suffer eternally for their sins . . . May their days be few and evil . . . and may their children be orphans deprived of every necessity."

Of the benefits the Orders conferred on Guatemala and of the many noble and heroic men and women among their thousands, it is needless to speak. Their schools and colleges, hospitals and hospices, their encouragement of the arts and crafts gave the raw colony a rich and permanent culture. Founded in a century of greed for power, they were the product of their time.

Rivalries and scandals developed within and between the Orders, notably between the Franciscans and Dominicans. Blood ran in the churches and the civil authorities had to be brought in to restore peace. When one faction or brotherhood was defeated, the victors serenaded the vanquished with wooden rattles, cymbals, drums and *marimbas,* singing *Vitores* (Hurrahs), in some cases so libelous that the King protested. Convents were treasure houses of silver and gold, tapestries, paintings, sculpture, jewels. Fiestas and ceremonies were prolonged miracles of splendor.

The poverty-eaten citizenry looked on, rarely daring in the face of such power and threat of the Inquisition to murmur. But in Spain the conquest of the Moors and the Americas had invigorated royal authority, made the monarchs conscious and jealous of their rights. Felipe II founded the Royal Patronage, centering ecclesiastical authority in the throne and making himself patron instead of servant of the Pope. Charles III, frantic to discover new sources of income for his empty coffers, sent a commission to the colonies which shortly increased his revenues forty times. Encouraged, he sought ways of reducing the influence and wealth of the Church.

The Orders became his enemies, the Jesuits finally challenging the sovereignty of the King. Whereupon Charles III banished the Company of Jesus from all Spanish America and confiscated its properties. On July 1, 1767, the Jesuits of Guatemala were escorted aboard the frigate *Thetis* to begin a weary odyssey around a hostile world. Six years later—before some of them had found a haven —earthquake, toppling the churches of Santiago to the ground, shattered the supremacy of the Church in Guatemala.

POLITICAL GUATEMALA

Hardly had the smoke of the Conquest cleared away when Spain imposed a system of isolation, restriction, rivalries, divisions of power, severity and cruelty on her colonies, all designed to make her own power omnipotent.

Although the Kingdom of Guatemala extended from Mexico to Panama and its governor had vested in him the same authority as the viceroys of Mexico and Peru, he was given the lower rank of Captain General and Governor, and his rule over trackless and undefined provinces was checked on every side. All affairs of state and all finances had first to receive approval of officials directly responsible to the King. Over all was the Real Audiencia or Supreme Court, an advisory but at times administrative body, permitted also to report directly to the King. Under it was a series of lower courts, each a further check on the authority of the Captain General. Throughout his term of office he was aware that the King's Visitador might arrive to investigate his actions and that when he stepped out of office, his administration would be investigated by *El Juicio de Residencia.*

No offices were elective and all appointments were made by the King to Spanish nobles sent out from Madrid. Even children born in the colony to pure-blood Spanish parents were considered creoles and eligible only to minor posts. This practice of imposing government from above was one of the first seeds of dissent sown by a nation that could acquire empires but never hold them.

Local government for Santiago and all other towns and settlements was administered by a Cabildo made up of *alcaldes* or justices, one for each group—Indian, mulatto, creole—and an Ayuntamiento of *regidores* (Board of Aldermen), its size determined by the size of the population.

Innumerable and meticulous laws were laid down to regulate every phase of life. Those who cheated apprentices or sold short weights of powder were fined; butchers received 20 lashes the first time they misrepresented the price or quality of meat, 40 the second; sale of arms and liquor to Indians was forbidden; regulations concerning the best way to make shoes, flour, etc., were formulated. On pain of 100 lashes and banishment for one year to the mines, no mestizo, mulatto, Negro, whether freedman or slave, or Indian could ride a horse. The Indians, all other weapons failing against their oppressors, resolved to bear no more children; twenty-five lashes, therefore, were given the man who failed in his conjugal duty.

Side by side with so much oppression lived the powerful few, noble officials and clergy, in riches, security and freedom. The result was that anarchy sometimes rocked the colony, and vices and crimes from Spain flourished among the masses already brutalized by the cruelties to the Indians and by living lonely lives in vast, unpopulated areas.

ECONOMIC GUATEMALA

Excitement swept Spain when ships from the new colony of Guatemala reached port with seeds of fruits, vegetables, grains and plants and trees; with new animals, birds, with textiles. Letters, from those of Cortes down, dwelt on Guatemala's wonders and begged for materials and equipment to be sent at once, both because the conquerors becoming colonists needed them and because they wished to surround themselves with the familiar things of home.

Spain responded enthusiastically. No ship, the King decreed, should sail without domestic animals, seeds, herbs, tools, and other supplies. And in all fortified centers and convents in the new land vegetables, fruits and trees of all kinds, both native and Spanish, were to be cultivated continuously.

Jiquilite or indigo, cotton, tobacco and cacao (from which chocolate is made), long known to the Indians, were extensively cultivated by the colonists. Balsam, sarsaparilla, quinine, gums, resins and a myriad other new products were found and developed for export. From the beginning of the seventeenth century, cochineal was a source of wealth, richer than some of the gold and silver mines or jasper, copper, opals and amethyst, or the quarries of marble and granite. Indian textiles were exported in quantities.

Sugar cane from the Canary Islands was imported for cultivation in 1536; platano from the Gulf of Guinea; wheat from Spain, grapes, olives, and other fruits and vegetables to create today's riddle as to which are products of the New World, which of the Old.

Hector de la Barreda arrived from Cuba with 30 heifers and a bull to settle in the lush valley still known today as the Valley of the Cows and found an industry that became so rich the owners of the vast haciendas did not know how many cattle they had, one man alone selling 8000 head at a fair. Francisco de Zorilla in 1630 brought sheep; others pigs and goats. Sheep and swine became so plentiful that distant and wider grazing grounds had to be found, and it was forbidden to charge more than 20 pesos for a pig. Hides, wool, animal fats promised a profitable source of revenue.

The Court of Spain, however, worked on the economic theory that gold and silver alone constituted wealth. Gold and silver it demanded in quantities far beyond the capacity of Guatemala's mines to supply. The alternative was taxes.

Taxes were imposed on all goods entering and leaving ports; poll taxes were placed on everyone, even the Indians already paying heavy tribute; a tithe of every income was required and a variety of charges and surcharges. Guatemala alone of all the colonies had to pay in addition an annual sum of 4000 gold ducats, and when Spain entered war with France and Holland, further heavy duties were imposed to support a squadron in the Caribbean.

Substantial prices were demanded for all offices, titles, privileges, concessions and grants in the Kingdom, thus concentrating the wealth and privileges in the hands of a few. No official from the Captain General down could take over his post until he had paid half the sum and given bond for the rest.

To prevent competition with her own industries, Spain prohibited the cultivation of mulberry trees and flax, of vineyards and olive groves, and, later, the manufacture of wine. This produced a situation very like prohibition in North America, with defiance strong against the crown and bootleggers an increasingly lawless section of the communities. The Kingdom's indigo export trade of almost 2,000,000 gold pesos a year, and its lusty sugar industry were cramped by labor restrictions and embargoes on machinery.

Further to protect Spanish industries, commerce between colonies and even within colonies was banned. Spain was the only market, and goods could be shipped or received only twice a year through the ports of Seville and Cadiz. Lack of roads and threat of pirates made transportation of products a great risk and overseas travel a cosmic adventure. The rare person who attempted it made his last will and testament, received the sacraments, and bade family and friends farewell forever.

Moved by the misery, despair and increasing crime, the local government of Santiago appealed to the King for relief. He turned a deaf ear, and, when pressed, sent a sharp reminder, "Well begins the week that has a hanging on Monday."

In his comprehensive account of Colonial Guatemala, Antonio Batres Juaregui summarizes the old fable of the goose that laid the golden egg:

> "Concentration of property in few and untried hands, rich con-vents, taxes, offices by purchase, tithes . . . centralized government, lack of laws adapted to circumstances, inequality of races, jealousies and hatred of one province for another, isolation, the horrors of the Conquest, decimation of Indians, ferocious intolerance buried the colonies in an immense tomb sprinkled with a few drops of Holy Water."

SOCIAL LIFE

During the first colonial decades, the people, chastened by dis-aster, always on guard against Indian attack, oppressed by Mother Country and Church, lived austere and simple lives. But when their public buildings and private homes were completed and there was leisure and greater security, in national and provincial capitals and on the country estates luxury and gaiety rewarded years of abstinence. For the nobility and aristocracy, that is; those fortunate ones who were entitled and whose children, legitimate and illegitimate, were entitled to use *don* before their names.

Social classes were numerous and their rights and privileges strictly defined. Next the nobility were the creoles, the Spanish-born of the colony, and very proud and exclusive they were, too. Then came the craftsmen and master artisans sent out from Eu-rope as wood carvers, iron, gold and silver smiths, couturières and boot makers to adorn the élite and their homes. Far below them were the mestizos (of Spanish and Indian blood), mulattoes (Span-ish and Negro), Negroes, freedmen and slaves; Zambos (Indian and Negro), and, lowest of all, the Indians, as slaves and substi-tutes for animals and machinery.

Homes, duplicating as closely as possible the luxury and comfort of those in Spain, were constructed about patios, gay with flowers and flowering trees and vines and cooled and quieted by an ornate pila of flowing water in whose shell-shaped background stood a sacred image. One entrance, the *zaguan,* gave admittance; an impressive affair with massive doors, studded and banded with iron or bronze and hung with three knockers, two on the upper half for those who came on horseback, one below for the humble who arrived on foot. Windows were high and barred with bird-cage grills of well-turned wooden bars. With outer walls from three to six feet thick, a man's home was literally his fortress.

About the first patio ran an arched corridor from which spacious rooms opened. Ceilings and walls were elaborately carved, inlaid and painted. Around the second patio were the bathrooms, walled and floored with hand-designed tiles and equipped with ingenious waterpipes; kitchens with wide chimney places and dutch ovens, storerooms and servants' quarters, and above them the pigeon loft. In the third patio were the stables and quarters for stableboys, grooms, and lackeys.

First patio rooms were extravagantly equipped with furniture of rare woods, carved and inlaid with silver and mother-of-pearl and upholstered with brocades and tapestries from the looms of Europe and the Orient. Paintings and mirrors in spectacularly carved and gilded frames adorned the walls, rare pottery and *objets d'art* covered walls and tables and filled ornate cabinets.

Spain at this time had brought carpet weaving to a high art, and deep-napped carpets from her looms as well as from Arabian, Syrian, Persian and Egyptian, carried to Spain during the conquest of the Moors, were imported by colonial *dons.* Velvets and tapestries draped the windows, held in position by moulded arms and hands of silver. Each home had its own oratory, each a treasure-house of silver and gold vessels, hanging lamps, sculpture, brocades, jewels. Silver and crystal chandeliers held scores of candles for illumination and decoration. In fact, the staffs of many homes included silversmiths, and rivalry was keen to possess the most beautiful plate in the colony.

Costumes and jewelry were ostentatious and magnificent; of velvets, silks and richly woven brocades, of emeralds, pearls and coral befitting a *hidalgo* (literally, "son of something") and his lady who had not only inherited the flamboyant tastes of their own country but had at their disposal the profusion of riches which Indian slaves could mine and grow in the new.

In such homes and costumes the social pattern set by the twenty young noblewomen Alvarado had brought from Spain with Beatriz was rigidly followed, and in all the rising cities and towns of the Kingdom as rigidly imitated; it is the pattern which determines the life of the conservative circles of the Republic today.

Young ladies were educated in music, elocution, embroidery and deportment; young men in the science of warfare and the duel. The most fashionable school for señoritas was that of Nuestra Señora de la Concepción. Outside its windows a fountain—Fuente de las Delicias—was the chosen spot for gallants to serenade them and fight duels for their amazement.

Public festivities took place whenever a new and noble official arrived, whenever some prince in Spain had a birthday, on numerous religious days and throughout Holy Week, and on July 25, when the founding of the first capital at Iximché was celebrated, and on St. Cecilia's Day, November 22, when both the Santiago of Almolonga and of Panchoy were founded.

Tournaments and games, bull fights and public executions were staged in the plaza while the Captain General and nobility watched from the balcony of the Palace. Above them was raised a crimson canopy and before them on the railing hung the banners and coats of arms of Spain, Guatemala, the capital and the Captain General.

Round the plaza were the canopied tents of the knights taking part, more banners and coats of arms. Costumes on these occasions were of gold and silver, brilliant satins, rich with rare laces, tiaras, headdresses of gold and jewels, plume-adorned cloaks, capes, girdles and hats for both men and women. Each knight was attended by at least six lackeys in showy liveries. And each tried to possess the most spirited and beautiful mounts, whose harnesses, lacquered in bright colors, were also sparkling with jewels and precious metals; the saddles were upholstered in velvets fringed with gold.

Drums, clarinets, trumpets, *marimbas* and other instruments provided music, and in the evenings fireworks, ingeniously breaking as trees, castles, and serpents, dazzled the eyes. Some fiestas lasted for days, some for a week or two.

The arrival of the mail once or twice a year was always greeted with pomp and ceremony. Then, with the postmaster at their head, officials and knights in dress uniforms and decorations rode out to receive and open it at La Cruz de Piedra—the Stone Cross—on the outskirts. This cross now stands before the church of La Merced in Antigua.

As the eighteenth century approached, this splendor reached its peak. Followed, aided by calamities and increasing economic and political tensions, the decadence that inevitably results when ornamentation for its own sake becomes paramount.

ARTS AND CRAFTS

Although the Kingdom of Guatemala had no public museums, art galleries, libraries, theaters or concert halls, few pioneer people have been so generally exposed to the arts. Churches, government buildings and homes of the élite were veritable treasurehouses of painting and sculpture, wood, stone, iron, gold, silver and bronze work. During the first century these were, of course, imported, but shortly the colony had artists of its own of every kind and degree.

Because their fields were limited by the overruling influence of the Church to religious or historical subjects acceptable to the Church, sculpture and architecture, whose language is not so well understood as that of literature, painting and music, were pre-eminent. Except for amateur efforts, the colonists had no drama, but they needed none. The ceremonials and processions of the churches were magnificent theater.

Monasteries and convents had their own orchestras, chorals and composers, music rooms and libraries of parchment scores; libraries and archives. To their memberships belonged many of the musicians, sculptors, painters, writers and master craftsmen.

The following pages can only suggest the scope and variety of the arts in Santiago alone, and in lesser degree those of provincial capitals and towns, and the reason why today architects and engineers and scholars from all the world are finding their way to the ruins of Santiago, now known as Antigua. Even laymen, remembering the isolation of this part of the world three centuries ago,

Biener

ANTIGUA AS IT APPEARS TODAY

Colonial capital of the kingdom of Guatemala, in the valley of Panchoy, sheltered by the volcano Agua

Biener

SURVIVOR OF THE GREAT EARTHQUAKE

Façade of the impressive ruins of the Colonial Cathedral, Antigua

Biener

ORIGINAL CAPITOL OF THE KINGDOM OF GUATEMALA

Now El Palacio de los Capitanes General, Antigua, housing the administration offices of the department of Sacatepéquez

Eichenberger

MONASTERY OF SANTA CATARINA MARTÍR

Archway erected to permit nuns to pass unseen from cloister
to cloister, incidentally making a perfect frame for Agua

MAIN PATIO AND CORRIDOR OF COLONIAL UNIVERSITY
San Carlos Borromeo, Antigua: today the Colonial Museum

RUINS OF THE MONASTERY OF SANTA CLARA
Whose double arcade and colonial fountain are considered among the most interesting ruins in Antigua

AN IMPOSING OCTET OF VOLCANOES

Agua, Fuego, Acatenango, Atitlán, Tolimán, San Pedro, Santo Tomás, Santa Maria

Biener

THE QUIET CHARM OF GUATEMALA

View of Lake Atitlán from the picturesque village of San Antonio Palopó

Osborne

EL SANCTUARIO, ESQUIPULAS,
SHRINE OF THE BLACK CHRIST

Osborne

SILVER FIGURE OF THE VIRGIN
OF CANDELARIA, CHIANTLA

view the towering walls raised by the hands and backs of men
with something of the same wonder and incredulity roused by the
Pyramids of Egypt.

SCULPTURE

Of all the arts, sculpture attained the highest and most enduring
fame. Its reputation spread to Europe and throughout the Americas (particularly Mexico), where museums and churches today
treasure many examples of colonial work.

The first piece of sculpture, a figure of Nuestra Señora del Socorro
(page 167) brought into the country with Alvarado's army in 1524,
was followed as soon as the Conquest was over by increasing numbers of sculptures and sculptors. Guatemala's own artists, however,
in time equaled and in some instances surpassed their masters.

Within the first fifty years, two men rose to recognition, Quirio
Cataño, creator of the Black Christ of Esquipulas, and Juan de
Aguirre, who, denied the hand of the señorita he loved, entered the
Franciscan Order and found solace in reproducing her face on all
his sacred figures. His most famous works are the Jesús de la
Candelaria and Justo Juez in Quezaltenango.

Outstanding in the later period were Alonso Paz (around 1640),
the third artist of that name in the Kingdom, and Evaristo Zuñiga,
a creole whose style resembled that of Paz. Examples of the work
of both are found in the churches and museums of Antigua and
Guatemala City. Several cults honor different figures by Paz. For
more than 200 years Holy Monday in Antigua has been dedicated
to the fiesta of his Jesús Nazareno. In terms of money it is valued
at more than $30,000, but in historical and religious significance it
is beyond price.

The figure of San José by Paz has its own story and place. In
1740 a humble shoemaker decided to erect a church to his patron
saint. Those were the days when the King had decreed that no
more churches or convents be constructed, and the shoemaker was
beset with a thousand obstacles. But eventually he had his chapel,
to which a devout señora gave the image of San José.

Other noteworthy sculptors of the period are Juan de Chavez,
whose figure of San Sebastián—now in the Cathedral in Guate-

mala City—is said to be the best example of colonial sculpture in the country; Juan Perales, known throughout Europe for his statues of Christ; Vicente España, creator of the image, El Señor de las Misericordias.

With them rank Bolaños and Guzmán, experts in *estofado,* the art of tinting flesh and robes. They had their own secret processes, learned in Mexico, and were in demand by the sculptors of both countries. To secure the delicate fleshlike tints which baffle modern critics, they first rubbed saliva into the wood with a rabbit's decomposed bladder.

Colonial sculptors worked in many mediums—marble, stone, alabaster, wood, ivory, stucco. Although their styles reflect European influences, a few developed techniques of their own. Of wood, for example, they used the roots of the cedar, orange and chicozapote trees, felled when the moon was full. These they left to soak in water for four years, dried in the sun for two. If the figures were to be finished in silver leaf, they were painted again and again with white; if in gold, with yellow. Each artist evolved his own methods of application and number of layers.

The columns and ceilings, altars and screens, fountains, medallions, coats of arms, the world of stucco figures on church and convent walls and stone figures before public buildings and private homes were all the work of the sculptors.

Modern Anglo-Saxon eyes find the lack of perspective allowed, the ornate robes of velvet and brocade encrusted with silver and gold embroideries, the jewels and gold crowns, and the backgrounds of real and artificial flowers confusing and the anguish and the blood oppressive. To understand colonial sculpture one must remember the century in which men suffered and inflicted suffering violently, and also that the statues are more than pieces of sculpture to Guatemaltecos.

ARCHITECTURE

One needs only to travel about Guatemala to appreciate the role architecture played in colonial life; one day's trail in remote valleys reveals from six to a dozen impressive churches and acres of crumbling convent walls. Santiago's churches and public buildings, of course, surpassed all others in the Kingdom in dimensions, grandeur, purity of style and taste.

In general, colonial architecture falls into three overlapping periods: Franciscan, during the sixteenth and seventeenth centuries; Spanish baroque in the eighteenth, and Roman-Corinthian, introduced toward the end of the eighteenth.

The Franciscan style with its strength and austerity placed stress on utility rather than esthetic value. Spanish monarchs concerned for the protection of their new empires decreed its use with the idea that churches and government buildings might serve as fortresses if need arose. Hence the lack of adornment, the four-to-eight-foot-thick walls, and belfries that could double as watch towers.

Civil and religious authorities did not agree with this opinion, and even before the baroque style crossed the seas, had begun to adopt decorative ideas from the Italian school. Spain, riches pouring in, was building too. Under the influence of her conquest of the Moors and of Renaissance architecture then sweeping Europe, her architects were evolving the style known today as Spanish.

Moorish influence is evident in the homes of colonial times and later. In the high, enclosing walls, corridored patios, intricately grilled windows, wide eaves, finely designed doorways, inner doors covered with bronze rosettes, amusing façades garnished with griffins and fanciful figures, sometimes with coats of arms, Moorish influence is plain. Every town had its public fountain, and the gardens and courts of churches and homes had several. The University of San Carlos (now the Museum) is an excellent example.

Spanish influence is apparent in plain outer walls, contrasting strikingly with the colorful and varied decoration within. Today street after street of such homes, their walls softly blended pastel stuccos, give charm and mystery and tranquillity even to modern cities.

Repressed on so many fronts, the colonists welcomed the churrigueresco style, covering once plain surfaces and austere columns, ceilings and façades with every known floral and geometric decoration. And the demure Indian, apt pupil of his masters, inserted

among the many strange devices, symbols of his own—the corn
plant, the serpent, and others.

Buildings became an orgy of ornamentation; the outstanding
example remaining today is the church of La Merced in Antigua.
When to sculptural ornamentation, sculpture, iron work, wood
carving and mosaics, quantities of silver and gold leaf, rich lacquers
and paints and massive paintings were added, the effect was—and
still is—dazzling.

Methods in some instances left much to be desired and the fact
that knowledge and experience gained in one part of the country
in the use and adaptation of native materials could not be passed
on readily to others was a handicap. One group, however, deserves
the credit awarded belatedly by Antonio José de Irisarri, who,
after traveling through all the Americas in the nineteenth century,
returned to assure the Indian masons of Guatemala that

". . . they appeared more intelligent than the mulattoes, zambos and
Spanish of other parts of the continent since they were infinitely more
skilled as architects than the masters of architecture seen elsewhere."

That he spoke truly is demonstrated both in the buildings of the
colonial period and of Guatemala today.

PAINTING

The rapidly rising churches, convents, and government buildings
offered endless invitation to all who could wield a brush. Massive
paintings and murals, scores of medallions to be inset in the carved
and gilded ceilings, were in demand. A single altar—and some
churches had a dozen or more—required from twelve to twenty
paintings. It was the golden opportunity for artists, and they
seized upon it with zest.

Viewing their work today, one is impressed with the fact that
though artists were plentiful, art critics were a phenomenon to
come. A theme treated in the proper religious light was a masterpiece. For one rich in conception and execution, pervaded by an
authentic and mystic reverence, scores are mediocre or worse, revealing clearly the sadistic and violent tendencies of their time.

Portraits of distinguished personages of the day and occasionally a historical subject—also with a religious flavor—provided the second source of themes. One, by Christopher Villalpando in the National Museum in Guatemala City, is typical. Its subject is that awful day in 1717 when the people of Santiago de los Caballeros gathered to await the end of the world. Among the figures are many representing colonial celebrities.

Contemporary life which artists arrive in shoals to paint today was an undiscovered mine, though Villalpando did sketch the Indians to secure facility in depicting expressions and attitudes for his series of 45 paintings of the life of St. Francis of Assisi. In an atmosphere of changing light and color that few countries in the world can offer, with trees and flowers and mountains and lakes of breath-taking beauty, colonial artists clung to the traditional backgrounds and pigments of Europe, ignored electric blue skies in favor of the sweetish blue of postal cards and wreathed saints and angels in the ever-blooming rose of candy boxes.

Among the artists whose skill has survived the test of time are Tomás de Merlo, of Portuguese descent, whose series depicting the Passion of Christ hangs now in the Museum of Guatemala City; Zurbarán, famous Spanish disciple of the Flemish school, and Antonio de Montúfar, whose paintings were sought by many churches and whose artistic fate is now a legend.

Commissioned to do the series of murals for El Calvario, his work was recognized as so original and brilliant that the day they were completed the highest royal and ecclesiastic authorities came to applaud and congratulate. As he left the church with them, he became suddenly blind, and the legend is that God blinded him because these paintings were sufficient to insure that his name should live forever.

Another characteristic story is told of the irascible Merlo, who, while receiving the last rites on his deathbed, opened glazed eyes to glare at the crucifix the priest offered him. "Why did you bring that image and where did you get it?" he demanded. "It has no merit. I do not like it and I have better ones." A member of his family hastened to bring a crucifix by Cataño. This Merlo accepted with pleasure, and, turning his back, ignored the baffled priest.

Many of the most valuable colonial paintings were destroyed by earthquake; others were lost or damaged in the transfer to Guatemala City. Many, many more have been bought by museums in Europe, North America and Mexico; others, unrecognized and uncared for, lie in isolated churches. The best of those remaining are in museums and churches in Antigua and Guatemala City.

LITERATURE

In 1659 a treatise on the Immaculate Conception by the Bishop of Guatemala, Payo Enriquez de Rivera, was published in Europe. It gave such offense to religious authority that he devoted three years to formulating a reply. More, by 1660, he had imported a printing press and a printer—Joseph de Pineda Ibarra, a Mexican creole—to give his opus to the world. This *Explicatio Apologetica,* dedicated to the King and printed in 1663, was the first book published in the Kingdom. As such it is a keynote to colonial literature.

It was not the first piece of printing, however. In 1641, the owner of an indigo plantation in the province of San Salvador wrote and published a small treatise, *El Puntero apuntador con apuntes breves,* on the cultivation of indigo. For this he made his own press, type and ink from primitive materials. The first three pieces to come from the imported press were two sermons and a vote of thanks to God.

That the Bishop's predicament should have made Santiago the fourth city in the western hemisphere to welcome the printing press—the others, Lima, Mexico City and Los Angeles (then in Mexico)—is one of history's major whimsies. A people who hardly dared think, much less speak their thoughts, had no enthusiasm for perpetuating them in black and white.

Until long after that first odd combination of wood, iron and leather arrived in Santiago, the life of a printer was exceedingly thin. Pineda de Ibarra, to survive, was given the right to print all public notices, a right inherited by his son, who, to keep himself from starving to death, urged an embargo on all books from Spain and Mexico.

Before the close of the colonial era, however, 2472 pieces of printing had rolled off the press. And the printers had their own guild and oath—"to work with Christianity and purity," and, possibly in memory of the Bishop who founded their livelihood, "to defend the mystery of the Immaculate Conception."

One newspaper served the Kingdom, the *Gaceta,* inaugurated as a monthly on November 1, 1729, and continuing as such until 1797 when it won a four-year struggle to appear weekly. War between Spain and England at that time, however, made paper prohibitive, so the Captain General suppressed the *Gazette.* Revived a year later as an official periodical for government and church notices, it was denounced by both State and Church as "pernicious." There were no magazines.

Prohibition of books, rigid censorship by Government, Church and Inquisition—*Don Quixote* had to be smuggled in—should have made for an avid reading public. But the majority of mestizos and creoles could not read, and those who could did not because prices of books were beyond their means.

The most prolific writers were the priests and Jesuits whose tomes on theology, mysticism, morality, witchcraft, miracles, apparitions and histories of their Orders and saints are too heavy and verbose for modern patience to endure. Most important were the chroniclers, trustworthy men appointed by the State. Few of their books were published during colonial times; many of their manuscripts were lost, only their titles surviving.

They wrote what they were permitted or told to write, and naturally from the preferred impassioned or partisan point of view. Perhaps it is for this reason that many historical or daily events of interest to readers today seem to have passed unobserved by contemporary eyes. Even letters of those days reveal in their unqualified approval of the Kingdom, the censorship guiding the feathered pens.

A soldier and a brave one wrote the best-known and most interesting of the independent histories, *The True and Noble Account of the Discovery and Conquest of New Spain and Guatemala* (1568). This was Bernal Diaz del Castillo, whose manuscript now lies in the archives in Guatemala City.

Antonio de Remesal, a Dominican friar, with *General History of the Occidental Indians* furnished what is considered today the cornerstone of historical knowledge of Guatemala. Published in Europe in 1619, only 200 copies were sent to the colony. Of these, 180 were ordered "thrown to the stables" by the Tribunal of the Inquisition. From one of the twenty surviving copies, a second edition was printed in 1932.

An English priest, Thomas Gage, who served in various parishes in Guatemala before he returned to England, recanted and became an Anglican, wrote there in 1645 a spicy account of his own life and those of his confreres, the Dominicans and Jesuits in the New World.

One of the rarest histories is *Chronicles of the Province of the Holy Name of Jesus of Guatemala,* written in 1714-16 by Friar Francisco Vazquez. Another is the *Recordación Florida,* by Francisco Fuentes y Guzmán, an official chronicler whose pages were appropriated by Father Domingos Juarros (1808) and ever since have been lifted from him in turn by later historians and writers.

During the second half of the seventeenth century, strong French and Italian influences crept across the seas to insert foreign phrases into the already florid style in vogue. The marked influence of Fernando de Herrera, a Spanish writer of exceedingly flowery style in prose and verse, did nothing to improve matters.

In this period, the first attempts at poetry were made by Pedro de Lievano, Dean of the Cathedral, and the last by Friar Matías de Córdova, who wrote in classic verse some fables whose title, *The Attempt of the Lion and the Success of His Enterprise,* suggests his style. One poet, famous today, was Rafael Landivar, a Guatemala-born Jesuit who, in exile in Italy, wrote *Rusticatio Mexicana,* the outstanding work of the colonial era.

The earthquake of 1773 and its aftermath, the unrest and confusion as the country worked itself up to declare independence of Spain, brought the literature of the Kingdom of Guatemala to a premature close. Out of disaster and political upheaval came several books whose style reflects the influence of those troubled times and one hair-raising account by Felipe Cadena, *A Short Description of the Noble City of Santiago and an Exact Account of Its Destruction.*

Music

If Indians and Spaniards can be said to have had a bond in common, that bond was music. From the first songs—Bible stories set to simple melodies—the *naturales* accepted eagerly the music of the Old World. Similarly the Spanish drew upon that of the New. Although not a period of creative music, it was an expressive one, with high and low taking part.

The first trained voice in the country was that of Friar Juan Zambrana, founder of the Mercedarian Order in the Kingdom. There were chorals of two and three hundred voices of boys; chorals for Indians who were apt and enthusiastic vocalists; chorals of priests and novices. Each church had its own choir, kept at high standards through rivalry: those of the Franciscans, Dominicans, Jesuits and Recollectos were the best in all Spanish America.

From the founding of the capital in 1543, all who could gathered each afternoon about the Hermitage of Santa Lucia to sing the Hymn of Praise (*Alabado del Obispo Marroquin*). When the Cathedral was ready for use, the service was transferred there and continued until the capital was moved to Guatemala City.

Everybody sang. When the *villancicos* (carols) arrived in 1539 from Spain, the vogue swept the country. Music was a part of each family gathering, the señoritas singing to their own accompaniments on the harp. And evenings were few indeed when somewhere gallants were not warbling and plucking guitars beneath the windows of lovely ladies.

The guitar and the banjo were the first instruments to arrive, brought out in the kits of the conquerors, but followed shortly by violins, violas, cellos, harps and clarinets. The Indians quickly adopted them, particularly violin and guitar, making crude instruments of their own. At the same time the Spanish took over and developed Indian drums and other instruments until now it is difficult to say what is the Indian contribution, what the Spanish. In the music for the dances of the Conquest and of the Toreadors, Jesús Castillo traces the evolution of the two styles into one. There are times, he says, when, though the melody is Indian, the rhythm is Spanish.

Masters of the violin, viola and harp were teaching in the capital by 1604 and during the late eighteenth century, economically straitened as the colony was, music schools continued to function. As early as 1548, the Cathedral not only had an organ but a noted organist from Madrid, Antonio Perez, who became one of the few colonial composers, as did his successor, Gaspar Martiñez. Priests and laymen composed sacred music, following closely the Toledo school, for voice and instruments.

Soon, too, the capital had its own instrument makers. Julian Lopez, using the organ of the Cathedral as his model, supplied many churches, including El Calvario at Esquipulas. A Jesuit, born in Guatemala and known widely as musician and mathematician, constructed the music box, later perfected in Europe.

With the possible exception of public executions, music was a feature of every public occasion. The day began with music when the sonorous bells of the churches, each in its assigned order, played over the city. First sounded the soft-toned bells of Santa Clara, followed by those of La Concepción, Santa Teresa, Santa Catarina, each rung more loudly than the last; then louder still the bells of the Capuchins and the Carmelites. Not until noon had the rounds been completed. At the hour of El Rosario or the angelus, all rang again, calling everyone to prayer, and finally in the evening they announced the end of day. One street in Antigua is still known as Street of the Bells.

These were no ordinary bells, but massively cast and decorated moulds of bronze, gold and silver to which devout señoras of the city had contributed by stripping rings from their fingers and pendants from their ears. In addition, the bells served as daily newspaper, announcing births and deaths, calamities and occasions for rejoicing.

CRAFTS AND GUILDS

The list is long and starred with names. This was the day of the master workmen, and each was jealous of the reputation of his own craft and each craft jealous of the others. By the end of the colonial period all had their own guilds or brotherhoods with strict regulations concerning apprenticeship and standards.

High on the list stood the engravers who brought their craft in Guatemala to an excellence surpassed in no other Spanish colony except Mexico. Beginning with a few craftsmen from Spain and several from Mexico, a numerous organization developed, its members skilled in every field—coins, medals, maps, illustrations.

They were especially skilled in working with wood and copper. Hardly a book or pamphlet of the time appeared without its woodcuts, the best perhaps those made to illustrate the volume of speeches and verse celebrating the coronation of Fernando VII.

The first copper engravings were made in 1714 by Baltazar España for Vasquez' history. Blas Avila, Francisco Cabrera who also managed to execute more than 1000 miniatures on ivory, Pedro Garci-Aguirre, engraver for the Mint, and one Indian, Manuel de Jesús Lopez, who began as a servant at the Mint, were masters of this craft.

In 1529 two silversmiths from Mexico made what are believed to have been the first silver pieces in the colony, but by 1550 a number of silversmiths and goldsmiths were doing a flourishing business in the capital. And when they set Indians to work as apprentices, they discovered with amazement that the pupils had little to learn from their masters.

From the time of the Maya, pre-Conquest Indians have been adept in working with precious metals. Many of their vessels, broken in sacrifice and hurled into the depths of the Sacred Well in Yucatan, are masterpieces of gold and silver, treasured now in the leading museums of the world. On the carved figures of Maya stelae, bracelets, anklets, chains and breastpieces of exquisite design are worn by nobles and priests. From Indians of such heritage came many of the beautiful altars of hammered silver in colonial churches and much of the silver and gold ware in the homes of the nobility.

Colonial craftsmen were greatly influenced by the Moors, particularly in their designs for jewelry. Jewels at that time were secondary to the art of the gold and silversmiths; emeralds, quantities of pearls and coral being employed merely to set off the delicacy and intricacy of the filigreed and embossed metals. Although this craft reached its peak in 1604, its masterpiece is the silver figure of Nuestra Señora del Rosario made in 1532 (page 170).

After 1560, wood carvers added their skill to making the capital resplendent. They worked in all styles from Franciscan to baroque, and in addition developed one, more restrained and distinctive, now known as Colonial, whose scrollwork and design suggest the Maya as their inspiration.

On altars and altar screens, beamed ceilings, furniture, chests and cabinets for the sacred vestments and vessels of the churches, they carved with incredible precision and sense of composition. To their art, the hardwoods of Guatemala were of no little assistance. In spite of climate and lack of care, many examples of their work can be found today even in crumbling and remote churches. Turned window bars and "linen fold" doors were their specialty, and some of them made sculptures in wood of the nobles for public buildings and posterity.

Tile makers developed the lowly tile into a work of art to line the wide eaves of houses, to floor and wall bathrooms, to embellish fountains and window frames. Iron workers wrought richly for doorways, windows and general ornamentation. Upholsterers employed brocades, velvets and silks, tufted and draped to line interiors of litters and, later, carriages in which the titled señoras traveled.

And the guilds watched with stern eyes the work of their members, determined that all should do honor to their profession. Each guild had its patron saint before whom new masters took the oath of integrity and new officers swore to maintain standards of workmanship and, incidentally, see to it that so worthy an organization received all the respect and privileges due it.

Many became so powerful that they exerted great influence. It was the privilege of the guilds to walk in the Corpus Christi procession. Each guild had its assigned place, the leading ones beside the priest. So sensitive was their honor that many processions ended in pitched battles as affronted guilds sought to improve their position. Keenest rivalry lay between the silversmiths and the fireworkers, each determined to march beside the priest; the silversmiths won the final decision.

So superior were the gold and silver smiths and so selective their guild that in 1745 the King of Spain had to step in to decree that all—even Indians, mestizos and mulattoes—who had worked steadily as apprentices for four years, passed with "seven marks of approval" examinations in theory and practice, and could prove good character, should be admitted. That is, provided, too, that each had sufficient means to post a bond in the royal treasury.

Their patron saint was San Eloy, and each year on his day the guild met to elect officers. The occasion was grave, for the authorities chosen would control all the silver and gold shops and the trademark of each smith, and would examine candidates for mastership and the quality of all gold, silver and precious stones furnished by a knight for some special piece of work. They would make sure that no smith dared to adulterate his metals or sell them at more than a just price. And they would impose the penalties, ranging from 50 pesos' to more than 1000 ducats' fine or banishment from the guild and capital for from three years to life.

In the church of La Merced in Antigua exists today a chapel to Saints Crispin and Crispiano, dedicated by the shoemakers' guild in 1676. Handicapped because they did not merit an altar and consequently could not celebrate a fiesta in honor of their patrons or receive new masters and officers with sufficiently awe-inspiring ceremony, the guild contracted with the Brothers of Mercy that in return for a small annual rental they would maintain a shrine "during all the years of the life of the Church of Jesus Christ" for the shoemakers' guild.

XIV

ANTIGUA

A star (*) indicates that the object so marked has been removed to Guatemala City

TO know Antigua and the old capital of Santiago de los Caballeros, one should have long hours to sit in the plaza or wander among the ruins and streets.   Then one will find the old homes still adorned with wooden grills and metal-studded doors and figures, more ruins of churches and public buildings than can be mentioned here, glimpses of patios and fountains and private oratories; quiet green squares with fountains and *pilas*.

The reader may be disappointed to find the exact locations of famous sculptures and paintings unspecified here.   These are changing times in Guatemala, when the treasures of libraries, archives, museums and churches are being reorganized and placed. A painting in a church in Antigua today may be in a museum in Guatemala City tomorrow.   Believing that it will be more truly helpful, we have mentioned the most valuable and historic pieces in connection with their original church in the old capital of Santiago and marked with a star those now in Guatemala City.

Although modern Spanish uses the words convent and monastery interchangeably, in colonial times a convent housed men, a monastery, women.   In the following pages we have kept the colonial significance.

THE CATHEDRAL

Magnificent even in ruin, the Cathedral was only one of the six resplendent churches that headed the list of eighty erected before the capital was destroyed.   Although begun in 1543, it was rebuilt continuously and may not have been completed even by 1773. Records of 1748 reveal that 25,000 tiles were still needed for its paving, that many columns still lacked their tortoise-shell sheaths, that the main altar was not completely lacquered with gold, and that twenty-five images of saints and evangelists were required for altars and pilasters.

Seventy windows lighted and seven massive arched and decorated entrances gave admittance to an interior 300 feet long by 170 wide. The three naves had eight chapels on either side, two of them, El Sagrario and Nuestra Señora del Socorro, large enough in themselves to serve as churches. Sixty-eight vaulted arches adorned with angels and coats of arms supported walls and roof, and sixteen columns, faced with tortoise-shell and further embellished with finely wrought bronze medallions, supported the dome, in each of whose curved triangles were statues of famous theologians of the Church. The dome itself supported an iron cross almost 70 feet high. Two square and lofty belfries contained ten bronze bells.

Above the portals of the façade was a statue of the Virgen de la Concepción, and above her the sculptured heraldry of the Cathedral. In eighteen niches stood stucco figures of saints.

Beneath the dome in the Royal Chapel was the main altar, designed by Mateo de Zuñiga, resting on a many-sided, laminated base of gilded bronze. Four sides were devoted to evangelists, the others depicted scenes from the Bible. The altar itself was lofty, intricately carved and inlaid with mother-of-pearl, ivory and silver. Its numerous images and paintings were the work of the best European and colonial sculptors and artists—Paz, Cataño, Merlo, Villalpando, Montúfar, and others.

Along the cornices were marble statues of the Virgin and apostles, almost three feet high. Every chapel and altar was similarly endowed with quantities of gold and silver, statues and paintings, though the architecture varied in style. Great branched candelabra and chandeliers, and crosses and lanterns everywhere were of silver.

Most famous and beautiful—in a distinctive style of its own—was the chapel of Nuestra Señora del Socorro. According to legend, this figure * was one of three tossed ashore in Spain after a heavy storm, the box in which they lay having been abandoned by some ship in distress. Legend ends and history begins when Francisco de Garay brought the image with him when he joined the Conquistadores in Cuba and Mexico. In 1524 Padre Godinez carried it to Guatemala under Alvarado.

Originally called the Virgen de la Piedad, she presided from an arched bower over the solemn mass celebrated by Godinez at the founding of the first capital at Iximché. Later she was to preside at the founding of the capitals in Almolonga and Panchoy. After the latter ceremony, she remained in the Hermitage of Santa Lucia from 1542 until 1620, when she was transferred to a shrine in the new Cathedral.

For years christening and marriage services were held before her, and she is credited with averting many disasters from volcanoes and drouth. It was only necessary for her to appear in procession, it was believed, for the rains to fall. Once her popularity lapsed, and lumber for the construction of another shrine was piled high before her. One day the Bishop was surprised to see a clear and lovely light shining through chinks in the lumber. Investigating, he found it came from the Virgin; never again was she neglected.

Figure and robes are carved of very fine cedar, but from colonial times she has been dressed in velvets and priceless jewels, one of them the celebrated lizard of emeralds given her by Francisco de la Cueva, husband of Alvarado's daughter, Leonor. Once a daring thief stole the lizard, and the Virgin herself assisted in its recovery. Beneath her altar was an empty tomb in which the thief took refuge. The Virgin saw to it that when he closed the entrance, a fragment of his cloak was caught, and from that he was identified.

After the earthquake, two chapels, El Sagrario and Guadalupe, were rebuilt and serve now as the Parochial Church of San José. Though its façade is practically new and its *decor* modern, many Cathedral relics link it with the past. Among these are the figure of Jesús del Perdón, by Quirio Cataño, considered one of the best sculptures in Central America, and a figure of the Virgin done in ivory. The pilgrimage and procession on the first Friday in Lent in honor of the Jesús del Perdón is one of the most impressive ceremonies in Antigua today.

According to traditional custom, famous personages of Conquest and colonial days were buried in the churches. In the Cathedral are Alvarado, his wife Beatriz, his daughter Leonor; her husband,

Francisco de la Cueva; Bishop Marroquin, Bernal Diaz, and many more.

At the right of the Cathedral is now an addition that was orig-inally the Episcopal Palace, seat of ecclesiastic powers and home of the Bishop of the Kingdom of Guatemala. From its balcony bishops, and after 1543 archbishops, blessed fiestas and processions. Three impressive entrances, studded with bronze and framed in sculptured stone, led to three spacious patios, ruins of which still retain their decoration.

In 1547 Bishop Marroquin built a palace and church on the slope of Agua which were show places of the time and whose ruins now provide magnificent views of valley and volcanoes. The site is known as San Juan del Obispo, is easily reached, and is very rewarding to visitors. The church, restored and modernized, con-tains some of its original carved altars and statues.

Church and Convent of Santo Domingo

In 1528 Friar Domingo de Betanzos founded a small Dominican church and convent in the capital at Almolonga. Six years later, Bishop Marroquin brought from Nicaragua Father Bartolomé de las Casas and three other Dominicans (page 16). As a reward for their services in conquering peacefully the Land of War, the Dominican Order stood high in the graces of Spanish and colonial authorities, and lavish concessions were made them, one a vast tract of land in the new capital at Panchoy.

They erected a church and convent that, though now crumbled ruins, startle the imagination with their splendor. Monumental walls of the church rose to a deep red dome and two belfries with large and sonorous bells. In one tower was the first public clock.

Gigantic columns and arches supported its walls, gilded and ornamented with arabesques and heads of cherubim. The main altar surpassed all others in the capital. Through numerous windows sunlight poured by day to set silver and gold and jewels afire; at night hundreds of candles in silver candelabra and chandeliers gave it brilliance.

A silver lamp hanging before the high altar required three men

to raise and lower it, says Thomas Gage, adding that there was
also a figure of the Virgin

> ". . . of pure silver, the size of a reasonably tall woman, which
> stands in a tabernacle made for it in the Chapel of the Rosary with
> at least a dozen silver lamps hanging before it."

After the earthquake this Virgen del Rosario * was proclaimed
patron saint of the city and by public subscription a gold crown
thick with jewels presented her. In this church too was a guardian
angel of great size made of gold and precious stones and a statue
of Santo Domingo by Alonso Paz.

Another chapel, that of Cristo Yacente,* though severe in style,
was rich with tortoise-shell and paintings. This figure was originally in England, but when Henry VIII founded Anglicism, it was
shipped to Peru. En route the ship was menaced near Trujillo,
Honduras, by a storm which forced the captain to throw many
large boxes overboard. When at last the figure was located, an
illustrious delegation made the long journey from the capital to
Trujillo to rescue it. They were so transfixed by its beauty that
they commissioned Pedro de Mendoza to make for it a carved and
gilded dais, inlaid with mother-of-pearl and enclosed with glass so
that it might be carried in the celebrated Holy Friday processions
of the Dominicans. Soon its chapel became the shrine of the most
distinguished families in Santiago.

This Holy Friday procession is one of the oldest ceremonials in
Guatemala (established before 1595) and during colonial times was
the most impressive of all. The flower of the city, political, social
and religious, and all the guilds, marched behind the Cristo Yacente until "so great the numbers, so numerous the images, so
severe the dress of the penitents and so solemn the cortege," wrote
Francisco Ximenez in 1721, "that it was one of the most devout
spectacles offered by humanity."

Within the walls of the convent nothing was lacking for pleasure, comfort or recreation, to quote Thomas Gage again:

> "In the lower cloister was a spacious garden, in the midst of which
> a fountain tossed up water, spouting it out of at least a dozen pipes,
> which fill two ponds full of fishes, and with this their constant run-

ning gives music to the whole cloister and encouragement to many waterfowl and ducks to swim and wash themselves there. Further within the cloister are two gardens for fruits and herbs, and in one a pond a quarter of a mile long, all paved at the bottom and a low stone wall about it, where is a boat for the friars' recreation who often go there to fish . . . and take from it as much fish as will give the whole cloister a dinner."

In 1547 this convent was made Priory for the Kingdom of Guatemala. One of the fountains now stands at the entrance to Antigua on the Guatemala City road.

In 1620 the Dominicans founded their College of Santo Tomás de Aquino here, the second college in the kingdom. From its inception it granted degrees; many of the most renowned men of the day were among its graduates.

The fame of church and convent is equaled by that of its first vicar, Bartolomé de las Casas. Born in Seville in 1474, he was the son of Antonio de Casaus (sic), who sailed with Columbus on the first voyage of discovery in 1492. Bartolomé's first contact with the Indians was the little Indian boy brought him as a present from that voyage.

The father returned to Hispaniola (Santo Domingo) to be one of the first settlers in the New World, and Bartolomé joined him there when he completed his training in law. While there, he accompanied the army of Diego de Velasquez to Cuba and witnessed atrocities which set him aflame for life. After this expedition he was himself awarded *repartimientos* of Indians. By 1514 his kindly treatment of them had won him the cordial hatred of the Spaniards.

Returning to Spain, he painted so black a picture of his countrymen's mistreatment of the Indians that the Pope made him head of an investigating committee of friars, and he was sent back to the New World with the title of "Protector of the Indians."

In 1517 he secured from Charles V one hundred leagues of land on the mainland of New Spain and fifty men whom he dressed in white tunics with a red cross on the breast. With them he established his colony, Cumaná, and put his theories into practice. Gathering hundreds of Indians to this land where no armed man

could enter, he taught them and treated them well. The colony
prospered, and its numbers increased until the Spaniards, unable
to fight him otherwise, supplied strong liquors to the Indians to
create disorder. The result was that when Las Casas went to
Santo Domingo to secure more men, the Indians rose and wiped
out the entire colony.

In despair at the news, Las Casas was comforted and advised by
Father Betanzos, a Dominican then stationed in Hispaniola, and
in 1532 entered the Order himself. As a Dominican and a fiery
one, he went to Mexico, then to Nicaragua, preaching always
against the mistreatment of the Indians and rousing with his reports many good people in Spain to support him.

At this time he wrote the historic treatise, *De Unico Vocationis
Modo,* in which he declared that the Indians could be conquered
peacefully. He proved his claims when he arrived in Guatemala
and brought peace to the Land of War. In 1539 he again returned
to Spain to complete his writings on *The Destruction of the Indians* and to assist in formulating the New Laws which revolution-
ized the management of the Indians.

Much against his will, he was made Bishop of the province of
Chiapas, but the resentment of the Spaniards was so strong that
his life was frequently endangered and even the Bishops of the
provinces of Guatemala and Nicaragua would not support him.
Forced at last to give up his work, he entered a convent in Spain
and wrote his *General History of the Indians.* In 1566, at ninety-
two, he died.

Nuestra Señora de la Merced

Because the Mercedarian Order was concentrating its efforts and
funds on the development of its work in Peru, the brotherhood in
Guatemala, from the arrival of the first priests in 1534 until the
completion of this ultra-baroque church and convent in 1760, lived
in modest and frugal quarters. Fully to appreciate the church one
must imagine their suffering as their bitter rivals, the Franciscans
and Jesuits, erected majestic structures while the roofs over their
own heads remained thatched with straw. One can appreciate too
the ironic justice that toppled their rivals' churches to the ground

in 1773 and spared this strong, new church though its convent was destroyed.

The massive façade is deeply carved with floral and abstract designs and further adorned with eight columns entwined with vines and flowers and geometric patterns. Ornate capitals, flying cornices, fancifully decorated niches, a recess above the main entrance to serve as background for Our Lady of Mercy, and seven smaller cubicles for the figures of saints. Two heavy towers adorned with angels and decorations in different styles contain the bells. Above all rises a dome guarded by gilded lions.

This churrigueresco style continues throughout the interior, which is divided into three naves by towering archways. The freshly gilded altar encircled by sculptured columns employs several different styles of carving and ornament. Centrally placed is the figure of Nuestra Señora de la Merced, wearing a gold crown set with many large jewels. Authorities say it is the work of a Spanish sculptor and imported in 1628, but an early chronicler gives a much less realistic origin.

A mysteriously sealed chest addressed to the Order of Mercy in Santiago de los Caballeros arrived by a ship whose captain knew nothing about the box. When the Brothers opened it, they were first greeted by a rare perfume, then by the sight of the figure which revealed a wound in one side from which came the scented liquid. Applied to the ill or maimed, it is said to have healing powers.

To the right of the altar is a chapel containing the celebrated figure of Christ carrying the Cross, made by Paz in 1616 for the Hermitage of La Cruz de Piedra, and another of the Virgen de Dolores, the work of Mendoza. The naves at either side contain six chapels, each with gilded and carved altars and figures by Paz, Martin Cuellar, Zuñiga and others. Throughout the church are massive sacred paintings in spectacularly gilded frames.

The convent was constructed on the same expansive lines to house the school which sent priests and lay brothers far and wide over the Americas, and was liberally equipped with cells, libraries, music rooms, and apartments for the priests and friars and novices. In the patio stood a fountain, one of the masterpieces of the period, called Fuente de los Pescados, because the Brothers carried on experiments in fish-breeding there. Restored in part after the earthquake, it is one of the "must" sculptures to see in Antigua. In the garden of the church is another old stone fountain and a bust of Bartolomé de las Casas.

SAN FRANCISCO

With the church of Santo Domingo at one end and that of the Franciscans at the other, the Calle de la Nobleza was a spectacle worth going to see on Sundays and fête days as the nobility poured out of their palaces and great homes that lined the street, churchward bound. The church and convent of San Francisco, begun in 1543, were even larger and more sumptuous than the Cathedral.

An extensive square enclosed by high walls, with a tall stone cross in the center, formed an impressive approach. The façade had eight columns and niches of various sizes in which stood stucco statues of saints, that of St. Francis of Assisi in the position of honor above the sculptured portals. The roof supported a series of domes, the main one lined with gold, and two towers, each with eight bells, and in one tower the inevitable clock.

Though the interior had but one nave, that one was lofty, its roof supported by colossal columns and arches. The main altar was proportionately high and impressive, with four recesses containing the figures of San Miguel, San Francisco de Asis, Virgen de la Concepción, all by Paz, and a guardian angel seated on a silver throne. Near it, and beneath the stained-glass windows, a fountain tossed its water ten feet into the air to catch the sunlit colors and reflect them in turn over the altar.

About the nave were several famous chapels, one containing the Virgen de los Pobres,* made by Aguirre in 1545, one of the oldest sculptures in America. Others were dedicated to the Third Order —a very large chapel rich in gold ornamentation, *retablos,* images and paintings; to Nuestra Señora de Loreto, its figure of the Virgin * dating back to 1570; to El Cristo de la Agonia, the figure by Felix de Mata, and to the Virgen del Coro,* also by Aguirre, made in 1558. A special chapel was also dedicated to Ecce Homo, the statue,* life-size, made of cork, with glass eyes, and seated on a silver base.

Among the jewels and treasure of this church were several unique and sacred reliquaries; one of gold enclosed a fragment of the Lignum Crucis, the True Cross. Here too were the head and arm of the Cristo de Trujillo,* all that was left of the figure after Spanish and Dutch pirates sacked the town.

The Order attracted many artists, and in the vaults of church and convent were buried such men as Villalpando, Merlo, de Liendo, and Alonso Paz.

The convent was monumental, with many dependencies, among them the famous college of San Buenaventura (established in 1595 as the first in the Kingdom), and its beautiful chapel, a library, archives, salons of music and art where paintings by artists of the Order were shown and Villalpando himself painted. There was a printing press, the second in the country, a Casa de los Estudios with schools of theology, philosophy, canons and, later, experimental physics and mathematics. One of the priests, a renowned scholar, had his own library of books, maps, globes and a laboratory with astronomical instruments, microscopes, barometers, etc. Today ruins of church and convent are among the most striking in Antigua, considered by many to excel all others in architectural grandeur.

This Order, too, had among its members men whose stories and personalities are inextricably linked with the history of the church. One was Brother Pedro de Betancourt; another, don Rodrigo de Arias Maldonado, respectively inspirer and founder of the Bethlehemites.

From his home in the Canary Islands where he was born in 1626, Betancourt, whose singleness of purpose compensated for his simplicity of mind, embarked for Cuba to see the New World. Arriving in Santiago de los Caballeros he entered the College of the Franciscans. After three years he gave up in despair, his mind unable to comprehend and retain what he had learned. Like Dick Whittington he walked out of the city. His London Bridge was the village of Petapa, in whose little church stood a Virgin of wood, bending forward as if to listen. To her he confided his

tragic failure and from her lips received encouragement to return
to the capital.

Back in the convent, he told his experience to his confessor,
through whom he was admitted to the Third Order. Retiring to
the Hermitage of Calvary to meditate, he became inspired to help
the sick. For a few pesos he bought a straw-thatched hut in an
Indian suburb for his first hospital and school for children. Working alone, he carried the sick on his back to this hut and cared for
them. Shortly he became known as the "Servant of God" and permission and funds to build a hospital and church were supplied
him.

About his hospital developed a group of the devout whom he
named Bethlehemites. They pledged themselves to bring in the
sick, if necessary on their own shoulders. The church became a
shrine, particularly at Christmas time when hundreds crowded to
hear his midnight mass and share the games and gifts that followed.

Among his assets was an unerring nose for scandal, and it became his custom to wander about the streets at night, ringing a
little bell to remind evil-doers not to lose their souls. In one of the
houses to which he gave his attention lived the most noble and
eligible of bachelors, don Rodrigo de Arias Maldonado. Only
thirty years of age, don Rodrigo had already served successfully
as governor of the province of Costa Rica, where he subdued the
troublesome Talamanca Indians so successfully that there was talk
of even higher posts in store for him. Called to Santiago on business, he remained to open a great house and live in reckless style.

What follows has many versions, the most authentic of which
seems to be that he fell in love with the wife of a high-ranking
official, and that one night when he was visiting her in her husband's absence she suddenly became lifeless in his arms. Unable
to rouse her, horrified and grief-stricken, he fled into the street. In
the distance he heard the tinkle of Hermano Pedro's approaching
bell. Running to meet the friar, he threw himself on his knees and
implored aid, vowing that if the young woman's life were saved,
he would devote the rest of his own to the Brother's work. Her-

mano Pedro was successful in restoring the lady. The next morning don Rodrigo entered the hospital.

Never was a man so tempted to break a vow. Almost immediately the King sent him word of his appointment as Marqués de Talamanca; he refused it. One of his tasks was to carry sections of raw meat on his back across the Plaza Real just at the hour when the fashionable world was promenading about the central fountain. Daily he was implored to return to his old life; persuasive government posts were offered him.

He was so faithful and resourceful that Hermano Pedro, physically exhausted from his arduous and ascetic life, though only forty years of age, leaned on him more and more. And when in 1675 Betancourt was dying, he passed on to his assistant, now called Hermano Rodrigo de la Cruz, the inspiration to found the Order of the Bethlehemites, prophesying that in time it would have branches in all parts of the world.

Brother Rodrigo finished the construction of the hospital and church, named them Belén, then sailed for Rome, where he received authorization to create the Order. Later he traveled through Mexico and Peru, founding hospitals and churches, and in 1716, when he died, his body was buried with great honor in the church he had established in Mexico City.

Pedro de Betancourt was buried in the Chapel of the Third Order in Santiago, and his tomb, accessible today, is still a shrine where the ill and the grateful come to pray and place small wax figures before the grill. And the superstitious come to touch the grill and make a wish, believing that all wishes made there will be granted. Near by is a curious figure made by a nun from cornhusks and therefore known as the Cristo de las Tusas. In 1735 and 1771 Betancourt was beatified by Pope Clement XIV.

Convent and church are in ruins, but the property, now in private hands, has been cleaned and planted to gardens, providing one of the most delightful and unexpected experiences for all who wish to visit them. The altar of the old church, now in the Chapel of the Third Order, is considered the most interesting example of colonial art in Antigua.

Opposite these gardens are the house of Pedro de Betancourt and

Guadelupe Church with its flamboyant and gaily painted figures
of the Holy Family in niches of the façade. As the King did not
grant permission for the erection of this church until 1793, it
escaped the earthquake and ruin of twenty years before.

COMPANIA DE JESÚS

In 1582 two Jesuits arrived in Santiago from Mexico to found a
modest church and convent for their Company. Modest hardly
applied to the results, for an entire block was needed to accommo-
date the church, convent and Casa de los Estudios. Additional
property had to be secured across the street for the Jesuit college
of San Marcos, later called San Francisco de Borja.

The church, of truly monumental proportions, completed in 1626,
boasted in its façade one of the largest windows in Spanish America; its walls were striking with unique designs stained red and
green. Two belfries contained the famous chimes which, with an
orchestra, accompanied the celebration of the mass. Towering
above them was the great dome. Doors of fine wood, patterned
with reliefs, opened to an austere but harmonious vista of tremendous columns supporting the vaulted arches of three naves. A
stately stairway led to the choir loft, the railings of both the pride
of the ironworkers.

The very wide main nave, with high, lavishly gilded altars, was
a veritable art museum with 70 images and statues and 40 paintings
by contemporary sculptors and artists on its walls.

Next the church were the two-story Casa de los Estudios where
many priests studied theology, philosophy and the sciences and
practised religious exercises, and the convent, built in the same
regal proportion and style as the church. Its college of San Francisco de Borja, founded in 1626, became immediately famous,
drawing scores of scholars and artists into the Order.

One of them was the Guatemala poet, Rafael Maria Landivar,
born in the capital in 1731. He took his vows in Mexico (because
of which he is sometimes called a Mexican poet) but returned to
Santiago to become head of the college. In exile he wrote in Latin
the poems that two centuries later retain for him the title of outstanding poet of Central America.

The house on the street of Santa Lucia where he was born was considered one of the handsomest in the city. Little remains of it now, but the powder works of his father, who was Commissioner General of Cavalry, situated on the same property, is still known as *La Polvora*. When, in 1767, the Jesuits were expelled, Landivar and two other Guatemalteco priests were exiled with them.

No visitor to Antigua should miss the Jesuit ruins, both because of their interest and beauty and for the setting they provide for the hundreds of Indians who find the spacious vaulted rooms and patios an excellent location for their wares on market days. In long rows they spread their textiles and vegetables, pottery, baskets, fruits, flowers, chickens and spotted pigs, unconcerned, if they ever knew, for the past which these soaring gray walls represent.

La Recolección

La Recolección in ruins is a sight which architects study and artists paint with admiration and wonder. Among the broken walls, six and eight feet thick and rising to a tremendous height, authentic style and proportions are still apparent, and above the tumbled stone rises one almost perfect arch.

The founder of this church and convent was Friar Antonio Margil de Jesús. Like Las Casas and Betancourt, he devoted him-self to the poor and oppressed, and the history of the Order of Recolectos in Guatemala is woven around his name and work.

Born in Valencia in 1657, he became a member of the Franciscan Order there, then chose the New World as his field. For years, with a friend and fellow friar, Melchor Lopez, he traveled on foot more than 1200 miles about the Kingdom of Guatemala, convert-ing the Indians by peaceful means, enduring cold, hunger, and hardship.

Hearing of their success, the Bishop of Guatemala begged their aid when the Indians of Verapaz rose in revolt. The two friars, like Las Casas, again succeeded in bringing order when military methods failed. As a result they were given permission to found a school in Santiago to which other members of the Order came from Mexico to assist.

This first college, built in 1701, was little more than a large hut, though it bore the imposing name of Propaganda Fide y Colegio de Cristo Crucificado de Misioneros. Approval and response to their work brought in alms and endowments with which they were able to construct the church and convent.

A wide square, in whose enclosing walls were beautifully proportioned arches, led to the church. Its three naves were divided by stately columns and hewn arches. Many images and paintings adorned chapels and altars, those of the main altar including the group by Bodega representing Christ Crucified * with the Virgin and St. John at the foot of the Cross.

Guardian angels, a Flemish *retablo,* a carved choir loft were among its treasures. The unusually large sacristy was hung with paintings by famous artists and furnished with fine examples of wood carving.

The convent, two stories high, included two large and two small cloisters. Among its dependencies were a library, archives, oratory, choir and music rooms, infirmary, pharmacy, study rooms, chapter room, and refectories. The library and archives were the best in the Kingdom. In 1908, a boat-shaped modern swimming pool was installed in one of its patios!

Friar Antonio Margil was made guardian of the convent, and its reputation soon brought requests from Panama and other places for chapters to be established there. The founder, believing that he had completed his work in Santiago, set off on foot once more, traveling up and down the country. In 1726 he reached Mexico, where, a few months later, he died. His body was buried in the church of San Francisco there.

BEATERIO DE LAS INDIAS

A Beaterio is a "house inhabited by pious women"; in this one, established by Bishop Marroquin in 1550, lived Indian women. The house was really a school under the patronage of Our Lady of the Rosary, in whose name large gardens of vegetables, fruits and flowers were cultivated to be given in charity to destitute Indians. By 1770 the school had become a cloistered convent with the Indian women wearing nuns' robes, living in cells. Word of this angered the King, who decreed that the convent should again be made a school, this time for Indian girls between seven and twenty-two years of age.

HERMITAGE DEL CALVARIO AND VIA CRUCIS

A simple structure of odd design, capped with three arched belfries, founded in 1618, destroyed by earthquake in 1717, rebuilt in 1720; its ruins are now deep in the silt of the Rio Pensativo, the massive cross before it still visible.

Here the artist Montúfar was blinded (page 157) and here also were works by Merlo,* a figure of the Virgen de Dolores by Bodega (on main altar), another of the Virgen de la Piedad by Cuellar, and Nuestra Señora de los Remedios, sometimes called the Virgen de la O.* Here Betancourt (page 175) retired to meditate and here lived the priests in charge of maintaining the Way of the Cross.

This Via Crucis had been marked out originally by the Third Order of the Franciscans with twelve wooden crosses, later replaced by small stone arches. It extended from the shrine of the Virgen de la Luz at the north end of the Calle de los Pasos to the Hermitage of Calvary at the end of the Alameda del Calvario. At Station 12 was a Cristo by Vicente España which is now the venerated Cristo de las Misericordias in Guatemala City. On Good Friday the procession moved slowly down these streets, stopping at each station.

On the way it passed also—on the east side of the Alameda—the parish church of Nuestra Señora de los Remedios, whose original church in the old capital at Almolonga was the second erected in the Kingdom. It is remembered now for its figure of the Virgen de la Esperanza (Hope) and for its legends. One of these legends —that at night the priests entombed in its walls left the church to stroll and meditate on the banks of the river—is thought to have been originated by wily men who returned to the valley in the nineteenth century to raise coffee, the object being to drive the inhabitants off the land. The ruins of the church are now embedded among the trees of a coffee finca.

La Candelaria

This church was also founded in 1550 by Bishop Marroquin and placed in charge of the Dominican Order. In 1754 it was made head of the vicarage of Candelaria, the scene of greatest havoc in 1773. Its only distinctive possession was the Jesús de Candelaria,* by Aguirre, one of the first and now most famous sculptures of the country. Almost destroyed in 1717, the church was restored by Father Francisco Ximenez, who, when he returned to Spain, left it many valuable historical documents. In the square before the entrance stood a stone cross: here the city market was first held.

Nuestra Señora del Carmen

This is perhaps the most-photographed church in the country. In its own day it was considered among the most beautiful of all the churches, and its ruins are still impressive. Fifteen of the sixteen Ionic columns of the façade are untouched, and above the entrance is the statue in stucco of Our Lady of Carmen.

Thick walls reinforced with bastions, vaulted arches and a dome —and two towers filled with chiming bells—made an imposing exterior, surpassed by the dazzling gold altar and the splendor of its services. The best preachers of the day filled its pulpits; a philharmonic orchestra and excellent choir accompanied the mass and brought people of all classes to its doors.

Founded by the Brotherhood of San Escapulario in 1686, the first church and convent were almost destroyed in 1717. Reconstruction improved the original plan, and when in 1728 the new church was opened with pomp and rejoicing, its vogue was assured. The inner walls were decorated with numerous arabesques, festooned with carved and gilded wood, and hung with valuable paintings by creole artists. In addition to its treasures of gold on the main altar was a statue of Our Lady of Carmen,* made in 1637, three feet high, and gorgeously robed in velvet and jewels. The side altars also were rich in precious metals and sculptures, one of them a Cristo de Esquipulas.*

The monastery was built on both sides of the church, forming an open square. Private homes occupy its site today, but in colonial times on the Day of the Virgin, July 16, fiestas were held in the square, with games and tournaments, and at night costly displays of fireworks and masked groups everywhere collecting alms.

Las Capuchinas

One of the most distinctive churches and monasteries in the Kingdom and most picturesque of the ruins today, Las Capuchinas is the site of the first Sisterhood in Central America. In 1725 the Bishop of Guatemala, Juan Bautista Alvarez de Toledo (himself unique because, born in Santiago, he had won honors and degrees abroad and was now the first creole bishop of the colony), sent to Madrid for five Capuchin nuns to establish their Order in Guatemala.

Their cloister had several unusual features. One was a complete sanitary system which modern engineers view with amazement. The novices lived on the first floor, the nuns on the second; each cell had its own bathroom. Also curious was the circular floor from which the cells opened.

In ample grounds were many corridored patios and fountains, an orchard, gardens of fruit, vegetables and herbs. In one garden stood a strange tower, Torre del Retiro, where each nun went into seclusion once a year. The irreverent called it the Tower of Martyrdom and told grim tales of the sufferings of the Sisters when they climbed its outside stairway and entered the formidable walls.

From the first floor rose a colossal column to support the second, which had an open patio in the center surrounded by eighteen cells. Into the supporting arches of the first floor were fastened large iron staples to which ropes were tied. On them was dried the linen of most of the churches, as the nuns were famous for their expert laundering of fine materials. The personal linen of the priests had to be dried in the dark to prevent its turning yellow: members of the Orders were forbidden to wear anything with bluing in it next the body.

The church, built solidly of stone, had in its possession several small oil paintings by Merlo.* In the glass-sealed recess of the altar stood the Virgen del Pilar, their patron saint, and also a painting of the Virgin * by Merlo. The church is gone now, but the cloister with its massive columns remains.

HERMITAGE OF NUESTRA SEÑORA DE LOS DOLORES DEL CERRO

Near the village of Santa Inéz Hortalanos in the outskirts of Antigua are the ruins of a small chapel built by a devout Indian, Sylvestre de la Paz. He began with an image of the Virgen de Dolores, by Manuel Chavez the younger, which he kept in his own house. So many came to worship before it, believing it possessed healing powers, that through contributions from the grateful and the hopeful he was able in 1703 to complete the Hermitage.

ESCUELA DE CRISTO

The first Brotherhood of the Kingdom was established by Bishop Marroquin in Almolonga in 1535 and its cloister named the Hermitage of Santa Vera Cruz. When the capital moved to Panchoy, the Bishop ordered a new Hermitage erected on the site of a shrine to San Miguel where the Indians formerly worshiped. This building Father Bernardino de Obregón y Ovando secured in 1664 for the Escuela de Cristo. Destroyed in 1717, a substantial church and convent were rebuilt on the site. Here the Brotherhood of the Oratory of San Felipe Neri carried on the work of converting Indians.

For this church Quirio Cataño created the figure of Cristo Crucificado—which when completed was so beautiful that Cataño burst into tears, overcome with emotion at its perfection—and a Christ bearing the Cross.* These two sculptures are among the most valuable in the country today.

Another fine work here was the Dolorosa by Mendoza. Here too was the painting, Adoration of the Magi, brought from Barcelona by some Capuchin monks, which, long erroneously believed to be the work of Murillo, was the source of excitement. A figure of San Felipe once owned by the Bethlehemites also was here. Over the door was sculptured the emblem of the Franciscans—two crossed arms, one bare, symbolizing Christ or divine power, the other clothed, symbolizing St. Francis or temporal power.

The Corpus Christi procession of this church was very famous and so was El Convite (The Invitation) held on the preceding day when a band of masked men paraded about the city satirizing leading citizens in verse and prose and inviting everyone to the fiesta.

The convent was a tremendous structure of two stories with a double tier of arches supporting the corridors surrounding the main patio. In the convent was a valuable collection of paintings by contemporary artists. Quirio Cataño was buried in this church.

Hermitage of El Espiritu Santo

These ruins suggest a feudal castle of the twelfth or thirteenth century rather than a sixteenth-century church. The Hermitage, one of the oldest in the capital, is memorable now only because some remarkable superstitions still cling to it.

Once the notorious bandit, Cayetano Figueroa, popularly called Chiquirin or The Cricket, took refuge in the church, and to keep his hiding place unmolested, emitted most horrendous groans and howls during the night. Eventually he was caught and shot. But from his tomb rose even more fearsome howls and groans. The city was panic-stricken; dire disasters were forecast and credited. A venturesome boy discovered that a blind cat, somehow imprisoned in the walls of the outlaw's tomb, was the source of the terror, but by that time the superstitions had taken lusty root.

La Concepción

One of the most famous churches of colonial times, now in ruins, its memory is perpetuated in the reputation of its Sisterhood, which functioned from 1578 until all Orders were banned in the mid-nineteenth century. In fact, the four nuns of noble Spanish birth, brought from Mexico to establish the Order, established also the pattern for women's life in Guatemala.

One of the four was an authority on church calendars and the saints; the second, an expert embroiderer; the third, an excellently trained singer and harpist; and the fourth, such a remarkable cook that illustrious personages from Captains General and Archbishops down considered it an honor to be served dishes prepared by her hands. Immediately their monastery became the goal of the

daughters of the aristocracy. By 1729 it outranked all other Sister-
hoods in Central America in reputation and wealth.

Much of this wealth was derived from the "portions," ranging
from 500 to more than 1000 gold ducats, which the young women
brought with them. These portions remained the property of the
Order on the death of the nuns and in time provided a notable
annual income. At times as many as 1000 women lived within the
cloister's walls—nuns, novices, children to be educated, and their
attendants and servants.

One of these nuns, Juana de Maldonado Paz, is remembered
today more for the sensation that rocked the city over her than for
a legend that she was the leading woman poet of colonial times.
Her father, a powerful noble and member of the Real Audiencia,
out of pride in his twenty-year-old daughter's beauty, wit and
talents as writer and musician, heaped her cell with costly cabinets
and ornaments of gold and silver, pictures and sacred figures and
gold crowns to adorn them. Then, although she had taken the
vows of poverty, he built for her luxurious quarters of her own
with private galleries, garden and chapel.

His devotion at length overriding judgment, he sought to make
his daughter Abbess over the heads of older and wiser nuns. The
result was mutiny in the Order and scandal throughout the city.
Climax and anticlimax were reached when all the church bells
clamored at once as they did in times of alarm and disaster. Everyone rushed to the monastery to defend or oppose Juana's appointment, only to learn that the young woman was not at all interested
in receiving the honor.

San Augustín

After erecting one church in a very unhealthy spot, the Augustinians took over the first church of Santa Catarina Martír and in
1615 built there a church and convent that shortly became the most
fashionable in the capital. With massive bastions supporting its
walls, a handsome façade with a great window above the entrance,
above that a statue of St. Augustine and round it figures of Augustinians and saints, and above everything a dome, it survived

until 1917 when earthquake left it in its present state, a still sightly ruin.

Behind once heavy cedar doors studded with bronze—now made of corrugated iron—the church boasted three famous paintings, St. Augustine, St. Peter, and St. John the Baptist, all by Montúfar. The main altar was of carved and gilded wood with a figure of San Augustín in the place of honor and a number of good *retablos*. The side altars also possessed several good images, the best, those of the Virgen del Carmen * and a life-size Cristo Crucificado.*

The chief claim of this cloister to fame was not in its architecture or treasure but in its membership. The most renowned philosophers and theologians of the Kingdom occupied its cells.

Santa Catarina Martír

After leaving its first church to the Augustinians, the Sisterhood erected this second structure in 1613 and settled down to compete with the Order de la Concepción for the honor of maintaining the best school and cloister. The rivalry soon became historic as aristocratic families of the Kingdom took sides.

One of the founders of the Sisterhood was Elvira de San Francisco, who when six years of age had been left at the door of la Concepción. At twenty she was already distinguished for her beauty and strength of character, but when she was made Abbess of Santa Catarina, and in spite of the fact that she was believed to be the daughter of a noblewoman, opposition rose because of her unknown origin.

The convent, one of the smallest in the city, was soon so popular that an addition was built across the street and the two buildings joined by an overhead archway so that the Sisters could go back and forth unobserved. This section of the city suffered most heavily in 1773, and the convent was badly damaged, but the archway, restored in 1833, is now one of the picturesque sights of Antigua.

The church, built in 1647, was originally called Santa Catarina Virgen y Martír. Very simple and austere in style, its façade was relieved by columns with decorative stucco capitals and an excellently sculptured coat of arms of Spain above the door. Its main altar and six side altars had many good statues. One of them was

a figure of Santa Catarina, by Cuellar; another, of San José, by
the Spanish sculptor, Juan Martinez Montañez, and a third, a
Cristo Yacente,* by an unknown artist.

Santa Clara

Founded in 1699, church and monastery of massive stone, carved
in pure Spanish style, survived the earthquake of 1773, only to fall
under later and less severe shocks. It differs from all other
churches in the city in that it faces its monastery so that nuns could
enter and leave either building unseen.

The church possessed a famous picture of Christ on the Cross,
presented by Bishop Alvarez de Toledo. Its main altar, in the
shape of an enormous miter, was richly carved of wood. On it
stood a figure of Santa Clara holding a guardian angel in her hands,
and a figure of Christ on the Cross, with Mary, Mary Magdalene
and St. John about the base, the work of Zuñiga.

The cloister was a popular choice for young women taking the
veil, as life there was a pleasure rather than a martyrdom. The
nuns, known as Clarissas, won a reputation for their cooking,
notably their bread, which was sold to the aristocracy for fête-day
feasts. The ample grounds occupied more than 225,000 square
feet; the main patio was the largest in any cloister of the city, and
in its center stood a beautiful fountain.

Church and cloister are in ruins now, though the façade with its
figures of San Miguel and San Gabriel stands and many find the
patio with its double tier of arches and the fountain one of the
most attractive spots in Antigua.

Santa Cruz

This was one of the first churches to be built in the baroque
style. Its façade, with a stuccoed group representing Christ on the
Cross with Mary and Mary Magdalene at the foot and six niches
holding figures of saints, was considered very fine. The atrium
opened on a square in which stood a stone cross and a 1732 fountain. Among its parishioners were many wealthy Indians.

On the main altar stood the Virgen del Rosario* by Alonso Paz,
and on another his Jesús Nazareno, now in the church of La

Merced. The church was celebrated for its procession of the Penitents in which marched from afternoon until midnight leading
officials and citizens, among them Pedro de Betancourt carrying a
heavy wooden cross. The ceremony took its name from Friar
Alfonso Sanchez (the Hermit of Chipilapa, for whom a street in
Antigua is named), a vegetarian in a day when men ate raw meat!
He lived in a straw-thatched hut, slept on a cross, and emerged
only to take part in this procession and attend mass. When he
died, civil and religious authorities walked behind his coffin, which
was interred in the Cathedral.

SAN GERÓNIMO

This little church was functioning some years before 1740 when
its college of Maximo Doctor San Gerónimo was built. It was an
imposing two-story structure, whose cloister, faced with a double
series of arches, enclosed a patio in which stood an octagonal fountain. Today it is interesting as a symbol of its times, for in 1718
arrived the royal decree prohibiting the establishment of further
Orders or churches, and in 1763, more than twenty years after the
college was opened, the authorities, discovering that the Brothers
of Mercy had not secured permission from the King for its erection, confiscated the property.

SANTA ROSA DE LIMA

At the end of the wide street of the silversmiths, now known as
the Alameda de Santa Rosa, and shaded by *amatle* trees, the ruins
of this church and beaterio suggest their ambitious size and style.
Today the church is almost forgotten and the beaterio is remembered as the "Convent of White Women" because of the high-born
and wealthy Spanish ladies who took their vows there, and for its
complete collection of paintings of the twelve apostles.

SAN SEBASTIÁN

After the severe earthquakes of 1565, the Ayuntamiento of Santiago felt the need of having a patron saint of its own. San
Sebastián was chosen, and on San Felipe hill on the outskirts of
the city a small church was erected in his name. Later city fathers

found both site and church too modest and distant, so in 1582 a
new and larger structure was built in the city. Shortly it became
a regular parish church and served as such until 1874, when another quake shook down all but the side walls and a portion of the
façade.

Its fame rests chiefly on its procession for San Sebastián on January 20. This became one of the main events of a colonial calendar crowded with main events. The sight of the highest military
officers in resplendent uniforms and decorations carrying the figure
of the saint on their shoulders, the corps of trumpeters that followed them, and the entire membership of the Board of Aldermen
following them, brought the city out in force. In the evening a
brilliant display of fireworks was set off before the church, after
which everyone danced.

SANTA TERESA

In 1675 the King of Spain granted permission to found the
Order of the Carmelitas Descalzas in Santiago and a monastery
for the nuns of Santa Teresa in connection with it. Bernardino de
Obregón y Ovando, who had already established the Escuela de
Cristo, went to Peru himself to secure three Carmelite nuns.

The church, begun in 1683 and completed four years later, had
the distinction of possessing the most beautiful and valuable tabernacle in the country on its altar. Made of the finest wood, inlaid
with golden arabesques, it contained a guardian angel adorned
with jewels. The building itself was a solid and majestic structure, with eight Ionic columns and six niches with stucco saints on
its façade and in the upper section an arched window in which
stood the figure of La Mística Doctora Santa Teresa de Jesús.

Gradually the houses, which the Bishop of Guatemala had left
on his death for the use of the Carmelites, were replaced by a
handsome cloister of two stories. When in 1717 the building was
almost destroyed, the nuns lived in huts in their orchard until it
was rebuilt. When it was more fully destroyed in 1773, the terrorized imagination of the people created many superstitions about it;
mystic songs could be heard there at night, they said, and slipped
in to listen.

Because of its strategic location, it witnessed most of the historic processions of the day—the Cathedral's procession, Las Palmas, on the Sunday before Easter; the procession *de los caballeros* when all the knights in a brilliant display of heraldry, banners, costumes and mounts rode past their doors in the Good Friday procession of the church of San Francisco. Before their doors, too, rode the Banner of the Tribunal the day the Holy Office of the Inquisition was established in Guatemala.

Plaza de Armas

The first cords marking the plan of the new capital of Santiago de los Caballeros in 1541 were stretched about a huge and almost perfect square to serve as the Plaza Real, the heart of the city. On the south side was then placed the site of the Palace of the Captains General; on the east, the Cathedral, on the north the Casas Consistoriales or Real Cabildo, the seat of local government, and on the west, the Portal de los Mercadores, street of the merchants. Leading off from this center were the first seven avenues and nine streets, to which locations for churches, homes and shops were assigned.

Immediately the plaza became the focus of the capital's life. Here were the spectacular pageants and processions, the bull fights and tournaments and jousts and games staged by the knights, and the dances given by the Indians for the pleasure of their conquerors. On one side were the gallows and whipping post where Spaniards and creoles during the first years—and after the death of Bishop Marroquin, the Indians—were hanged and lashed. From the balconies of government buildings and the Episcopal Palace, the royal and ecclesiastic authorities looked on.

In the center after 1614 stood the fountain about which the Indians gathered on market days to spread themselves and their wares on straw mats and erect others for shade above them. And every afternoon the social world came to circle round and round on foot or in carriages to see and be seen.

Today, deep in shade trees and bright with flowers, it drowses in the sun, its silence broken occasionally by the shouts of children playing under the eyes of passive Indian nursemaids. Now it is known as the Plaza de Armas because the headquarters of the military face upon it.

EL PALACIO DE LOS CAPITANES GENERALES

The first seat of government for the Kingdom of Guatemala in the new Santiago de los Caballeros was the Casas Reales (Royal Houses) built in 1550 under the direction of Bishop Marroquin, to serve as headquarters for both State and Church. Its construction was so faulty that finally engineers and architects were commissioned to erect a new one—entirely for government purposes—that would endure. Completed in 1764, it did endure for nine years, when the earthquake of 1773 laid it low. Its façade, however, has been restored to its original Spanish Renaissance purity and enough of the interior rebuilt to suggest the scale of its plan and decoration.

The finest piece of construction in all the Kingdom in 1764, it was named Palace of the Captains General, and, perhaps in celebration of that event, the Captains General and Governors were given the additional title and authority of President of the Real Audiencia.

The façade has a double arcade of wide corridors and 54 arches, 27 above, 27 below, whose huge pilasters are hewn of single pieces of stone. In the center of the façade was sculptured the royal arms of Spain with a large stucco lion on guard at either side. Above and to one side were the arms of the capital, and on the other a long inscription concerning the building's erection. Today the crest of the Republic of Guatemala has replaced them.

Colorful and varied are the records of the thirty-six Captains General—from the second to the thirty-seventh—who ruled the Kingdom from the Casas Reales and the Palacio. At one extreme was Mayén de Rueda, whose tyranny and corruption roused the wrath of the Franciscans. He personally pursued the confidential assistant of his predecessor into the sanctuary of their church, and when an aged priest protested his brutality, first insulted, then struck, the priest. The Franciscans closed their doors and prepared to move to Mexico. All the Orders closed their churches, convents and schools in sympathy. The scandal spread to the surrounding country and threatened to end in rebellion. At last the Real

Audiencia persuaded the Franciscans to reconsider; Mayén de Rueda was removed from office and returned to Spain. He may have gone mad there, or possibly hatred was father to the thought; at any rate, violent legends, recorded as fact, assert that he went mad in Santiago and for the rest of his life roamed the fields naked, living on herbs and charity.

At the other extreme was Diego de Avendaño, whose seven years of government were ruled by such wisdom and justice that when, some years after his death, his tomb was opened, his hands were found to be as natural as in life, the reason, of course, being that they had never mistreated man or beast or touched a dishonest penny.

The sala of the Real Audiencia in the Palace was a sumptuous place of carved walls and furniture and portraits in oil of kings and queens, popes, archbishops and bishops, famous priests and other colonial personages. Doubtless the members of the Audiencia saw in its costly elegance assurance of their permanent location in Santiago de los Caballeros.

In 1549 they had been transferred from Gracias a Dios in Honduras, to Santiago; after fourteen years, as a result of scandals in connection with the Captain General of the time, they were ordered to Panama. Bartolomé de las Casas (page 171), an old man of ninety then, as almost the last act of his life, hurried to Madrid and won from the King restoration of the Supreme Court to Guatemala.

Also within the block-square walls of the Palace were the offices of the royal tax, the exchequer, of the balls and tournaments, of the knights, of the military headquarters of the army and the barracks of the dragoons. The prison was there—the best one in Spanish America at that time—and the department in charge of Indian slaves. In the heart of the building were two large patios, each with its colonial fountain. Today the Palace houses the offices of the Department of Sacatepéquez.

THE MINT OR CASA DE MONEDA

After two centuries of struggling to reconcile money from Mexico and Peru with a little gold from Spain, the Kingdom of Guatemala won the right to mint its own currency. In February, 1733, with music and with banners flying, the capital's authorities rode out in procession to welcome the director, his five assistants, and the necessary dies and equipment arriving from Mexico. A little more than a month later, silver doubloons, Guatemala's first coins, were minted, and a *bando*—a military officer accompanied by a trumpeter—announced from all corners of the Plaza that thenceforth they were to be accepted as legal currency.

On one side of each doubloon was the royal arms of Spain; on the other the bust of Felipe II, and on both, legends in Latin and the date, 1733. A year later, dies and silver from the mines of Honduras were ready to turn out pesos. Of these more than 4,000,000 were minted, their irregular contours winning them the name of *macacos* or "pieces of eight." They were in circulation until the late nineteenth century.

In time the colony had a complete system of coinage, based on the *real* as the unit of value:

Ocho escudos	16 reales	$2.00
Doubloon	8 "	1.00
Peso	8 "	1.00
Toston	4 "	.50
Peseta	2 "	.25
Real		.125
Medio real	½ "	.0625
Cuartillo	¼ "	.0316

Silver had greater value than gold in colonial times. Gold pesos were in demand by wealthy Indians for necklaces for their wives, and *macacos* and *cuartillos* also in quantities found their way to the necks and wrists and ears of the Indians. Many of these chains are still worn today.

As there were no banks in the Kingdom, men hid their wealth—frequently in water jars buried in gardens, patios and walls, sometimes in false backs of furniture. These hiding places were buried under the ruins in 1773, and, discovered generations or a century or more later, have created a wealth of legends of fortunes found by newcomers. The largest known amount to be found totaled $30,000.

Palace of the Real Cabildo

From the time the capital was set up at Almolonga, two *alcaldes* or justices were elected annually to administer the city government, and when the capital was moved to Panchoy, a *corregidor* (mayor) and *regidores* (aldermen) shared the little building known as Casas Consistoriales.

One of these aldermen, elected *regidor perpétuo* because of the honor in which he was held, was Bernal Diaz del Castillo. A rough-and-tumble youth of almost astronomical naïveté, he left his home in Medino del Campo in Spain in 1514 when he was twenty-two and set off to find adventure, fame and fortune in New Spain. Adventure he had, fighting 119 battles, according to his own tally, under Pedrarias Davila, Cortes and Alvarado in Panama, Mexico and Central America. Fortune he never won, but the devotion of his contemporaries and fame he gained beyond his dreams.

The Conquest over, he chose Guatemala as his home, settling down in Almolonga and then Panchoy with Teresa Becerra, daughter of another conqueror, as his wife. At seventy, irked beyond endurance by the inaccuracies and misrepresentations of the histories of the Conquest, he resolved to write one himself. The result was his *True History of the Conquest of New Spain and Guatemala,* which he completed when he was eighty-four. He left it as a legacy to his children. Two of his descendants picked up his pen; Fuentes y Guzmán (page 160) and Antonio Batres Juaregui, to whom later writers are something more than reasonably indebted.

In 1743 the Casas Consistoriales was replaced by the Palace of the Real Cabildo. It had been planned to erect a building that would complement the Palace of the Captains General and also occupy one full side of the Plaza Real, but funds ran out and the rest of the area was left for a Portal de Nagueras (Portal of the Skirt Traders) and houses in one of which the first printing press of 1660 was set up.

Two stories high, built entirely of stone with a double arcade of 24 arches and a tower, the Cabildo served until an earthquake destroyed the need for it. Fortunately, about the middle of the

nineteenth century it was restored and remains today as the seat
of the municipal government for Antigua and headquarters of the
civil government. On its façade can be seen the coat of arms
of Santiago de los Caballeros. Frequently it is called the Ayuntamiento, though its official name now is Intendencia or City Hall.

Here in colonial times, in addition to the offices and auditorium
of the city fathers, was the new city jail, an immense room, large
enough to contain 80 prisoners. The jail had its own chapel, on
whose simple altar was a figure of Santiago Apóstol and an oratory
with a life-size Cristo Crucificado, with the Virgen Dolorosa at the
foot for the solace of prisoners condemned to death. Here too
were the archives, a multitude of documents and records of great
historical value, including maps of the city and of the sources of
water supply.

Its auditorium and some of its offices were hung with paintings
of illustrious personages of Spain and Guatemala. A crayon sketch
of Las Casas, an oil of Columbus, and the portrait of Pedro Cortés
y Larrás, the Archbishop who led the fight to retain the capital in
Santiago, are still there. So are the archives, though neglected and
with many documents lost, destroyed or stolen.

University and Colleges

If Bishop Marroquin's petition to the King in 1559 had been
granted, Guatemala would have had one of the first three universities in all the Americas. On his death in 1563, the Bishop left
funds for a building, but the indifference of the King and the
opposition of Jesuits, Franciscans and Dominicans, who wished no
rival for their own colleges, delayed authorization until 1676.

Two years later the College of Santo Tomás de Aquino of the
Dominican Order was elevated to university standing, and under
the new name of La Pontificia y Real Universidad de San Carlos
Borromeo and in a $100,000 building of its own, was opened amid
much public rejoicing. For a time the aristocracy tried to limit
its students to those of pure Castilian descent, but this was over-
ruled and many men of all classes, five of whom became Bishops
and one, surgeon to the King, were graduated.

The curriculum included various branches of theology, philosophy, canons, law, medicine and the Cakchiquel language. On its faculty were many distinguished ecclesiastics, writers, scientists. Rivalry between the university and the colleges of the Orders kept standards high. In 1687 the university was granted all the privileges given those of Mexico and Peru, among them the right to award degrees and for graduates to wear hoods. So to the pageant of ecclesiastical robes, military uniforms and bright and varied Indian costumes were added the colors of the hoods, white for theology, green for lawyers (because of which the wearers were called *pericos,* parrakeets), blue for philosophy, yellow for medicine, etc.

The building was a striking example of Moorish architecture with fretted arches and hexagonal windows set into thick walls. Its original façade had a beautifully wrought and huge portal, adorned with mortar and stucco angels holding in their hands books and symbols of the sciences. On the walls were large shields bearing the coats of arms of Spain and pontifical heraldry. The façade, restored after 1821, now bears the coat of arms of the old Federation of Republics of Central America and the words

"Academy of Public Instruction, whose existence is due to the benevolence of Mariano Galvez, stimulated by the Municipality of 1832."

The patio was very large with seven archways on each side, all twenty-eight trefoiled with terra cotta, framing four wide corridors. In the center was a large fountain. Ten lecture halls were well lighted and well proportioned.

The auditorium was spacious and richly furnished. Among its works of art were portraits of Spanish monarchs, popes, Bishop Marroquin, and others. The chapel boasted three excellent statues of the patron saints of the university, San Carlos, Virgen de la Concepción, and Santa Teresa de Jesús. Library and archives were filled with books and manuscripts by Spanish writers and later with Indian grammars, histories and records and accounts of *costumbres,* written by faculty members and graduates. (Next door was the chapel of San José whose beautiful doorway still remains.)

In its day the university was the foundation of learning and the focus from which radiated the cultural, moral and intellectual life

of all Central America. Today its building is the Museum of
Colonial Antigua.

Although most important, the university was not the first institution of learning in the colony. In addition to the Dominican
Colegio de Santo Tomás de Aquino, the Jesuit Colegio de San
Francisco de Borja and the Franciscan Colegio de San Buenaventura, all the Orders had schools for children. Early in the sixteenth century the Colegio de Indios de Nuestra Señora was opened
for the education of Indians. Of it little has been recorded—on
the assumption, as Victor Miguel Diaz puts it, that "when so many
mestizos could not read, it is easy to imagine the enormous number of ignorant Indians who would rebel at receiving lessons from
the whites who had always treated them as slaves." Later the
school merged with the university.

In 1596 Felipe II commanded that seminaries for the Indians be
erected in all the Bishoprics of New Spain, and four years later
the Real Audiencia established the seminary of La Asunción de
Nuestra Señora in Guatemala. Only young men of noble Spanish
families were admitted, however; the faculty was poor, and little
more than Latin grammar and theology was taught. In 1767 the
King ordered that sons of Indian chiefs should be admitted, and
for their instruction the Colegio Tridentino was formed within
the seminary. The chapel of this college is still in a fair state of
preservation and can be seen in the corner house in the same block
as the Museum.

MUSEUM

The spacious halls of the University of San Carlos now house
many of the art treasures of colonial days both from the old capital
of Santiago de los Caballeros and from crumbling churches and
homes about the country.

Here are paintings by Merlo, Montúfar and Corea originally in
the Cathedral, and the painting, Salvador de Horta, a relic from
the first capital at Almolonga; portraits of officials and nobles from
the Palace of the Captains General, and two paintings in the style
of Murillo. In a special closed cabinet hangs the portrait of the
nun, Sister Berengaria, who, after twenty years as cook and menial
in the Convent of Santa Clara, was suddenly elevated to the post

of Abbess because the jealous sisters could not agree to elect one
of themselves. Her face still reflects bewilderment or perhaps awe,
for during her first night in office the shades of all her predecessors
rose from their graves to come and congratulate her.

Numerous examples of colonial crafts—carved wood, stone, iron
and leather work, and furniture, as well as the architecture and
decor of the Museum itself—enable the visitor to reconstruct something of the life of the old capital.

HOSPITALS

In Almolonga a crude hut under the name of Misericordia served
as the first hospital, but in Panchoy six hospitals were founded,
three of them in charge of the Brotherhood of San Juan de Dios,
established in 1641, two under Pedro de Betancourt (page 175).

The first and largest was El Real Hospital de Santiago, erected
in 1553 by Bishop Marroquin with his own funds to care for Spaniards and creoles. Two centuries later it was a substantial building
of two floors, with long, wide corridors enclosing four patios where
six fountains provided abundant water, and large and well-lighted
sick rooms.

The second was the Hospital de San Alejo, maintained by the
Dominicans for the Indians. Erected and supported by alms, it
was soon so crowded that, even with beds side by side, room was
insufficient until the Real Audiencia provided an annual pension
of 600 pesos. Bishop Marroquin tried to combine this hospital with
the Royal Hospital, but neither Spaniard nor Indian would consider being ill under the same roof, so this idea was abandoned
until 1685.

San Pedro Apóstol, the third hospital, built in 1660, was very
small, and limited admission to priests, deacons and subdeacons.

And the fourth was the Hospital of St. Lazarus for lepers. Lep-
rosy, like many other virulent diseases, was unknown in Central
America until the arrival of the white man. When some cases
appeared in the capital, no attention was paid them. By 1638 the
disease had spread alarmingly and an extensive tract of land was
set aside on the outskirts for hospital and church, which from 1640
to 1773 were in charge of the Brotherhood of St. John. The church

had a fine image of St. Lazarus by Alonso Paz. Lepers were permitted to cultivate their own herb, vegetable and flower gardens and orchards, but were forbidden under severe penalties to approach the city. The cemetery of Antigua occupies this land today.

Colonial hospitals were supported largely by charity. The poverty of the few doctors available, says Miguel Diaz, was equaled only by their ignorance. Their fees of two reales (25 cents) for visits by day and three by night were condemned as exorbitant, and on their reduced charges they could scarcely buy necessities.

By 1773 the practice of medicine and care of the sick had advanced, but that the early patients survived the hospitals is a tribute to man's will to live. Beds were of wood, provided with a thin pallet of straw and a heavy wool blanket, changed when they fell to pieces. In the center of each room was an open pitcher of water, lighted at night by candles, for the use of all. The diet for every disease and injury consisted of tortillas, soup, potatoes, and unsalted mutton. Medical instruments were of wood and tin.

On an open shelf were the hospital supplies: syrups, oils, purgative seeds, roots and infusions. Salves were made of suet. Pink honey from sugar cane was prescribed for all pulmonary troubles.

In front of the hospital of San Juan de Dios today is Union Park, with shade trees and a fountain; but in 1680 any patients fortunate enough to be conscious had the privilege of hearing the first bull fight in the city.

STREETS AND AVENUES

In colonial times each thoroughfare was named for a saint, some predominating activity or feature; with the Republic those colorful titles were replaced with numerals. In 1938, however, the city government, influenced by the increasing tourist travel, began to restore one by one the old names, and now decorative tile plaques are set in the walls as guides.

Though the Calle de la Nobleza (Street of the Nobility) was the center of wealth and trade, lined on both sides with palaces and mansions and important commercial houses, the Calle Ancha de los Herreros (Wide Street of the Blacksmiths) was the most famous. In 1536 a spark from a blacksmith's forge almost wiped out

the capital at Almolonga, and to prevent similar fires the city
fathers ruled that in future all blacksmith shops should be erected
outside city limits.

The capital in Panchoy soon expanded to include their street,
and it became the main artery of traffic, with carriage makers and
carpenters, liquor shops and many others nudging out the forges.
Also many fine homes were built here, with carved wood grills
at the windows and peepholes in the doors. At the end of this
street stood the Stone Cross where the Postmaster and officials met
the mails from Spain. Now houses and shops are deep in the silt
of the Pensativo.

The city, both as Santiago de los Caballeros and as Antigua, has
always been blessed with ample supplies of clear water, thanks to
the skill of colonial engineers. They brought water from the hills
in three brick aqueducts (still doing service today) to masonry
towers or *alcantarillas* located at strategic points in the city. From
these water was distributed to individual buildings and, by ingenious pipes, connected with bathrooms and *pilas*. Some of the *alcantarillas* still stand and, of course, the number of public and private
fountains from colonial times is legion.

Certain corners of Santiago were designated as the points from
which official announcements would be made. At such times a
bando would make the rounds, and when the trumpeter had collected the neighborhood, an officer would read the proclamation
aloud; his rounds completed, the new regulation was in force.

Today the streets are lighted by electricity, but colonists ventur-
ing out at night moved in darkness, except where householders
kept a lantern or candle burning beneath a small sacred image in a
niche in the wall. Occasionally a knight or official passed, his way
made brilliant by blazing torches in the hands of numerous lackeys.

RESTORED COLONIAL HOMES

In recent years the restoration of old colonial homes has added
to the charm and interest of Antigua. Of these, the first and most
widely known is the Popenoe House.

Built in 1634 by don Luis de las Infantes Mendoza y Venegas,

Justice of the Supreme Court of the Kingdom of Guatemala, situated on the Street of the Nobility, it passed through many hands until acquired by Dorothy and Wilson Popenoe.

It is an impressive structure, Renaissance-Moorish in style, with vast rooms (the sala or reception room is 90 by 92 feet) and several patios. In addition to its restored walls and colonial furnishing, one of the patios is devoted to orchid culture, and some varieties are in blossom in all seasons.

In the sala is a collection of portraits by colonial and modern artists of personages who contributed to the history of Antigua and the house itself. Towering above the roofs is the Capuchin cypress, planted in 1850, from which the house derives its local name, Casa del Capuchino.

Other restored colonial homes include the "House of the Bells" on the street of that name, owned by Mr. and Mrs. Lewis Palmer, and El Alcázar, an inn. El Alcázar occupies only part of the once enormous and sumptuous mansion of the wealthy Chamorros family, who for their housewarming substituted wines from Spain for the water flowing into the large fountain in the main patio. Later the family of the poet, Pepe Batres, lived here.[1]

[1] Casa Rodil, Casa de los Sirenas, so called because of the stone sirens guarding its entrance, Casa de los Leones, originally the property of the high-ranking Alvarez and Toledo family, may also be of interest, though little or nothing has been done to restore or preserve their colonial character.

THE REPUBLIC OF GUATEMALA

XV

THE MOVEMENT FOR INDEPENDENCE

THE influences contributing to the bloodless revolution which won the Kingdom of Guatemala freedom from Spain can be set down in a neat little row—the American Revolution; the French Revolution; Spain's economic, political and religious tyranny; the Jesuits, who after their expulsion from Spanish America in 1767 had striven to rid the New World of Spain; the unofficial aid given by England, Spain's hereditary enemy, to refugees and revolutionaries in London. Together they do not add up to the one great cause, the sacred fire, lighted early in the colonial régime.

This was Spain's policy of giving the *chapetones* (those born on Spanish soil) precedence in all things over the creoles, those of pure Spanish blood but born in Guatemala. The creoles' hatred of the *chapetones* was Spain's undoing. And in South America, Simon Bolívar, "Liberator of Spanish America," had, in freeing Venezuela and founding Colombia, proved that Spain could be undone.

Spain was unhappy also in her appointment of Captains General before 1821. The last of these, Brigadier don Gabino Gainza, a weak man from Spain's standpoint, was an astute one from the colonial. Aware of the wall of hatred against Spain from the Straits of Magellan to the Rio Grande, confident that Mexico would win her freedom, above all interested to maintain his own position, he did little to restrain rebellion in Guatemala.

The last straw was the abdication of Carlos IV from the Spanish throne and the substitution of José Bonaparte of France. Spaniards and creoles whose loyalty had held them aloof from Independence, saw now no reason why Guatemala should be ruled by a Spain that could not rule itself. Remained to the Royalist Party then, only the Officiales Reales, the Church authorities, and their satellites.

No country could have been less prepared for Independence. The entire Kingdom was ridden by wretchedness and poverty. Only a fraction of the population could read and write; the majority—the Indians—could not even speak Spanish. Nor were there among the Independents any who had had either theory or practice in the art of government. All lacked faith in themselves and one another. The final handicap was the ill will of one province for the others and their common resentment and jealousy of the capital.

And the Indians, dominated for 300 years by Spanish tyranny, descendants of survivors of the Conquest whose heritage for centuries had been to submit to Indian autocrats, were sunk in a vast mire of misery, ignorance and apathy. A few could grasp the idea of winning freedom from Spain; none could understand the abstract principle of liberty.

Here and there after 1810, when echoes of the Grito de Dolores— the cry of the priest, don Miguel Hidalgo y Costilla of Mexico, who led his congregation against Spanish authorities in the village of Dolores—reached the colony, spasmodic revolts and conspiracies were attempted, first in Salvador, then in Nicaragua. In the Convent of Belén in Guatemala City a priest lent his cell to a group of prominent men who under the pretense of playing chess plotted revolution. But Spain's eyes and ears were everywhere and conspirators were either caught or betrayed.

Such was the situation on the morning of September 15, 1821, when a meeting of all royalist, Church and creole officials was called in the Palace of the Captains General. They were to consider an important document which had arrived from the province of Chiapas, the first state in the Kingdom to declare its independence of Spain.

This document was the Plan de Iguala, formulated in the village of Iguala, Mexico, by Emperor Augustín Iturbide and the Royalist Party there. Sometimes known as the Plan of Three Guaranties, it provided (1) that Mexico and the Kingdom of Guatemala should invite a Prince of Spain, preferably Fernando VII, to come to the New World and rule them jointly as an independent empire; (2) that the Catholic Church should be the supreme and only religious authority; (3) that *chapetones* and creoles should bury the hatchet and live in peace and harmony forever.

Surely that meeting of September 15 was unique among the gatherings in history to consider the subject of Independence. In addition to the Captain General, the Royal Officials, the Archbishop and church officials, there were the leading creoles and such representatives of the provinces as had conquered the impassable roads. And as word of the meeting spread, corners of the audience chamber and the corridors filled to overflowing with men and women of all classes.

Outside other agencies were busy. One was Maria Dolores Bedoya de Molina, a leader in the conspiracy for many years. To create the impression that the Royalists underestimated the demand for Independence, she gathered *marimbas* and fireworks in the Plaza to attract a mob of the curious but politically apathetic. Another was El Calvario Church, whose curate set the bells ringing. Other churches followed suit. And the populace, understanding little, but responsive always to excitement, shouted and cheered, and their numbers increased.

In this bedlam the debate in the Palace proceeded. Early, Royalists and Church realized their cause was lost; the creoles and citizens crowding the doors had but one idea—liberty. And in the streets the uproar mounted until first the Archbishop, then the Royalists sought the safety of their own homes. Gainza's suggestion that the meeting endorse the Plan de Iguala was howled down. Independence of Spain, Mexico and every other country alone would satisfy.

A lawyer, don José Cecilio del Valle (El Sabio, "The Wise") dictated then and there the Act of Independence of Central America. Gainza and twelve men, now known as the Proceres de la Independencia, signed it. The Act merely established the fact of Independence; it left the field open for republic or monarchy to follow.

Shortly the Act disappeared, and until a few years ago was believed to have been spirited to Europe—as have been many other valuable records—and sold to the British Museum. In 1934, don Joaquin Pardo, secretary of the Sociedad de Geografía é Historia, found it between the pages of an old manuscript in the archives.

XVI

ONE HUNDRED AND TEN YEARS OF TURMOIL

HARDLY had the Act of Independence reached the assemblies of the various provinces for ratification when the governors of Nicaragua and Honduras, ambitious to demonstrate their equal authority with the capital, secured votes of adherence to the Plan de Iguala and to separation from Guatemala. Chiapas had already joined Mexico; Costa Rica was indifferent; Salvador then and forever after declared its independence of Guatemala and all other nations.

In Europe, too, the new Guatemala government encountered difficulty. Its monarchies, disturbed by the Spanish-American trend toward democracy and eager to divide the disordered states among themselves, delayed recognition. The only encouragement came from the United States, which recognized the government as soon as Congress convened and, aware both of Europe's interest in Central America and Russia's in Alaska, formulated the Monroe Doctrine, sometimes called the real Declaration of Independence for Central America.

In Mexico, Emperor Augustín de Iturbide was in no mood to allow these small states to balk his ·dream of an empire extending to the Isthmus of Panama; by force or persuasion he succeeded in annexing all but Salvador, but in 1822 his empire collapsed. With the exception of Chiapas, the little states then united as the Republica Federal de Centro America, though in all but geographical location they were as separate as the poles.

Their first General Congress in 1823-24 adopted a constitution modeled on that of the United States, providing for a president to administer the Federation and a chief of staff as a governor of each state; abolished slavery and instituted other reforms. Its greatest achievement, however, was in stimulating each state to mix in the affairs of the others. The result was that revolution followed revolution with individual greed for power rather than national interest the object.

Party hatred within each state was equally bitter; each had two major parties, the Liberalists who opposed the Church, and the Conservatives (made up of landowners and merchants) who supported it. They became so irreconcilable that, except in Guatemala and Salvador, each state had two capitals.

The first president of the Federation, General Manuel José Arce, a Salvadorean, set the example. Shortly he quarreled with his party and founded a government of his own. This roused Salvador, Honduras and the Liberals of Guatemala, who, united under the leadership of the Honduranian general, Francisco Morazón, overthrew Arce and made Morazón president.

The chief of state for Guatemala under Morazón was Mariano Galvez, a Liberal far in advance of his times. He abolished the religious Orders, introduced the Livingston Code which did away with the death penalty, provided for trial by jury, civil marriage, and other reforms inimical to the Church. He also established a general school system, and when a cholera epidemic swept Central America, forbade burial within city limits. When he tried to fight the plague, the ignorant people in the districts suffering most heavily declared that the doctors he had sent them were poisoning their water supplies. Uniting under a twenty-three-year-old outlaw, Rafael Carrera, they set off for Guatemala City.

Followed a period of turmoil and civil war that by 1839 resulted in there being no national government at all. Morazón was finally defeated, and Carrera, ignorant, lawless and inexperienced, became President! He acknowledged no authority save the Church, and the Conservatives, though they feared and hated him, swarmed to his support. So long as they did not interfere with him and his Indian hordes, he allowed them to do as they pleased. They were pleased to abolish all Galvez' laws, restore the religious Orders, particularly the Jesuits, and reinstate all the old Spanish institutions and titles.

To add to the confusion, European bankers, eager to gain control in Central America, offered large loans on little or no security to whatever faction faintly resembled authority. England, for example, as soon as Morazán was in office, offered the Federation a loan of seven millions. Less than a million had been advanced when the Federation fell apart, but each of the five states was saddled with its share of the debt.

Guatemala was made responsible for one-third, or the lion's share, and to this in later years more and more millions were added in English and German loans, until with defaults, refundings and special taxes on coffee and other products given as security, the finances of the country were in chaos until 1913. Then arrangements were made for definite payments and interest on loans acquired by irresponsible and sticky-fingered politicians a century before.

Carrera accomplished two things. He subjugated the highlands of Guatemala, which under the title of Estado de los Altos had seceded, and in 1847 he established Guatemala as a separate and independent Republic. As its first President, he was also the first of a long line of dictators, making and unmaking Presidents in the other Central American states at will. Banished for a few years, he returned to be elected President for life.

Carrera died in 1865, and much to the disappointment of a country weary of poverty, tyranny and inefficiency, Cerna, another Conservative, became his successor. Two years later the first Liberal revolt broke out, led by Serapio Cruz. Defeated, he fled to Salvador, but his effort inspired two young Liberals in the Department of San Marcos. One was Justo Rufino Barrios; the other, Francisco Cruz.

Three unsuccessful revolts, three periods of refuge in Mexico, and they separated, Barrios remaining in Mexico, where he met Garcia Granados, another Liberal refugee. Then at Palencia in January, 1870, the government troops captured Serapio Cruz and hung his head in the chapel of the cemetery at Guatemala City. Barrios and Granados began another revolutionary advance on the capital with an "army" of 45 men.

This time they had an aroused country behind them, and their forces swelled as again and again they met and defeated government troops. At Patzicia, success assured, they stopped to draw up the Liberal platform (El Acta de Patzicia) and elect Granados provisional President. After a decisive victory at San Lucas, a village on the outskirts of Guatemala City, they marched into the capital on June 30, 1871, and placed the Liberal Party in the control of the government it holds today.

Although Granados was the first Liberal President, Barrios, succeeding him in 1873, really inaugurated the Liberal program and became known to history as the Reformer. Gathering the most notable men in the Republic about him, he made sweeping changes —the establishment of a national bank, more equitable distribution of wealth, plans for railway lines and ports and for a national school system. He transformed confiscated church properties into public buildings, substituted a university and normal school for the two Catholic colleges, and granted freedom of worship to all religions. Under his administration, the various lotteries were merged and legalized as a government monopoly for the support of charitable institutions, a source of revenue still used for the same purpose today.

In 1878 the Constitutional Assembly gave him dictatorial powers and formulated the Constitution of the Liberal Party. Barrios had two major ambitions; one, to settle the boundary disputes between Mexico and Guatemala; the other, to unite the Republics of Central America once more in a Federation. In the first he was successful. In attempting the second, he was killed and his dreams of federation died with him.

He had, however, given stability and direction to the government sufficient to carry through varied régimes [1] until 1892, when José Maria Reina Barrios became President. Under Reinita, as he was called because of his small stature, the first national printing press was established, social life and the arts encouraged, domestic and foreign trade stimulated, and to that end the idea of holding the first Central American Exposition generated for 1897 in Guatemala City. The Exposition was a success, but national finance suffered a terrific loss which, added to Reinita's introduction of paper currency, brought business to a standstill.

[1] Note 11.

Because of that and the policies inducted by President Manuel Estrada Cabrera, made President on Reinita's assassination in 1898, life in the Republic until 1921 was very much subdued. A shrewd lawyer, Cabrera managed to tide over the financial situation, to complete and merge the railways joining the capital to the coasts, to further education, and to add Guatemala to the Allies during the World War; but, like many of his predecessors, he developed a lust for power. Completely ruthless, he maintained himself in office without the aid of either party until 1920, perhaps the longest term of any President in Central America.

When Revolution overthrew him, the country found emotional relief in preparation for the celebration of its first century of freedom in 1921, but no political relief until ten years later when, in a general election, General don Jorge Ubico, a Liberal, became President and a new and modern era was begun.

President Ubico's administration has been marked by progress in every direction. Business and foreign trade have been studied and developed; currency stabilized; diversified farming introduced, with experimental stations to study new crops and assist the farmers to cultivate them. Highways and bus lines, railways and airways, both local and international, are opening up the country rapidly, and cables, telephones, telegraph and radio, as well as mails, are bringing it into close communication with the rest of the world.[1]

Towns and villages have been cleaned and beautified, schools opened everywhere, a sanitation and health department built up with jurisdiction extending to the most isolated finca. Athletics and the arts alike have been supported. Labor laws, liquor laws for the protection of the Indian, and laws in general for the protection of individual and property rights make Guatemala today an orderly and peaceful country.

General Ubico was overthrown on June 24, 1944, in a "peaceful revolution" ("Manifestación de los Brazos Caídos"). He was succeeded by General Federico Ponce Vaides as Provisional President. In 1945 Dr. Juan José Arévalo Bermejo was elected as President and in this year also Guatemala adopted a new Constitution, which is considered the most liberal in the history of the country.

[1] Notes 12 and 13.

XVII

GUATEMALA TODAY

Population—Of a total population of 3,283,209,[1] it is estimated that from 55 to 60 per cent is Indian or of Indian blood. Of the remaining ladino population, 10,860 are foreign residents, representing 45 nationalities. Germany, Great Britain, Spain, Mexico and the United States have 1000 or more nationals in Guatemala; China has 901. Great Britain's representation is largely composed of Negroes from Belize and Jamaica employed in the ports and on the banana plantations.

Government—As in the United States, the government of Guatemala is vested in three chief authorities—executive, legislative, and judicial. A President is elected by popular suffrage for a term of six years and is assisted in an advisory capacity by a Council of State and the Secretaries of Agriculture, Finance, Foreign Affairs, Interior, Public Education, Public Works and Communications, and War. The National Legislative Assembly is composed of Deputies elected by popular vote, each one representative of 30,000 inhabitants or fraction exceeding 15,000. The Supreme Court includes five members, appointed for four-year terms by the Assembly.

Departments—The country is divided into 22 Departments, each under both civil and military authority. The Governor or Jefe Politico is appointed by the President and the Commandante de Armas by the Minister of War.

Each Department is divided into Municipios (counties or townships) with headquarters in a designated town or village center. Each Municipality is governed by an Intendente or Mayor, a ladino appointed by the national administration, and a board of *regidores* (aldermen) whose numbers depend on the size of the Municipio's

[1] Census—1940.

population. Two of the aldermen serve as *sindicos* or district at-
torneys. If the Municipio is small, the Intendente may be either
Indian or ladino. He is assisted, not by a board, but by a ladino
secretary equipped to pass on local legal questions.

Department	Sq. Miles	Population	Capital	Population
Alta Verapaz	4,472	291,210	Cobán	8,808
Baja Verapaz	1,206	103,077	Salamá	4,456
Chimaltenango	764	191,376	Chimaltenango	9,108
Chiquimula	917	162,544	Chiquimula	12,447
Escuintla	1,693	185,250	Escuintla	6,876
Guatemala	821	363,652	Guatemala City	198,137
Huehuetenango	2,857	209,758	Huehuetenango	6,305
Izabal	2,371	89,742	Puerto Barrios	17,155
Jalapa	797	138,397	Jalapa	11,355
Jutiapa	1,243	222,372	Jutiapa	7,623
Petén, El	13,843	12,254	Flores	1,804
Progreso, El	742	73,523	El Progreso	3,573
Quezaltenango	753	245,438	Quezaltenango	37,230
Quiché, El	3,235	187,412	Santa Cruz	4,143
Retalhuleu	726	75,686	Retalhuleu	7,566
Sacatepéquez	180	87,940	Antigua	14,495
San Marcos	1,464	228,138	San Marcos	4,399
Santa Rosa	1,141	186,331	Cuilapa	4,482
Sololá	410	94,427	Sololá	3,904
Suchitepéquez	960	196,783	Mazatenango	15,398
Totonicapán	410	101,995	Totonicapán	6,932
Zacapa	1,039	156,778	Zacapa	15,856

Education—Under the Secretary and Department of Education,
a national system of education is maintained from kindergarten
through university. All schools follow the same curriculum, meet
the same standards, require Spanish as the official language, segre-
gate boys and girls in different classes or buildings. Education is
compulsory for all children between the ages of seven and fourteen.

Free primary schools in every town and village include six grades.
Kindergarten schools are conducted in connection with the primary
schools or independently. Finca and plantation owners are required to provide rural schools on their property for children of

Indian employees; their curriculum must include reading, writing, arithmetic, agriculture and simple crafts.

Three choices are offered graduates of the primary schools: (1) Normal School (in Guatemala City, Antigua, Quezaltenango and Chiquimula) for a four-year course and diploma as teacher in primary, kindergarten or rural schools; (2) Secondary School (in the above four cities) for a four-year course in preparation for the university or a one-year course which enables the student to enter the university and prepare there for the particular college he wishes to enter; (3) Technical Schools. These include a Commercial School, School of Physical Education, National Academy of Fine Arts, National Conservatory of Music, and a Language School, all in Guatemala City, and a School of Agriculture in Bárcenas.

Of the Normal Schools, the Escuela Normal Central de Señoritas or Belén is a model of its kind in Central America. Housed in the historic Belén Convent, it is modern in equipment and methods. In addition to the required training for teachers, its curriculum includes courses in domestic science, sports, and modern languages. Primary and secondary classes are also provided for day and resident students. Normal students wear smart dark blue and white uniforms, and as future leaders of their communities, lead the processions during the annual review of the schools by the President.

The National University in Guatemala City offers matriculation in the Humanities, Law, Social Sciences, Engineering, Natural Sciences, Medicine. Buildings, methods and equipment are modern, standards high. Its summer sessions are attended by students from the United States.[1]

Hospitals and Charities—Guatemala maintains nineteen government hospitals. The General Hospital, Leper Hospital (La Piedad), Hospital for the Insane (San José) and Hospital for Venereal Diseases are in Guatemala City; so is the Military Hospital, though this is under military jurisdiction. The remaining hospitals are located in various Department capitals.

The General Hospital occupies an enormous building, all on one floor, its departments and wards separated by gardens. An annex

---

[1] Foreign language schools function in the capital (Instituto Guatemalteco-Americano; Anglo American School; Alliance Francaise) and in some of the larger towns.

serves paying patients. An average of 16,250 patients is cared for annually. The equipment is extensive and modern, including radium and X-ray installations. The staff includes a director, appointed by the administration, physicians who have been graduated from the National University, nuns and lay nurses. Hospitals for tubercular cases and for the aged are now under construction.

Independently owned and operated hospitals include the United Fruit Hospital at Quiriguá to serve its employees primarily, though outside patients are also admitted. Its director is Dr. Neil Mcphail, the malarial expert; its nurses are British and American graduates. The Tiquisate Hospital at Tiquisate was established and is maintained by the Compañia Agricola Nacional, an affiliate of the United Fruit. Its chief work is the subjection of the malaria menace in the lowlands. Between 1926 and 1938, it succeeded in reducing positive blood reactions in malarial cases from 50 to 10 per cent.

The American Hospital in Guatemala City, established and maintained by the United States Presbyterian Board of Foreign Missions, serves an average of 1160 patients a year in its clinics and wards. It also maintains a training school for nurses and an Ambulance Clinic which visits various parts of the country each year. In 1937, at its station in El Rancho, 700 patients were attended. The director of the hospital is Dr. Charles Ainslee; its physicians are American or American trained; its superintendent of nurses is an American, and the nurses are graduates of the Hospital Training School.

The Roosevelt Hospital, donated by the U.S.A., will furnish, when completed, every modern equipment for attending 1000 patients.

The Casa del Niño (House of the Child) of the Sociedad Protectora del Niño is another Central American model of its kind. Philanthropic women of Guatemala City raised the money for its foundation and contribute their services to its management. The Casa includes not only a small hospital but clinics and playgrounds for children, a training school for children's nurses—where working mothers leave babies and small children during the day, and clinics and lectures on child hygiene are held regularly—and four branches in densely populated outlying sections.

Foto Alvarez

THE NATIONAL PALACE IN GUATEMALA CITY

Elste Weil

ANTIGUA IN FIESTA DRESS

GUATEMALA CITY FROM THE AIR

The volcanoes Pacaya and Agua and Lake Amatitlán are seen in
the background: the dark outlines about the city are deep ravines

A CAPITAL BUILT ON AN ISLAND

Flores, capital of the Petén, headquarters of the chicle, rubber and lumber industries in the unbroken tropical jungles, on Lake Petén-Itza

Sanchez Latour

METROPOLITAN CATHEDRAL, GUATEMALA CITY
As seen from the corridor of the Portal del Comercio

Eichenberger

AVIATION BUILDING, AIRPORT, GUATEMALA CITY

Eichenberger

UNION STATION, GUATEMALA CITY

In the foreground is the bronze statue of President
Rufino Barrios, on the site of the former bull ring

Biener

NATIONAL MUSEUM, GUATEMALA CITY,
ORIGINALLY THE CHURCH, EL CALVARIO

Dr. J. J. Dozy

FOOTBRIDGE ACROSS ONE OF THE
STEEP STREETS OF QUEZALTENANGO

TWO VERY RARE PHOTOGRAPHS

Dr. J. J. Dozy

WITCH DOCTORS IN SESSION

Burning incense and candles before traditional
Mayan crosses at Lake Chicabal (See page 291)

Srta. Marguerita

THERE ARE YOUNG PARROTS!

Mother parrot and baby son ruffling brilliant green
and yellow plumage under the tropical sun of Iztapa

Biener STELA E, QUIRIGUÁ

This monolith, 35 feet in height, is believed to be the tallest stone quarried and carved by the Maya

Biener STELA I, QUIRIGUÁ

Brilliantly carved and unusual in detail: cross-legged figure found only here and at Piedras Negras

Army—Although small, Guatemala's military forces are very complete, including infantry, artillery, cavalry, motorcycle corps, and airplane fleet, all with modern equipment. The regular army is made up of men between 18 and 30. Every man between 18 and 50 must serve one year. Volunteer battalions of higher rank and privileges are composed of men returning to give one year or more of service. Other volunteer battalions are made up of Indians, each battalion from one tribe, uniformed in colorful tribal costume.

Army officers are trained in the Escuela Politecnica, the West Point of Guatemala. Cadets include 115 Guatemaltecos, selected by competitive examination, a few cadets from other Central American countries to whom admittance is granted as a matter of international courtesy, and a limited number of Pensionistas who pay a moderate monthly fee. Cadets are known as Pensionados and their tuition and expenses are paid by the government. In time of peace they are required, at the convenience of the government, to serve twice the time in the army they have spent in the school; Pensionistas may serve but are not required to.

For degrees of Officer Graduate or Graduate in Science and Letters, the course requires three and a half years. The teaching staff of thirty includes instructors in English and French. Admission is highly prized, as the cadets are well disciplined and receive excellent physical and character training which prepares them to serve not only in the Army but as leaders, community and national.

XVIII

ECONOMIC OUTLOOK

ALTHOUGH practically self-sustaining and potentially a rich or at least a well-to-do country, Guatemala at present is poor, due to unsettled world and local conditions which until recent years have prevented the development of her resources and transportation facilities.

It is and must remain an agricultural country. Lack of fuel resources and the high freight rates not only make industrial production costs high but the character of the people for years to come will preclude a mass-production market. The large Indian population is or can be independent. Of the remaining population, one half forms a low income group with but limited buying power. The entire country, it is estimated, cannot consume at present as much manufactured goods as one city of 35,000 people in the United States.

Foreign Trade—Foreign trade is developing and normally shows a favorable balance. The United States is Guatemala's important export market, taking most of the coffee, all of the bananas and chicle, her three main products. Canada and Switzerland rank second and third. Most-favored-nations agreements are held with the United States, Germany, Canada, France, Belgium, Italy, the Netherlands, and Sweden.

Imports include lard, wheat, flour, leather, cotton fabrics, fiber bags, paper, rubber goods, gasoline, iron and steel manufactures, machinery, hardware, chemicals.

Coffee and bananas are the chief exports, together totaling about 90 per cent of the value of exports. In normal years coffee represents about 70 per cent of the total value. Chicle is the only other agricultural export of importance, though some honey, sugar, broom root, essential oils and hides are exported.

When Brazil drastically altered its coffee export policy in November, 1937, the immediate reaction on world market prices changed the economic outlook in Guatemala at once. However, because Guatemala coffee is considered one of the finest grades in the world (almost all of it is grown at altitudes of 2000 feet and over), the entire 1938 crop was sold readily and the future of her market assured. The average annual crop averages 1,000,000 quintals (1 quintal = 100 pounds), with a value under normal conditions estimated at $10,000,000.

Banana plantings and exports have gained steadily in the last few years. The value of exports is arbitrarily calculated at 50 cents a bunch or stem, with 8,604,053 stems exported in 1937, and 9,502,123 in 1938. Though *sigatoka* and Panama diseases have made heavy inroads on production on the east coast, intensive preventive measures indicate that the pest may be controlled. The new and extensive plantings on the Pacific Coast are responsible for the increase and also for the tricky problem in transportation solved by the banana itself.

Bananas must be grown under tropical temperatures and picked green; they must not be allowed to ripen until they reach their market. The trip "over the hump" from the Pacific slope to Puerto Barrios on the Caribbean (from which all bananas are shipped) includes long areas both of tropical temperatures and of cool or cold. In the absence of refrigerated cars, the banana leaf has proved itself the perfect insulator.

Chicle promises to become more profitable as its market increases. At present two United States consumers absorb the entire production. The vast forests of the Petén are rich in sapote trees, which when once tapped for chicle cannot be tapped again for seven years. All the lands are government-owned, therefore, and concessions leased to contractors. A unique feature of the industry is the law requiring all chicle to be shipped from Puerto Barrios. As the only means of communication between the Petén and the port is by air, every pound—and in 1937 there were 1,387,879 pounds, valued at $306,362—travels by plane to the ships.

Domestic Trade—Corn, wheat, sugar, beans, pepper and tobacco play the leading roles in home commerce. Corn is grown in all sections, with a normal production of 3,000,000 quintals and an approximate value of $4,500,000 annually. In years of crop failures, as in 1936, the government, to prevent price speculation, imports and sells corn at a reasonable increase. One failure insures a bumper crop and lower prices the following years, as every hut will have at least one small patch around its door.

Wheat is grown in the highlands, but to date its production (around 100,000 quintals) is not sufficient to provide flour in quantity and quality for local demands. Flour is therefore imported and a law requires that all bread products contain a minimum of 25 per cent of the local flour.

Sugar, grown in the lower altitudes, is by a mutual agreement of the producers limited to a production for local consumption, since not enough can be cultivated to make competition in the world market profitable. In 1944, about 543,100 quintals of white sugar was produced.

Beans, primarily the staple black beans or *frijoles,* are grown everywhere, something like 175,000 quintals, according to the Department of Agriculture, being produced annually. Such figures are incomplete, however, as numerous small growers of beans and other products make no reports.

Tobacco is also grown widely, particularly in the Departments of Zacapa and Santa Rosa, to meet the increasing market for cigarettes and cigars. Some 19,000 quintals are produced today, roughly valued at $300,000. A limited amount, approximately 10 per cent, of light tobacco is imported for the manufacture of "Virginia" type cigarettes. Less than one per cent of the cigars are made of imported leaf. About half a billion cigarettes, hand and machine made, and 100,000,000 cigars are manufactured annually.

Because the white tissue used for cigarettes is a government monopoly, only colored tissues may be sold for other purposes. The tourist planning a trip to Guatemala can save himself from possible embarrassment by seeing to it that his baggage contains no white tissue paper.

Livestock figures are incomplete. Perhaps it is sufficient to say that except for a limited importation of cattle from other Central American countries for fattening, Guatemala is self-sufficient. At present neither scientific breeding nor feeding of stock is generally practised, though a few individuals are importing blooded cattle for the improvement of their herds.

Guatemala is rich in minerals; somewhere in the country is a little of everything except coal. No complete analysis of its mineral resources has been made, and gold, lead, sulfur and salt are at present the only minerals exploited. From the standpoint of exports, gold is the only one of importance, 4598 ounces, for example, being shipped in 1937. Sulfur is very plentiful, but, owing to the expense and difficulty of transportation, imported sulfur is less expensive than domestic.

It is possible that shortly Guatemala may emerge as a potentially rich source of petroleum. In May, 1937, the Compañia Guatemalteca de Petroleo (in other words, the Shell Oil Company) contracted to explore petroleum rights in the Petén, Alta Verapaz and Izabal, and surveys are now being made to determine the areas in which exploitation rights will be requested.

Manufacturing industries, as has been said, necessarily must be limited in their production. As yet, although numerous household articles sufficient to supply the majority of requirements—textiles, wearing apparel, flour, soap, candles and such necessities—are manufactured, none has reached a point of production where the question of exportation has arisen.

Banking and Finance—Commercial banking is concentrated in the Banco de Guatemala, established by decree in 1946 (the only bank of issue), and in the Bank of London and South America. Other banks include the Banco Central de Guatemala, the Credito Hipotecario Nacional and Banco Hipotecario.

Total amount of currency in circulation as of July 31, 1947, was Q.62,314,990.

XIX

THE ARTS

FROM the high peak reached in the seventeenth century, colonial arts plunged into a period of decadence and inertia that endured until this last decade of modern history. This was due not only to the normal rhythm of rise and fall on which creative arts move always, but to the poverty, political uncertainty and general isolation of the country from the rest of the world. With no outer stimulus and no inner incentive, artists grew stereotyped and stagnant; masters imitated one another and pupils faithfully reproduced their masters.

Names—notably those of José Milla, historical novelist, Antonio Irisarri, author of the autobiographical *El Cristiano Errante,* and Pepe Batres, poet—rise above the murk, but such names are few and their work subject also to frequent retrogressions to European influences.

The picture now is changing materially. All the arts, save the dance, are showing signs of renaissance, the result of a continued period of stability, a growing sense of national unity and independence, and the development of communications between the Latin American countries and the rest of the world.

Professor Yela Gunther, Director of the National Academy of Fine Arts in Guatemala City, is optimistic for the future, foreseeing a general development of the arts in the rise of young men and women of this generation and those to come, freed at last of the domination of colonial and European influences. They are already beginning to sow, he finds, the seeds of a national culture.

And he points out that it is in Mexico, Peru and Guatemala, once the three great centers of Aztec, Inca and Maya civilizations, that interest and work in the arts are most alive today. The ancient Indian artists were inspired by the beauty of their lands to

222

create, and their arts reflect the physical characteristics of the scenes about them. He points out, too, the effect of the physical features on the character of these nations and their art techniques.

The Aztecs, and the Incas in a lesser degree, were virile and harsh in nature, ferocious warriors, devoted to human sacrifice and torture. The Maya, on the other hand, were not warriors, did not sacrifice human life, were peaceful and orderly, devoted to the development of agriculture, their science and arts. They were decidedly mystic and moved to the same "suave and dulce" rhythms as the rolling mountains, the smoothly rounded cones of the volcanoes, the curving rivers and valleys about them.

Young Guatemala artists today are responsive to these same influences, the same beauty of surroundings and atmosphere that inspired the Maya and the artists of ancient Greece. They too are revealing tendencies toward mysticism in their work, and their techniques are smooth and flowing rather than rugged and bold.

Of the Guatemaltecos whose work is winning recognition today, Carlos Merida is counted among the foremost Latin American painters, and one of the few to employ abstract themes. Humberto Garavito and Alfredo Galvez Suarez are also well known. In the field of sculpture, Yela Gunther is preeminent and perhaps typical of the modern movement in Guatemala. His father was a sculptor, disciple of the European and the colonial schools. The son, though eager to model, was unhappy and dissatisfied with his work. He did not find his métier until he encountered a pupil of Rodin. Today he is creating a significant form of his own, entirely subjective, and, as a teacher, is encouraging his students to do likewise.

Modern music has one creator, Ricardo Castillo, whose recent impressionistic compositions reveal clearly their roots and rhythms in Guatemala. Literature, the most prolific of the arts, is represented by the fiction and non-fiction of Flavio Herrera, Rafael Arevalo Martinez, Carlos Samayoa Chinchilla, Fernando Juárez Muñoz, Carlos Wyld Ospina, José Rodriguez Cerna, David Vela, and the poetry of Alberto Velasquez.

Without either theaters or audiences, dramatists had little encouragement while the country was in disorder or in later times when the motion picture was happy to supply the public's need.

Guatemala does have one playwright, however, Drago Braco, and
the development of the national radio stations has lured Little
Theater groups from seclusion to create a demand for the legitimate drama which will be supplied on the completion of the new
Municipal Theater in Guatemala City.

In spite of the fact that Guatemaltecos, like all Latin Americans,
have an inherent love and instinct for rhythm, the dance alone has
found no supporters. This is due, according to Professor Yela
Gunther, to the fact that "the inspiration for the dance would have
to come from the Indians, and the Indian dance, though dramatic
and significant, is not artistic"—a statement which is potent in its
revelation of the influence of the Indian and his culture on modern
Guatemala.

XX

SPORTS AND RECREATIONS

SPORTS are by no means localized to the golf courses and tennis courts in Guatemala City. The possibilities of mountain climbing, hunting and fishing have only been scratched as yet; one day the sportsman may be seeking Guatemala as he now turns to other and less well-equipped but more fully exploited lands.

Mountain Climbing

Agua (Water) . . . 3752 meters (12,393 feet)—Ascent starts from village of Santa Maria de Jesús near Antigua and requires five hours. Horses and guides can be secured in village.

The most popular time for the ascent is during the dry season, particularly in January, at full moon. One can leave Antigua or Santa Maria in the evening, climb or ride to the rest huts, and, just before dawn, climb to the summit for the sunrise. A magnificent panorama of mountain peaks, east, west and north, rises out of the mist, and to the south, across a hazy plain, is the Pacific Ocean. Following the coast, almost shoulder to shoulder, stands a range of volcanic cones; near by are Fuego and Acatenango. Occasionally climbers are rewarded with the sight of the spectacular shadow of Agua projected on the atmosphere high above the volcano.

Agua's own crater is elliptical, 105 by 75 meters (344 x 245 feet); in depth, 130 meters (427 feet). Access to its interior is not difficult; resthouses are provided within it for overnight stops. Half way to the summit is the old crater.

Acatenango (Place of Reeds) . . . 3960 meters (12,970 feet)— Ascent starts from the village of Calderas, Chimaltenango. The eight-hour climb may be divided in two by stopping for the night

225

or a rest on the *meseta* or plateau. The climbing is difficult and should not be undertaken without guides. This volcano has two cones, the smaller, Yepocapa (3850 meters—12,630 feet), whose crater, due to rock formations, cannot be entered, and Acatenango, whose crater, 490 feet in diameter, is easy of access.

Fuego (Fire) . . . until 1932, 3835 meters (12,581 feet)—Ascent can be made by the longer, harder route via Alotenango, a village, or by way of the volcano Acatenango. Until 1932, the year of the last eruption, this was the highest of the three volcanoes overlooking Antigua. Then its cone was destroyed and its summit is now inaccessible. Both Fuego and Acatenango can be climbed on the same expedition by making the ascent of Acatenango first, returning to the *meseta* for the night and climbing Fuego the next day. Views from both volcanoes are superb, sweeping over the same country as seen from Agua. Climbers should secure guides.

Pacaya (Palm) . . . 2544 meters (8344 feet)—Reached by another village of Calderas (Department of Escuintla) where guides may be procured. Volcano offers four accessible peaks, the eastern one easily reached in two hours on foot. The crater of the peak, Calderas, is now filled with water. From here one can climb to the ridge of an old crater and then to the present cone. The western peak, Cerro de Agua, is the most difficult to climb and provides the best sport. Vegetation on the slopes is luxuriant except on the southeast where there are lava fields. The entire trip and return can be made from Guatemala City in one day.

San Pedro . . . 3024 meters (9921 feet)—One of the volcanoes overlooking Lake Atitlán, its ascent can be made in five hours from the village of San Pedro, where guides are available. Thick forests obscure the view and the ascent is difficult but good sport. The broken crater on the southeast slope is horseshoe-shaped.

Atitlán . . . 3525 meters (11,565 feet)—Another lake volcano, reached from the village of San Lucas Tolimán. The crater is 820 feet in diameter, 165 feet deep. A hard climb, requiring at least ten hours because of the deep ravines. Views of lake and country are magnificent.

Tolimán . . . 3130 meters (10,270 feet)—Also reached from the lake village of San Lucas Tolimán. The climb requires six hours and is not difficult. The elliptical crater is 820 by 490 feet, the depth, 197 feet.

Tajumulco (Hill of the Ancestors) . . . 4210 meters (13,812 feet) —In the Department of San Marcos; is the highest volcano in Central America. Guides should be secured in the town of San Marcos, from which the start is made. Travel by motor to the village of San Sebastián, from there on horseback to Horqueta (about 13,000 feet) between the volcano's twin peaks; from here one must climb on foot for two hours to the lower or eastern peak and the old crater. The elliptical crater, 230 feet below the summit, is the favorite meeting place for witch doctors and their ceremonies. From here to the summit, the going is hard.

Tacaná . . . 4064 meters (13,335 feet)—Also reached (with guides) from the town of San Marcos; a very difficult climb, but worth it. The crater, 1640 feet long, is located on the southwest slope, 627 feet below the summit.

Santa Maria . . . 3768 meters (12,361 feet)—Ascent starts from Quezaltenango (where guides are secured) and is reached by way of Suipache. A hard climb, but interesting for the luxuriant and beautiful vegetation. The main crater, about halfway to the summit, is in almost continuous eruption, though since 1928, when it devastated some coastal villages, its outbreaks have done no serious damage. The smaller crater, Santiaguito (Little St. James) was formed then. From Suipache, the ascent to the summit requires four hours on foot.

Zunil . . . 3533 meters (11,588 feet)—Reached from Zunil. (See Quezaltenango, page 283.)

Tecuamburro . . . 1946 meters (6383 feet)—Ascent is made from village of Ixpaco, Department of Santa Rosa. The twin peaks are easily climbed. The crater appears like a broken horseshoe.

Moyuta . . . 1684 meters (5525 feet)—Ascent can be made on foot from the village of Moyuta in three hours. Large rocks and trees make climb arduous, but view from summit includes volcanoes in Guatemala and Salvador, mountains in Honduras, and Pacific Ocean. The crater is round, with break on western slope. In it the Indians now cultivate corn.

Fishing

San José on the Pacific Coast and Puerto Barrios on the Caribbean Sea provide deep-sea fishing that rivals Florida's famous waters. At San José, barracuda, sailfish, roosterfish, etc., offer excellent sport either for still fishing or for trolling. The rivers, Maria Linda and Michatoya (Fish that Leave), which flow into the Pacific here, also offer good sport, particularly to trollers, while the winding channel of the Chiquimulilla Canal is a fisherman's paradise for fly fishing—perch, bass, mangrove snappers, red snappers, snook, robalo, jack or amberjack. Boats with outboard motors, boatman and bait can be secured for about $5.00 a day.

At Puerto Barrios, Amatique Bay and the nearby islands provide magnificent sport with tarpon, barracuda, sailfish and other deep-sea fish. The Rio Dulce, Lake Izabal, Canal Inglés and Rio Graciosa, within short distance and easily reached, are also popular for fishing expeditions. Boats and launches can be chartered by the day or week.

Almost any river above 1500 feet in altitude contains fish that resemble the mountain mullet, offer good sport, and are as delicious as trout. In the Petén, the rivers, Pasión, Salinas, San Pedro Martír and their tributaries which flow into Lake Petén abound with fish, some as yet unclassified. The streams about Tecpán contain carp due to the fact that two years ago the beds of the carp hatcheries there overflowed during the rainy season and eggs and small fish were carried down into brooks and rivers.

Lake Amatitlán contains the *mojarra,* a small but very delectable fish. It was first introduced to the lake in 1549 by the Dominican Father, Diego Martinez, and in 1573 the municipal government of the village of Amatitlán brought fish from the Pacific Coast to stock the waters. Since early times when the Dominican Order lost its claim to exclusive fishing rights in the lake, fishing has been free to all.

Lake Atitlán also contains the *mojarra* and another small fish, *triponcito*. Lake Petén is filled with a variety of fish, many unidentified. One, the *sabalo,* provides both good sport and good health when eaten, as it supplies the same properties as are found in cod-liver oil. During Lent and especially during Holy Week, the lake is the scene of a great fishing fiesta of the Indians. While the men fish from rafts, the women erect mat shelters and dry and salt the fish over open fires.

Hunting

In almost any part of the country, but particularly in the dense forests of the Pacific Coast and in the Departments of Petén and Jutiapa, deer, wild hog, tapir and jaguar offer good hunting. The highlands, in addition, have the puma and *coatemundi*.

Thousands of teal duck on their way south during October, November, and December stop to rest on the Esteros, the swamps and marshes near San José. (In April, when they return north, the marshes are dry and they pass on.) Wild pigeons, quail and wild duck are found in profusion on lakes and marshes during the dry season. Lake Ayarza offers rich rewards to the hunter, as it has been given little attention thus far by sportsmen.

Guns may be brought into the country on permits obtained with one's visa at the Guatemala consulates. Hunting trips can be arranged in Guatemala City or in any of the larger towns. If one knows the owner of a coffee finca, however, his problem is solved. Fincas usually are well provided with dogs, guns, guides, all the essentials and most of the luxuries of hunting.

Swimming

Guatemala offers a wide range of swimming. Most popular is sea bathing at San José and Champerico and Puerto Barrios. At

Iztapa, near San José, are both sea bathing and fresh water in the rivers Maria Linda and Michatoya. Almost all lakes, but particularly Amatitlán and Atitlán, and almost any river provide excellent sport. During holiday seasons and week ends, hundreds of people leave Guatemala City by train, bus, and motor car for the various beaches.

In addition, in and near the city are several swimming pools with exceptionally moderate rates—Finca el Sauce, a large pool in excellent picnic grounds, with facilities for sports; Ciudad Vieja, within walking distance of the city (on Sundays and holidays buses can be secured at Central Park); Lo de Bran, new pool in northwest section of city; also El Tuerto and El Administrador have pools.

Guatemala is rich in thermal springs; many provide excellent swimming pools. Near Guatemala City, the best are Las Monjitas on the slopes of Pacaya, at Escuintla, Antigua, and Chimaltenango. These can be reached by bus or motor in an hour or two and are popular both for swimming and because of the medicinal properties in their waters. Travelers and motorists traveling over the country need only inquire at their hotels or pensions to discover these thermal pools. Many are mentioned in connection with various towns (page 254).

Riding

Guatemala is the horseman's delight. Trails web the country, and usually through breath-taking scenery. Guatemala City has several stables and a riding academy, and trails through Aurora Park and neighboring ravines provide an endless variety of excursions. Most large centers have horses (and guides) which can be secured through the hotels or local government authorities. Maya Inn at Chichicastenango has its own stable. For long trips, pack mules and complete camping equipment should, of course, be taken.

Motoring

With almost 5000 miles of completed highways and some 900 and more miles under construction, long and short trips via interesting Indian villages and frequently through spectacular scenery are possible. Good motors, with chauffeurs, can be secured by day or week at rates depending not on time but destination, and, if made in advance, moderate.

For suggestions for trips from Guatemala City, see Amatitlán, Chinautla, San Raimundo, San Pedro and San Juan Sacatepéquez (page 254), from which the Pan American Highway can be followed to the Motagua River for swimming and picnicking, Escuintla, San José or Iztapa, Antigua, Rio de los Esclavos.

This River of the Slaves takes its name from the fact that after the Battle of Jumay here, the conquerors branded the faces of Indian captives as slaves. The Pan American Highway crosses the river on a bridge built in 1592 by Francisco Fuentes y Guzmán; with only slight repairs it has done duty through the centuries. In the stonework of the bridge can be seen a footprint, said to be the Devil's.

Racing

During the National Fair in November, races are held daily in the Hippodromo del Sur, with horses entered from Salvador, Mexico and Belize as well as Guatemala. Races are also held frequently during Christmas Week. Bicycling and motorcycling, year-round sports, take the form of races during special fiestas.

Games

Football, baseball and basketball are also year-round attractions, with various contests between schools, Departments, and private teams. During national fiestas, Central American teams compete.

Central America holds its own Olympic Games every four years with athletes entered from the five republics, Mexico, northern South America, and the Caribbean Islands.

Golf

Guatemala City has two excellent golf clubs—Guatemala Country Club and Mayan Golf Club; each has a good nine-hole course and a handsome and fully equipped clubhouse. Sponsored travelers and visitors are extended the courtesy of the courses on payment of moderate weekly or monthly fees.

Tennis

The Guatemala Tennis Club and the Hercules Sport Club in Guatemala City have several courts each, and other sport facilities. The Guatemala Club provides badminton and squash courts and a swimming pool; the Hercules, a gymnasium and basketball. Both clubs extend courtesy cards to sponsored travelers.

Photography

Photography must be considered as a major recreation in a country where scenery, atmospheric effects and Indian life are the delight of professional and amateur. A filter is recommended—particularly during the rainy season—for the spectacular cloud effects. It is forbidden to photograph the forts.

Clubs and Organizations

The American Club, founded in 1896, with a membership including all nationalities, boasts one of the finest clubhouses in Latin America, with library and reading rooms, bowling alleys, billiard room and ballroom. Other social organizations include the Guatemala Club, with a membership limited primarily to Guatemaltecos, Lions Club, which sponsors a hospital for tubercular children, Rotary, founded in 1925, and the Masonic Temple. For young people there are the Boy Scouts Guatemaltecos, with headquarters in Guatemala City and a recreation ground on the outskirts, and Girl Guides —*Muchachas Guias*.

XXI

THE CAPITAL: GUATEMALA CITY

VISITORS viewing the clean, well-laid-out capital where more than 164,000 people live and work, like to speak of its "Old World atmosphere" and imagine that the city has existed since its founding in the quiet order of today. They are mistaken. The peace and order are the reward of a city that for a century and a half has been the scene of revolution, war, epidemics, explosions, intrigues and earthquakes.

When in September, 1773, Captain General Mayorga and his retinue of 4250 officials and followers left the stricken valley of Panchoy and threaded the mountain trails to the Valley of the Cows, they settled in the village of La Ermita at the foot of El Cerrito del Carmen (page 241). Founded in 1620, La Ermita then boasted a population of 1668. Here a provisional capital was established while surrounding valleys and mountains were studied for water supplies and a permanent site.

This site was found in the neighboring Valley of the Virgin, named in honor of Nuestra Señora de la Asunción, whose image stood in the little church erected by Indians who had arrived in the valley on the eve of the Virgin's Day more than a century before. Soon Our Lady of the Ascension was venerated throughout the region and became the patron saint of the new capital, which by royal decree was named in her honor, Nueva Guatemala de la Asunción.

On January 1, 1776, Guatemala City was officially inaugurated, and on the following day the city fathers held their first official meeting to elect officers and promulgate decrees for the city's administration.

Construction was pushed rapidly with Luis Diez de Navarro and José de Sierra as the engineers in charge of the city plan and

later Antonio Bernasconi directing all construction. As in the two
earlier capitals of Santiago, the Plaza Real was the first considera-
tion, with the location of the Cathedral, the Palace of the Captains
General, the Ayuntamiento, Commandancia and the Portal del
Comercio about it. From this center, a city fifteen streets long and
fifteen wide was laid out.

Originally all streets acquired characteristic names. First Avenue
was the Street of the Hospital; Second, the Street of the College
for Women; Fifth, the Street of the Snail, and Sixth, the Street of
Shade Trees. In 1877 numerals were substituted (although the
old name plaques imbedded in many walls are now being uncovered one by one), and only short intersecting streets bear names.

Homes built then still survive in the suburb, Parroquia Vieja
(Old Parish). The construction of some was very ambitious, one
achieving a total cost of $180,000. The principal churches were
erected little by little. By 1800, in spite of the reluctance of the
citizens of Santiago de los Caballeros to move to the new capital
and of the epidemics of smallpox and cholera, Guatemala City
presented an established form and aspect. Its population, however,
was scarcely 25,000.

During the next twenty years, under the burden of political disorder and economic tyranny, the newness wore away until by 1821,
when Independence was won, the capital was a place of apathy and
poverty. The square of El Sagrario beside the Cathedral was filled
with charcoal makers and their mules, and beyond the center of
the city, weeds and rubbish filled the vacant areas and water stood
in the streets. "Shops selling meat were fetid; factories of tallow
candles putrid; tanneries infested all sections, and dirty people and
hungry dogs gave the capital the appearance of a slum in Con-
stantinople." At night the streets were dark, except for a few candles burning in wall shrines before figures of saints; numerous
criminals and a few police were all who ventured out.

Social life and romance could not be completely discouraged,
however. In the late afternoons following vespers, family parties
gathered to gossip and sip chocolate. Gallants braved the danger-
ous streets nightly for rendezvous, becoming so bold that barred
windows as well as doors bore locks. Even so "from time to time

slander made known that some maiden had lost to the passionate and blind god the white flower of her pristine purity."

Though the Church and the Orders had lost much, they still retained great wealth and were the center of what social and cultural life there was. A few royalist families tried to retain the ostentation of life in Spain, but for the majority, existence was simple, frugal and languid.

As the capital of the Kingdom, of the Republic, of the Federation of Republics, and finally of the Republic again, Guatemala City was the center and butt of political turmoil. Fighting on her streets was frequent, and public buildings, including the Cathedral and University, served as battlefields.

With the victory of the Liberal Party in 1871, life for the first time assumed a measure of stability. President Rufino Barrios stimulated new construction and commercial enterprise, and President Reina Barrios encouraged lavish social festivities.

But in the highlands another city was growing in size and influence. By the end of the nineteenth century it was in all but name the capital of the country. This was Quezaltenango, whose strategic location and proximity to the coast made it the logical commercial and shipping center. In 1902 an earthquake destroyed both city and rivalry, however, and instead of remaining to rebuild, many of its leading families moved to Guatemala City.

The darkest hour before dawn arrived for the capital in 1917 when for more than six weeks—from Christmas Eve, 1917, until January 31, 1918—the city was shaken by an almost continuous series of earthquakes, and all the horrors of 1773 were repeated. When the last one shivered away, Guatemala City lay in ruins.

This time few residents deserted the city or heeded the incipient agitation to move the capital once more. Everyone, as soon as calm was restored, hurried to rebuild homes and business houses on a firmer and more ambitious scale.

The revolution of 1920—known as the Week of Tragedy—which released the country from the domination of Cabrera, and the approach of 1921 with its celebration of the first Centennial of freedom from Spain, gave reconstruction impetus. Churches were rebuilt, new public buildings erected, and the city generally was dressed to receive distinguished guests from all parts of the world.

On this foundation the administration of President Ubico has built steadily and rapidly a modern city with paved streets, parks, bus lines, numerous and impressive public buildings. New residential suburbs have been opened, slum districts destroyed, and attractive colonies of workingmen's homes erected. Because the capital is so modern, visitors find colonial Guatemala or Indian Guatemala more colorful and interesting; but for general living, no city in Central America excels its variety of convenience and recreation.

PARKS

Central Park

Central Park is divided by Sixth Avenue into two parts—Parque del Centenario to the west, where a large fountain plays, at night brilliantly illuminated, and the Plaza de Armas, once the Plaza de la Constitución, to the east. In the latter the Military Band or Symphony Orchestra plays in an acoustical shell several times a week. Both have gardens, vine-covered pergolas, and malls.

Originally (1778) the Parque del Centenario was the site of the Palace of the Captains General, where many historic events, including the signing of the Declaration of Independence in 1821, took place; the Garrison of the Dragoons, the Real Audiencia, and just round the corner, the Mint: all destroyed in the 1917 earthquake. For the 1921 Centennial, a temporary Palace was erected to house the celebrations. Popularly called El Palacio de Cartón, because built of beaver board, it served its purpose, then went up in flames. Now on the spot stands the fountain surrounded by gardens.

The Plaza de Armas began its history as the public market. Here now stands a statue of Christopher Columbus, the work of Thomas Muir, commissioned by President Reina Barrios, and installed in 1896. The Discoverer stands on a sphere representing the world, and the world rests on the shoulders of three figures— Science, Constancy, Courage. The quetzal, of course, symbolizes Guatemala.

Here too is the monument—the work of Justo Gandarias—

presented by the Spanish colony in the capital in honor of the Centennial. Medallions depict scenes from the memorable day at Iximché in 1524 and reproduce Alvarado's words as a stake was driven into the ground to indicate possession:

> "Write down, Scrivener, that I, by virtue of the powers vested in me by the Governors of His Majesty and by the resolution of the authorities here present, appoint and settle on this site, the capital of the Province of Guatemala."

High above them is the coat of arms given the Kingdom of Guatemala in 1532 by Charles V.

North of Central Park, a great modern Palace is now rising to house all government offices and a municipal theater. To the south still stands the old Portal del Comercio—street of shops. Its architecture and corridors suggest the scene in colonial days when three sides of the park were faced with these arched structures. On the fourth is the Metropolitan Cathedral.

Aurora Park

A vast and beautiful area offering many interests in addition to views of the surrounding volcanoes and countryside. Here are the aviation fields, government and private, the zoo, the Archeological Museum, National Observatory, and the race course—Hippodromo del Sur. A favorite spot for residents on Saturdays and Sundays, and for motorists at all times for its miles of good roads. The park is a tribute to the efforts of don Salvador Herrera, a former Minister of Agriculture.

Minerva Park

Surrounded by deep ravines, dotted with cypress groves and gardens. Here is the Temple of Minerva erected by President Estrada Cabrera, primarily as a place for the school children to celebrate the close of the school year. The park also is a center for parades and other public events, and for the race course, Hippodromo del Norte.

Here too is a unique and useful work of art in concrete—the Relief Map of Guatemala. Within an area of 2500 square meters, boundaries, mountains, rivers, forests, lakes, towns and other features of the country are laid out to scale. Interesting in itself as a difficult piece of work accomplished under difficult conditions, it is an invaluable aid to the newcomer to the country. The map was designed and executed by a Guatemala engineer, don Francisco Vela, 1905.

Morazón Park

Formerly Parque Estrada Cabrera and a city landmark. In it stands the famous ceiba tree under which for many years the August fairs were held and Indians congregated daily on their way to and from the city.

Carmen Park

Cerrito del Carmen, the hilltop on which stands the old church of Nuestra Señora del Carmen (see Churches), laid out to lawns and gardens. A favorite spot to visit at sunset for views of city and country.

Parque Gómez Carrillo

A city square and popular playground. During Carnival, one of the officially approved sites for public celebrations.

El Parque de los Niños

This strategic site overlooking the capital, until 1944 dominated by the historic fort, *Castillo de San José,* is now a playground for children.

Other Parks

Small areas or squares are found in various sections of the city, bright with gardens and flowering trees, cooled by fountains— Plaza Barrios, Isabel la Catolica, San Sebastián, San Francisco, Navidad, Galvez, Plaza de España, Universidad Nacional, Plazuela Benedicto Saenz.

MONUMENTS

In the Plaza de España: *Charles III.* Once a stone fountain, this statue of the King of Spain and circling horses originally adorned the Plaza de Armas. After the Declaration of Independence, the public undertook to destroy it and succeeded in damaging it badly.

On the Reforma Boulevard:

General Miguel Garcia Granados, by Durini, erected by President Reina Barrios to celebrate the Liberal victory in the 1871 Revolution.

President Reina Barrios, erected by President Estrada Cabrera.

Padre don Miguel Hidalgo y Costilla, the Mexican priest who is credited with initiating Independence for Mexico and Central American Republics.

Benito Juarez, another Mexican who contributed to the cause of Independence.

Dr. don Lorenzo Montúfar, Guatemalteco philosopher and writer.

Father Bartolomé de las Casas, Dominican priest (page 171).

Monumento del Ejercito—a column erected to honor the Army; at the base are busts of President Rufino Barrios and President Reina Barrios and statues of Liberty, Justice, and Guatemala.

In Concordia Park: *José Milla,* famous historical novelist, who wrote under the pen name of "Salome Jil"; and José Batres Montúfar, author and engineer.

In Morazón Park: Busts of *Beethoven* and *Robert Fulton.*

In Botanical Gardens: *Carlos Linneo,* Swedish naturalist.

In Parque Isabela la Católica: Statue of *Queen Isabel.*

In Minerva Park: Bust of *José Antonio de Liendo y Goicoechea,* a Franciscan priest who was both doctor and educator during early nineteenth century: statues of *Rafael Landivar* and *Matias Córdova.*

La Torre, a reproduction in steel of the Eiffel Tower, visible from almost all parts of the city. Erected in honor of President Rufino Barrios. A bell on its summit is rung only on June 30, the anniversary of the triumph of the Liberal Party. Its light is an airplane beacon.

Facing Union Station:

President Rufino Barrios, a bronze, said to be one of the most beautiful statues in Central America. (This square was once the site of Guatemala's first bull ring, built in 1823 of solid stone, destroyed in 1917, and until then the fashionable place to spend Sunday afternoon.)

Churches [1]

Catedral Metropolitana

The first stone was laid with great ceremony on St. James' Day, 1782, but the structure was not completed until 1868 when two towers were added. More than 300 feet long and 100 wide, it is an admirable example of colonial church architecture. Three naves, crowned by oblong domes; 86 windows; 16 altars, many of them covered with gold leaf. The basilica is said to be the finest in Central America. Although seriously damaged in 1917, the Cathedral has recently been restored, and in 1937, a pipe organ was installed, the first in the country.

Its chapels contain numerous art treasures, including the figures of San Sebastián, by Juan de Dios Chavez, considered the best in the city; San Francisco de Paula, by Alonso Paz; the San Pedro (1642), by Antón Rodas, in the hands of which, on St. Peter's Day, the keys of the Cathedral are placed; San Juan, by Juan Perales, and the Cristo de los Reyes, all formerly in Antigua. Here also are the Virgen de la Concepción de los Espinos (1852), by Ventura Ramirez; Virgen Dolorosa (late nineteenth century) by Santiago Ganuza; Virgen de Lourdes (1878), by Mariano Ganuza (all artists of the new Republic), and jewels and vessels of gold and silver, the gifts of parishioners. To the left of the altar is the chapel, El Sagrario, famous for its tabernacle and sacrament of pure silver. To the right is the chapel of the Virgen del Socorro (page 167). Among the numerous paintings on walls, altars and columns are many from the original Cathedral in Antigua, but as yet they have not been identified and catalogued.

To the left of the Cathedral stands the Palace of the Archbishop of Guatemala, a striking example of the colonial home and one of the few remaining. Behind its nail-studded entrance, grilled win-

[1] Although the Catholic Church is preeminent in Guatemala, the Constitution provides freedom of worship to all religions, and scattered about the city are churches and chapels of other denominations, including the Presbyterian Mission Church, which holds services in both English and Spanish, the Episcopal Church, the Jewish Synagogue, and the chapel of the Seventh Day Adventists.

dows and carved façade, are guarded many treasures of the Church.

To the right is the Colegio de Nuestro Señor San José de Infantes, founded in 1781 as a training school for choir boys, and ever since celebrated for the quality of its musical instruction. In its patio is one of the first statues of Christopher Columbus on the American continents.

Nuestra Señora del Carmen

As the sixteenth century drew to a close, Juan Corz, a humble friar of the Order of St. Francis of Assisi, returning from a pilgrimage to Jerusalem, chanced to pass through the village of Santa Teresa in Spain. Sisters of the convent of Avila there, impressed with his piety, begged him to go to America and carry with him an image of the Virgin then enshrined in one of their cells.

About 1604, Juan Corz and the image appeared in the Valley of the Cows (Valle de las Vacas) in Guatemala. In one cave he established himself, in another the image. Soon word of this devout hermit and the fervent prayers heard rising from the cave of the Virgin spread among the cattle haciendas and the Indians. Miraculous powers were attributed to the figure, and the great families, over the protests of the hermit, erected a chapel for it. In the night, however, the image returned to the cave by supernatural means.

Juan Corz then offered to build a Hermitage on the little hill near his cave, which he called El Carmen, because it resembled the hill of Carmel he had seen on his pilgrimage to the Holy Land. Hardly had the figure been placed within it when slander rose against the hermit, so bitter that he called on God and the Virgin for aid. Suddenly an immense ball of fire fell from heaven on the little hill, setting the hay that grew there afire and destroying the new chapel; only the image was saved. Believing the meteor a punishment on their calumny of the good friar, the valley dwellers arranged a fiesta to restore his reputation.

Corz then began another chapel, La Ermita del Monte Carmelo, and at the foot of the hill a hermitage for Indians from the village of Canalitos who were to care for the building. They arrived on the eve of August 15, 1620—the Day of Our Lady of the Ascension —when a fiesta was to dedicate the new chapel. On that day Juan Corz disappeared, and though he was sought from Mexico to Nicaragua, he never was seen again. On that day, too, the village of La Ermita, named in his honor, was founded.

The chapel Corz constructed was destroyed in 1917 and the present church, patterned on it, erected. It resembles a feudal castle more than a humble hermitage, and at one time its towers were fortified. In it hangs a portrait of don Juan José Morales Roa y Alfarol, by Rosales; don Juan, a wealthy member of the Third Order of El Carmen, was largely responsible for the recon-struction of the first church.

The low enclosing wall about the church and the great stone cross are modern. Not so the palm tree which towers above it; it was there when Juan Corz arrived. The Corpus Christi celebra-tion of El Carmen is the gayest in the city. On the afternoon of Independence Day, September 15, a special fair and fiesta for chil-dren are held.

Nuestra Señora de la Merced

Known for its magnificent jewels, particularly emeralds, which form the church treasure, and for the richly brocaded robes of its priests. The Virgen de la Merced is the patron saint of the Col-lege of Law in Guatemala, and her Day, September 24, is cele-brated by the lawyers with much ceremony. Another figure, the Virgen de la Concepción, by Ventura Ramirez, is one of the prized sculptures in the country.

Here too are the figure of Jesús Nazareno, by Zuñiga, and the largest painting in the city, La Apoteosis de la Orden de la Merced (1759, artist unknown, restored by Rosales), and a series of sculp-tures illustrating the life of San Pedro Nolasco, by Alonso Paz, all from Antigua, as are the altars. Another prized painting of the Apostles, by José Valledares, hangs on the central column.

After the 1917 earthquake the church was reconstructed and improved by the removal of two heavy bell towers. Its carved doors and *decor,* its cupola with the characteristic lions of the Order, are of interest. Under the main altar were once the subterranean tombs.

Santo Domingo

For almost ten years before 1792, the Dominican Order worked on plans for the enormous church and convent that once stood here; ten years more were given to their construction, the convent patterned on the original in Antigua. After 1917, the ruins were reconstructed to their present proportions. Though a few doors and arches of the convent remain, the site is now occupied by private homes and government buildings. October is celebrated here as the month of the Virgin of the Rosary; the widely venerated silver figure was crowned "Queen of Guatemala," January 28, 1933, when her crown of silver set with jewels was presented her.

Art treasures include El Apoteosis de Santo Tomás de Aquino (artist unknown), by many critics declared the finest painting in the capital; Martyrdom of the Dominicans in Sandomir, Poland, by Mariano Pontaza; Apparition of the Virgin to Santo Domingo de Guzmán, by Rosales; paintings of the Apostles, attributed to Zurbarán but actually the work of several artists; sculptures of San Pedro, San Francisco, and Santo Domingo, by Alonso Paz (all from Antigua); also the famous figure of Cristo Yacente (page 170). The choir room has some excellent carving, including a music rack with antique parchment choral scores.

The Holy Week procession of this church is famous throughout Central America for its adherence to tradition.

San Francisco

Begun in 1780, but due to political and seismic disturbances not completed and consecrated until 1851. Built in the shape of the Latin Cross on a pedestal. To insure permanence, cane syrup, cow's milk and white of eggs were mixed with the mortar instead of water. Until 1917, one of the imposing churches of the country; still one of the most fashionable. Its subterranean chapel, where the Holy Sacrifice and mass on All Saints' Day were celebrated, and the tombs of many illustrious men were totally destroyed.

Many of the paintings and relics of the original church in Antigua are here; the fragment of the True Cross; the Sacred Head from Trujillo; the cork figure of Ecco Homo; the figures of Nuestra Señora de Loreto, Nuestra Señora del Coro, Virgen de los Pobres (by Aguirre), San Francisco de Asis, by Paz, and San Sebastián, by Vicente España. Among its treasures of the Republican period are the Niño de Jesús, blessed by the Franciscans in Jerusalem in the crèche where Christ was born; El Corazón de Jesús (Heart of Jesus), by Ganuza, and El Salvador del Mundo (Savior of the World), a sculpture brought from Spain in 1916.

During the earthquakes of 1917, one of the great arches, falling, revealed that long ago the priests had used the roof as a secret vault for books and manuscripts under political ban.

La Recolección

Neo-Ionic in style, consecrated in 1845, this church until 1917 was another of Central America's impressive buildings. Its pure-toned bells, thick walls, some of the many paintings it once housed, remain as reminders of the riches and political power of the priests of this Order. Two of the four stucco figures of the evangelists, the work of Ramirez, still balance on ruined arches.

Among the Antigua treasures in the partly reconstructed church are Christ Crucified, by José B. Bodega; Christ Recumbent, by Vicente España; Santa Gertrudis, by an Indian sculptor, Blas Rodriguez (about 1723), to which the Spanish artist Manuel de Corral applied gold leaf. In the parish house adjoining are also many treasured paintings and relics.

Las Capuchinas

Of the original church and convent consecrated in 1789, only a small part remains. The reconstructed church, however, has ten carved wood altars from Antigua, which are among the best examples of colonial carving extant; the coat of arms of Dr. Cayetano Francos y Monroy in the rosettes of the ceiling; red lacquer doors. A painting of the Virgen del Pilar, said to be by Thomas Merlo, hangs in the vestry.

Guadalupe

Completely destroyed in 1917, a large new church is now under construction. One of the most colorful events of the year is the celebration of Guadalupe Day, December 12. Hundreds of children dressed in Indian costume take part in an all-day procession when the Virgin of Guadalupe is carried through the streets, accompanied by music, chants, rockets. Streets and homes en route are picturesquely decorated with arches of fruits and flowers.

Nuestra Señora del Carmen el Bajo

Begun in 1784, this church stands as a testimony of man's gratitude. Its construction was largely financed by the Marqués de Aycinena in gratitude for receiving the title; the work was largely done by slaves who, to show their appreciation of the Royal Edict of 1785 forbidding further branding of slaves on face or body with the seal of the owner, contributed their services every Sunday. The present reconstructed church is a favorite for fashionable weddings.

Its figures of the Virgen del Carmen, El Cristo de Esquipulas, and Santa Teresa are from Antigua.

La Capilla de Nuestro Señor de las Misericordias

Privately built with gifts from wealthy families as the chapel of the General Hospital; modern in style. Contains the figure of Nuestro Señor de las Misericordias, famous for miracle-working powers; originally in Antigua. Hundreds of pilgrims visit its shrine every Monday.

Nuestra Señora de los Remedios

Now houses the old Calvario Church. Contains a copy of the image of the Virgen de la O or Virgen de los Remedios, made in Antigua during colonial days. Also from Antigua, the figure of the Virgen del Rosario from the Santa Cruz church; a Cristo Yacente; Virgen de la Piedad, by Cuellar; Virgen de Dolores, by Ganuza, and a large crucifix.

Nuestra Señora de las Angustias

Small, ultra-baroque church, privately built by don Felipe Yurrita, in the style of the Cathedral of Toledo, Spain, and still incomplete. Repays detailed study of its stone work and of its strikingly beautiful altar of carved wood, the work of an Indian.

Nuestra Señora de la Candelaria

Built in 1861; known for its ceremony and procession on Holy Thursday. Here are Aguirre's Jesús de Candelaria and the Virgen de Dolores, by Chavez, from Antigua.

Parroquia Vieja

Formerly La Ermita de la Cruz de Piedra (Hermitage of the Stone Cross). Contains image of Jesús con la Cruz, by Quirio Cataño from the Escuela de Cristo in Antigua, and a Cristo from the Hermitage of the Cross of the Miracle.

Nuestro Señor de San José

Erected 1783; contains Jesús Nazareno, by Alonso Paz, and Nuestro Señor de San José from Antigua.

Santa Catarina

Here is the Cristo Yacente from the Antigua church, now the subject of a legend. Pedro de Betancourt (page 175), it is said, while walking along a road came upon the figure and received from it a sign that it was to be carried to the church of Santa Catarina. There it remained until 1773, performing many miracles.

Santa Rosa

Served as Cathedral for 26 years until the Cathedral was ready for use; chief treasures, several sixteenth-century paintings from Antigua.

Santa Clara

One of the capital's fashionable churches; contains the sculptured group, Christ, Mary Magdalene and St. John, by Evaristo Zuñiga; stained glass windows have recently been installed, the work of the Guatemalan artist Julio Urruela Vásquez.

Beatas de Belén

Painting of Niño Jesús del Nacimiento, by Alonso Paz.

Nuestra Señora de la Asunción

Houses figure of the same name, the patron saint of Guatemala City (page 233), Escultura Sevillana.

Corazón de Jesús (formerly known as Santa Faz)

Contains figure of Christ Crucified, by Evaristo Zuñiga, from the church of Santa Clara in Antigua, also a group of the Dolorosa, St. John, and Mary Magdalene, said to be Zuñiga's work.

San Augustín

Contains Antigua figures of San Augustín and the Virgen del Carmen; a painting of San José, by Montañez, and a nineteenth-century painting from Italy.

San Sebastián

Image of Nuestra Señora de Dolores, from the Hermitage of Dolores del Cerro in Antigua.

Private Chapels

Many families still living in their ancestral homes hold services for family and friends on special occasions in their private chapels. Some of these chapels are very beautiful in design and rich in sacred figures, vessels of gold and silver, the work of early Spanish and colonial craftsmen.

Shrines

In colonial and early days of the Republic, many homes also maintained a niche in an outer wall in which stood a sacred image or patron saint of the household. Flowers and burning candles or lanterns, constantly renewed, gave interest to the streets by day and illumination at night. Only one remains now—the Divino Rostro (Divine Face), at the corner of Seventh Avenue South and Fourteenth Street.

MUSEUMS

National Archeological Museum

A rare collection of some 3000 pieces from the Maya sites of Uaxactún, Kaminal Juyú, Piedras Negras and others, and from the Pipil region on the Pacific Coast, including some magnificent jades, polychrome pottery, stelae and ornaments, excellently arranged and classified. See Nebaj, page 300.

National Museum

Established in 1935 in the former church of El Calvario; demolished to give way for the extension of 6th Avenue South. The massive and dramatic paintings by Merlo and Montúfar are being restored to the church of El Calvario in Antigua. The Museum in Antigua will acquire some arts and crafts of the colonial period.

In a building in the Aurora Park—Guatemala City—are to be collected the arts and crafts of the post-colonial period—1776-1821— and another section will be dedicated to those of the Republican period—1821 up to date.

The rare books and incunabula, among them eighteen of the nineteen volumes of the *Biblio Maxima* translated into Spanish and published in Paris in 1660, and brought to Guatemala in 1718 by the Bishop of Chiapas as a gift to the Escuela de Cristo (Antigua); the ten-volume *Biblia Poliglota,* written in seven dead languages, published in 1645 (the only other copy extant is in British Museum), have been transferred to the Bibliotéca Nacional (see p. 249).

ARCHIVES [1] AND LIBRARY

Archivo General del Gobierno

A collection of 109,577 documents concerning the Kingdom of Guatemala, classified and catalogued by señor Joaquin Pardo; and a collection of documents of the Republic, perhaps as large, on which work is only begun. A *Bulletin,* issued occasionally, lists new manuscripts and documents filed.

[1] Eventually all archives will be catalogued and assembled in one building.

Sociedad de Geografía é Historia de Guatemala

Founded May 15, 1923; maintains its own building, in which is housed a reference library of geographical and historical works and documents on Central America. Has published fifteen volumes of new editions and first editions of unpublished manuscripts. Ranks as the Academy of Arts and Sciences of Central America. Issues quarterly bulletin, *Anales*. Among the rare documents in its guardianship is the Declaration of Independence. Arranges lectures by distinguished visiting archeologists, historians, and writers, and occasional exhibitions.

Intendencia (City Hall)

Custodian of the original manuscript of the *True History of the Conquest,* by Bernal Diaz del Castillo, 1568; the Minute Book in which the first decrees and laws of the Kingdom were recorded; the manuscript of the official chronicler of the Conquest, Francisco Antonio de Fuentes y Guzmán, written in the late seventeenth century, the last volume published in 1933, are also here; the original manuscript of the *Testament of Pedro de Betancourt* (page 175); the illuminated parchment of the Act of Foundation of Guatemala, 1524, and many old letters and documents relating to the history of Guatemala.

Escribania del Gobierno

A collection of government documents, edicts, and laws.

Bibliotéca Nacional (National Library)

A representative collection of the works of modern Guatemala and Central American writers on all subjects and in all forms; also some rare first editions, including the *History of Guatemala,* by Remersal; the 1782 edition of Landivar's poetry; Vicentius Bellovancensis' *Speculum Naturale Venetüs;* Hermann Lichtenstein Coloniensis, May 15, 1494; and A. P. Maudsley's *Biologia Centrali Americana,* London, 1889, one of the most complete classifications of Central American flora and fauna, and a superbly illustrated account of archeological sites.

GARDENS

Botanical Gardens

Every variety of flora that flourishes on Guatemala's various soils and climates is being assembled here. In hothouses are plants from the lowlands; in pools aquatic plants, and everywhere trees and flowers. Director of the Gardens is Professor Ulises Rojas, author of the three-volume study, *Elementos de Botánica General,* a detailed classification of Guatemala flora.

Experimental Gardens

Under the direction of the Ministerio de Agricultura; experimental gardens for the promotion of diversified farming and the introduction to Guatemala of new grains, fruits, vegetables, and for the development of coffee. Seeds are distributed free to farmers; coffee served to all visitors, and souvenir bags presented. Pamphlets, *Publicaciones para la Agricultura,* issued.

Orchid Gardens

Although the private gardens of don Mariano Pacheco Herrarte, visitors interested in orchids may secure permission to enter through the offices of the Experimental Gardens. Rare begonias and indigenous medicinal plants also grown here.

Aurora Park Gardens

Supplementary to the Experimental Gardens.

MARKETS

Guatemala City's three public markets would delight any community. The Mercadito or Little Market, on the south side, is popular for its wide variety of fresh vegetables. The second, known as Colón because it occupies the site where the fashionable Colón Theater once stood, spreads through a tree-shaded square. All year round it provides excellent pottery, gourds, baskets, as well as grains and other farm products and the *metate* or corn-grinding stone. But just before Christmas it becomes the Christmas Market, crowded with fir trees, palms, moss, orchids and flowers, and with aisles of booths selling ingenious and minute figures and decorations for Christmas trees and *nacimientos*. An excellent place at any time to see Indians of all tribes and costumes.

The Mercado Central occupies a vast building that fills an entire block and is the largest market under one roof in Central America. Hundreds of Indians arrive daily, laden with vegetables, fruits, flowers, and other wares typical of every section of the country. Later in the day, the Indian venders are replaced by *regatones,* men and women traders who have bought out the Indian stocks. Every Indian tongue and almost every European, the Spanish predominating, of course, can be heard in some part of the building, and high above them all, the raucous voices of parrots.

Flowers, tropical and those familiar to northern climates—among them masses of orchids—are piled high on tables and floor along the central aisles: a brilliant and enchanting sight. Tables and baskets and floor are heaped with vegetables of all shapes, sizes, colors, the variety of chile-peppers alone dazzling the eyes.

Here are *frijoles,* or black beans, the staple of every menu; *platanos,* in appearance very like bananas, but in reality a vegetable that can be served in a score of ways; large and fragrant vanilla beans, all the way from Verapaz; *huicoy,* a miniature pumpkin of delicate flavor; *huisquiles,* prickly green pears; *miltomates,* whose spicy flavor is used in sauces; *caibas,* which look like sweet peppers and are as delicious stuffed; *flor de izote,* a cluster of white blossoms of subtle flavor much in demand during Lent; *aguacates* of all sizes and textures; *chipilin,* whose leaves are used like sage, and a score of others.

Oranges and bananas identify the fruit section where unfamiliar but delectable fruits are legion: *papaya,* a melon-like fruit both yellow and orange-red; *caimito,* something like a plum; *mangoes,* from green to gold, in all sizes—best in May and June; *mamey, zapote, chico,* all of the same family and excellent raw or in conserve; *pitahaya,* a cactus fruit of American Beauty shades when opened and as beautiful as a flower; *tuna,* another cactus fruit of most delicate flavor; *acerola,* a tart cherry; *membrillos,* large and excellent quinces; *granadas* or pomegranates; *anonas,* custard apples; *granadillas,* the fruit of the passion flower, and luscious; and peaches, strawberries, cherries and other northern fruits in season.

Special booths contain herbs, roots, barks for cooking, medicines and potions. One section is devoted to meats, including the armadillo and iguana, and fish and crabs.

Lining the walls are booths with hand-loom and foot-loom textiles, and yard goods, baskets, pottery, tinware, sandals, hats, leather goods, blankets and raw materials, and lining the outside of the building are *tiendas de jarcia,* shops of ropes, hammocks, and other fiber products, and also shops with every other product, particularly blankets and textiles. Almost anything made or grown anywhere in Guatemala can be found in some nook or corner of the market.

One section of the building is worth a special visit. This contains the restaurants where primitive charcoal stoves cook savory Guatemalan dishes—rice fried with vegetables; platano patties with frijol hearts; enchiladas with cheese or ground meat and spiced with pickles; tortillas and more tortillas. The diners sit on benches before the brick table-like ovens and eat from gaily decorated clay dishes, using a tortilla as knife, fork and spoon, and drinking coffee from tiny pottery jugs.

PUBLIC BUILDINGS

In architecture and equipment many of Guatemala City's public buildings compare with those of larger or older cities in Europe and North America. Among those the visitor will appreciate are

The President's Palace

The Government Palace has murals by Alfred Gálvez Suarez and stained glass windows by Julio Urruela

The Department of Justice

The National Assembly

The National Printing Press and Radio Station (Typografía Nacional y la Radio Difusora TGW)

Department of Health and Sanitation (La Sanidad)

Department of Communications

Aviation Building and Airport (one of the finest in the world)

The President's Tribunal on the Campo del Marte, where military maneuvers, the annual review of the army and schools, and other celebrations and parades are held

The Customs House (Aduana)

Colonia 25 de Junio—a colony of workmen's homes built to replace
slums, admirable in construction, design and arrangement

The Cavalry Barracks

Other structures of interest include the two forts, Matamoros and
San José; the viaduct over Las Vacas River, built by the International Railways (743 feet long, 229 feet high, it is the largest in
Central America); and the Aqueduct which still, after more than
200 years of service, is bringing water to the capital from the hills
about Mixco and Pinula. Also of interest are many of the lega-
tions and residences along Reforma Boulevard and in the surrounding Santa Clara district.

XXII

TOWNS AND VILLAGES

TOWNS and villages included here have been selected for their accessibility and importance or interest; they do not include a complete roster.

Because highways, hotels, pensions, bus lines, air lines and other accommodations for travelers are at present progressing so rapidly, it is impossible to give complete information. Hotels, tourist offices, steamship and airway lines, however, as well as municipal officials outside Guatemala City, can supply details concerning hours, schedules, etc.

In general, it is sufficient to remember that a good highway joins Guatemala City with the capital of each Department except Petén and Izabal; that each such highway has a regular bus service, and that from each Department capital, roads, trails or waterways lead to all villages of that Department. Plane service also links national and Department capitals, and train service connects the national capital with each coast. (Road map, between pages 256-257.)

Train distances are calculated by miles; figures supplied by International Railways. Highway, trail and waterway distances by kilometers (1 km. = ⅝ mile): figures supplied by the National Department of Highways. When *by trail* is specified, access is possible only on foot or on horseback.

For condensation, the following abbreviations have been used:

* Situated on Pan-American Highway
E. Elevation, according to National Office of Statistics
F. Fiestas or ceremonial days
H. Hotel with some or all conveniences
h. Small inn
MD. Market Days
P. Size of population and classification. Population figures are according to progressive calculation, based on 1940 census, and

estimated for 1946 by the National Office of Statistics. On page
214, the population figures of the capital cities of the twenty-
two Departments are listed. As the town serves primarily as a
trade or religious center for a population living throughout the
municipality, figures for the municipality are given here.

Classification of Indians according to nation is based on preferred authorities. Although Guatemaltecos of pure Spanish
lineage are correctly *criolles* (creoles) and those of mixed
blood, whether 10 or 90 per cent Indian, are *mestizos,* the
popular term to include both groups is *ladino,* and in that
sense it is used here.

Spanish priests early established the custom of prefixing the
name of the patron saint chosen for each village to the name of
the village: in the following pages, the saint's name is inserted in
parentheses *after* the name unless use has made it an integral part
of the official title.

Aguacatán, Huehuetenango. E: 1594 meters (5228 feet). P: 11,096—
Aguacateca tribe. F: Aug. 3. MD: Th. and Sun. From Huehuetenango, 25 kms. (15⅝ miles).

"Place of abundant avocados," at the foot of the Cuchumatanes
Mountains; established after Conquest by merging pre-Conquest
village of Chalchitán with settlement of Aguacatecas of the Quiché
nation, a small, dark, shy people, unlike types in neighboring villages; still functions as two separate settlements. Modern church
houses interesting relics of colonial church which lies in ruins beside
it.

Near by is historic site, Pueblo Viejo, another pre-Conquest village, and three burial mounds. From neighboring gold mines,
Indians said to have made bricks of solid gold to present to King
of Spain in return for permission to retain their lands. Within a
mile, a large and beautiful spring gushes out of rock to form source
of San Juan River and irrigate the fertile fields of onions, garlic, and
other vegetables grown here.

Amatitlán (San Juan), Guatemala. E: 1245 meters (4084 feet).
P: 10,255—ladino. F: May 2-3 (page 39). From Guatemala City,
27 kms. (17 miles).

"Under the Amatle Tree," the village, is chiefly interesting for
its 1635 church, whose miracle-working figure, El Niño de Atocha,
is goal of an annual pilgrimage, and for its thermal springs—
Aguas Termales—beneficial for arthritis, rheumatism, and general
health. Woolen goods and felt hats manufactured here.

Original pre-Conquest village is three miles distant. At end of
lake is colony of week-end and summer cottages and bathhouses.
Good swimming, boating, hiking, with marked trails and rest
houses for hill climbers to El Filon Park, where observation post
in midst of gardens commands sweeping view of lake and country. A delightful scenic highway circles lake.

Antigua (Guatemala), Sacatepéquez. E: 1533 meters (5029 feet).
P: 24,235—ladino. F: Holy Week (best processions in country)
and San Felipe Pilgrimage (page 50). MD: best on Th. and Sat.
From Guatemala City, 39 kms. (24⅜ miles). H.

For complete account of history, background and sights (pages
136-202). Good hotels, roads, motor cars, guides and other facilities for seeing city and surrounding country. If time permits, two
or three neighboring villages should be visited for their interest
and for the drives which lead through coffee-finca country between
aisles of *cushin* and *gravilea* trees used to shade coffee. On the
road to San Felipe is a pottery factory. From these villages come
the vegetables, fruits, particularly good oranges, and other products
sold on the Antigua market and the quantities of castor beans
which make Antigua the center for castor oil manufacture.

1. *Alotenango* (12 kms.—7½ miles)—A pre-Conquest village of 7132,
   where now live descendants of the Tlascala Indians who were Mexican allies of Alvarado, and of the Manches. Colonial church erected
   by Franciscan Order. One route for ascending Fuego starts here
   and passes through extensive lava fields, Rio de Lava. F: June 24.
2. *Carmona*—Historically interesting as site of quarries which supplied stone for colonial builders, the best bulls for the bull fights,
   and silver from the now extinct mines of Cucurucho near by.
3. *Ciudad Vieja*—Pages 132-135.
4. *Dueñas* (San Miguel Milpas)—Founded 1553, by Dueñasin, a
   Conquistador who bought the land from the Indians for 23 meas-

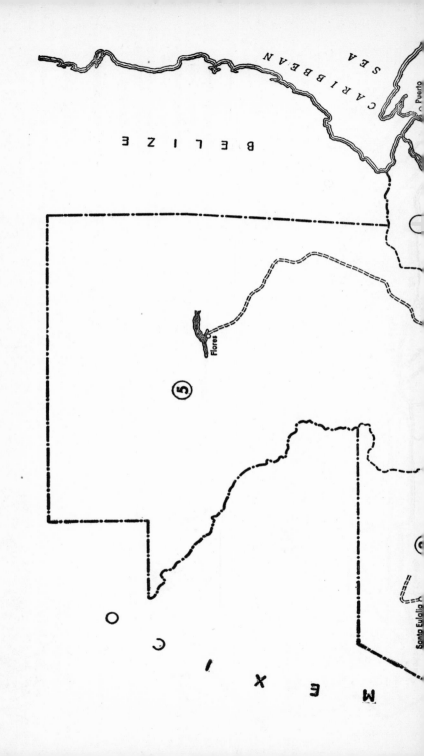

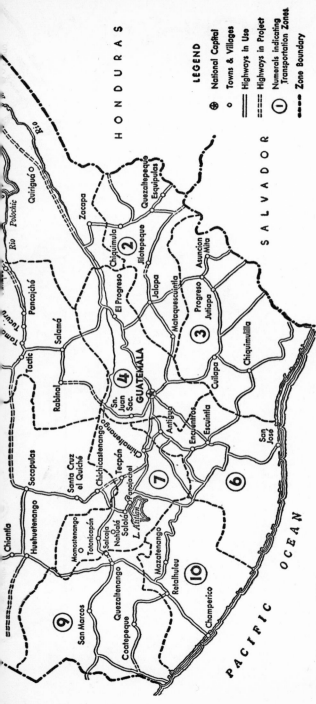

National Department of Highways

NATIONAL HIGHWAYS OF GUATEMALA

The physical outline of Guatemala, concentration of population in the southern area, and the fact that many national and Department boundaries have been redefined only recently make reproduction of a completely authentic map a difficult problem. The above Road Map of 1938, though incomplete as to Department boundaries, is accurate as to routes and towns and villages.

LEGEND

⊕ National Capital
○ Towns & Villages
━━━ Highways in Use
=== Highways in Project
① Numerals indicating Transportation Zones.
━ ━ Zone Boundary

ures of corn and 20 chickens. Its original *milpas* or cornfields are
now planted to coffee.

5. *Magdalena-Milpas Altas*—Still a village of "high cornfields"; interesting textiles.

6. *Pastores*—"Place of the Shepherds," founded by Alvarado in center
of his grazing grounds for sheep.

7. *San Antonio Aguas Calientes*—Page 286.

8. *San Juan del Obispo*—Page 169.

9. *San Cristóbal el Bajo*—Especially on July 31 when the Fiesta of
the Chauffeurs is celebrated.

10. *San Pedro las Huertas*—Especially on St. Peter's Day, June 29.

11. Various thermal springs are located within short distance, delightful for bathing and picnics; the best are El Cubo and Medina.

* **Asunción Mita**, Jutiapa. E: 600 meters (1968 feet). P: 26,329—
ladino, Pokomán. F: Aug. 15, and Fair, Dec. 6-10. From Jutiapa,
city, 31 kms. (19⅜ miles).

Established 1449, according to Indian records; captured 1550 by
Spaniards, and named Mitlán, "Place of the Dead"; Mita is a contraction. In colonial times was a large trading center, as Royal
Highway to Panama passed through here, and commerce with
mule trains was brisk. Colonial cemeteries visible from highway.
Now a ladino trading center and starting point for Atatupa Hot
Springs, for temples and pyramids of ancient archeological site,
and for fishing in Lake Güija. Train stops at flag station, Mita,
16 kms. (10 miles) from village.

Ruins of the early Indian settlement extend to hilltop above village; many interesting objects found among them. Temple on
summit, says legend, was erected in honor of the Feathered Serpent, Quetzalcoatl, by an old man and young girl who rose out of
the lake; for centuries has been the scene of annual *mitotes* or
Indian dances.

Atitlán (Lake) Villages, Sololá

* *Panajachel* (San Francisco)—E: 1580 meters (5184 feet). P: 2521—
Cakchiquel. F: October 4—with Indian dances. MD: Sun. From
Sololá, capital, 8 kms. (5 miles). H.

Panajachel, "Place of the Tree-Killing Vine," includes within its
borders Tzanjuyú, historic "nose of the mountain," where the

Tzutuhil warriors were crushed by the Spanish; within the municipality is a settlement of Patanatic Indians, branch of the Quiché, from Totonicapán. The colonial church, built in 1737 by the Franciscan Order, contains some good silver. The Indian women wear blouses of brown (undyed) cotton, those of the married women elaborately embroidered.

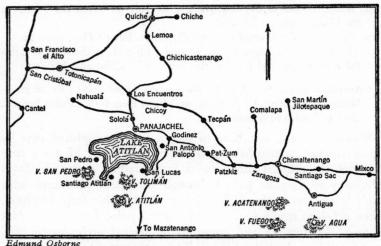

Edmund Osborne
Villages and Volcanoes near Lake Atitlán

Although, strictly speaking, not one of the lake villages, Panajachel is the center from which all of them may be reached by highway, launch or trail. Facing across the Lake to three volcanoes and rolling mountain ridges, it occupies one of the most beautiful settings in the country. Good hotels, bathing, horseback riding, boating, fishing, mountain climbing make it a popular tourist headquarters and week-end resort.

From nine to seventeen Indian villages are dotted about the lakeshore, according to different classifications, their inhabitants, descendants of the three great nations—Quiché, Cakchiquel, Tzutuhil —that once ruled this region. Each village has its own individuality and special form of industry. Unfortunately their names refute the popular belief that there are twelve villages, each named for one of the apostles. Some are accessible by highway, others by trail, but all can be reached by launches from Panajachel. Following is a table of the distances by water from Panajachel to nine of the villages which can be visited in a "round trip of the lake."

	Kilometers	Miles
From Panajachel to Santa Catarina Palopó....	3	1⅞
Santa Catarina Palopó to San Antonio Palopó.	7	4⅜
San Antonio Palopó to San Lucas Tolimán...	12	7½
San Lucas Tolimán to Santiago Atitlán.......	16	10
Santiago Atitlán to San Pedro la Laguna.....	14	8¾
San Pedro to San Juan la Laguna............	1	⅝
San Juan to San Pablo la Laguna............	4	2½
San Pablo to San Marcos la Laguna..........	5	3⅛
San Marcos to Santa Cruz la Laguna.........	8	5
Santa Cruz to Panajachel...................	8	5

* *San Andrés Semetabaj*—E: 1946 meters (6385 feet). P: 2691— Cakchiquel, ladino. MD: Tues. F: Nov. 30, Dec. 1. From Panajachel, 6 kms. (3¾ miles).

Name signifies "St. Andrew of the Round Stones." Artichokes, asparagus, strawberries grown here. Impressive ruins of colonial church.

San Antonio Palopó—E: 1658 meters (5438 feet). P: 3031—Cakchiquel. F: June 13; Th. and Fri. of Holy Week; St. Nicholas Day, Sept. 10.

Although perched high on rocky slopes of the lake, St. Anthony-by-the-Sea villagers never acknowledge its presence for practical purposes; they neither fish nor travel its waters, always going by trail. Most typical of the lake villages, with really spectacular views. Colonial church contains naïve, unpainted wooden figures. Large areas of onions and anise seed cultivated. During coffee-picking season, village almost deserted. Men's costumes unique— long, pure wool tunics with red sashes, very patriarchal in effect.

San Lucas Tolimán—E: 1530 meters (5018 feet). P: 5892—Tzutuhil. F: Oct. 17-19. MD: Th. and Sun.

Quaint, clean, and peaceful village, important as embarkation point for Indian traders from Pacific Coast who take launches here for Tzanjuyú and thence by trail to Sololá and other highland markets. Tolimán means "Where the Reeds Are Gathered," and from the reeds of the lake the men weave mats. Textiles colorful and good.

San Pablo la Laguna—E: 1585 meters (5200 feet). P: 1171—Tzutu-hil. F: June 30.

Center of rope-craft industry and one of few places where dyes are used in bags, hammocks, and other wares which are traded all over the country. Name means "St. Paul of the Lake."

San Pedro la Laguna—E: 1606 meters (5268 feet). P: 2823—Tzutu-hil. F: June 29. MD: Th. and Sun.

One of the largest villages on eastern shore; built on volcanic ash and up-and-down slopes of volcano San Pedro. People faithful to old rites and costumes; very industrious. Weave textiles and mats for many villages; cultivate corn; build dugout canoes from cedar and avocado wood of trees felled high on the volcano. The dugouts have square sterns and built-up sides, characteristic of all lake boats. Village has several *temaxcals*—vapor baths. Men wear colored shirts, red sashes, and trousers whose cuffs are embroidered with animals and flowers.

Santa Catarina Palopó—E: 1599 meters (5249 feet). P: 708—Cakchi-quel. F: Nov. 25-26.

Men weave mats from Lake reeds and fish for crabs and snails with curious basket contrivances as nets.

San Jorge Panajachel—A very small Cakchiquel village, settled by refugees from the 1773 earthquake in Antigua. Interesting at fiesta time—Apr. 24—for Indian dances and always for its views of the Lake and the nearby waterfall, Cascada de San Buenaventura. Corn cultivated chiefly.

Santiago Atitlán—E: 1530 meters (5018 feet). P: 10,878—Tzutuhil. F: July 25-26. MD: daily, 5-7 P.M., also on Mon., Tues. and Sat. A.M.

Largest and most important of lake villages, stands on site of original Tzutuhil settlement, in shadow of volcano Atitlán. Established by Franciscan Order and its church (1566) made *Guardiana* or "local superior of the convents of the Order." Very typical and colorful village with walled compounds of thatched mud huts on winding streets from central plaza, circled by towering mountains and volcanoes. Cultivate cotton, fruits and vegetables, build canoes. Women wear bright red, tightly wrapped skirts, white *huipiles* and the celebrated halo headdress; men, white shirts, short white trousers embroidered with small figures, red sashes and straw hats. Holy Week customs are an interesting mixture of Christian and pagan ideas.[1]

Ayampuc (San Pedro), Guatemala. E: 1485 meters (4880 feet). P: 8400—Cakchiquel. F: June 29 and first Friday in Lent. From Guatemala City, 28 kms. (17½ miles).

Site is part of land-grant awarded Bernal Diaz del Castillo, soldier-historian of Conquest. Colonial gold mines worked here. As reward for help this village gave Cakchiquel nation in pre-Conquest tribal wars and in battles against Alvarado, its men have the privilege of leading all processions in which Cakchiqueles take part. Through March and on May 3, pagan ceremonies are held here to ask the gods for rain and good corn and bean crops, as the soil, due to lava deposits and volcanic ash, needs every assistance. Women's textiles good in techniques and colors.

Ayutla, San Marcos. E: 21 meters (69 feet). P: 4015—ladino. From Guatemala City, 177 miles by train. h.

Terminal of International Railways and port of entry for travelers arriving by way of Mariscal, Mexico, terminal of Mexican railways. Suchiate River, which serves as boundary, crossed by bridge. Also terminal for branch line to Ocos, small Pacific port, 12 miles distant; trains, Sun., Tues., Fri. Climate very hot.

---

[1] For those with time and inclination, three little-known lake sites offer beauty and interest: (1) La Cristalina, between villages of San Pedro and San Pablo in Bay of San Pedro; (2) La Rada de Atitlán, on inlet beyond Santiago Atitlán; (3) Zunaná (Water of the Hummingbird), near Santa Cruz.

Bananera, Izabal. E: 42 meters (139 feet). P: about 2000—ladino. From Puerto Barrios, 37 miles by train.

Modern town, built by United Fruit Company as headquarters for offices and staff; residents chiefly American and English. Indian village near by. Similar town, Tiquisate, Suchitepequez, serves as Pacific Coast headquarters of Fruit Company.

Barrios—See Puerto Barrios.

Cantel (San Buenaventura), Quezaltenango. E: 2286 meters (7498 feet). P: 10,873—Quiché. F: Fair, Aug. 14-18; Easter Sunday when Passion Play given. MD: Sun. From Quezaltenango, 5 miles.

Originally known as Chuijullub, "On the Hill," takes modern name from Cantel Factory, one of few cotton mills in country. British machinery—1500 spindles; German dyes; American and Guatemala cotton; Indian operators; manufactures thread and trade materials, especially *manta de Cantel,* a white cloth in demand for Indian clothing. Factory worth visiting for itself and for beautiful setting and gardens. Village church interesting for peculiar façade, silver lamps and ornaments, images, altar.

Chajul, El Quiché. E: 1920 meters (6298 feet). P: 7871—Ixil. From Santa Cruz, 88 kms. (55 miles).

Established in colonial times by merging eleven Ixil settlements into one village, Chajul is one of the three villages of this tribe in the country. Its Indians are very reserved, keep strictly to themselves, and have their own rites, traditions and language. Their costumes are very interesting and vivid, a combination of Indian and Spanish ideas of dress, the red coats of the men being an imitation of the coat of Spanish officers. Village is notable for the figure of the Christ of Golgotha (Pilgrimages, page 51).

Champerico, Retalhuleu. E: 6 meters (20 feet). P: 2808—ladino. From Retalhuleu, 39 kms. (24⅜ miles).

An open roadstead on the Pacific Coast which serves as port for highlands and the Costa Cuca and Costa Grande coffee regions;

also as port of call for ships on the San Francisco-New York route. Customs House at Retalhuleu. A popular Holy Week resort when thousands visit beach for bathing and fishing.

Chichicastenango (Santo Tomás), El Quiché. E: 1965 meters (6447 feet). P: 32,666—Quiché, ladino. MD: Th. and Sun. From Guatemala City, 146 kms. (103¾ miles); from Santa Cruz, 18 kms. (11¼ miles). H.

One of the most interesting and colorful villages in the country. Settled in 1524 by refugees from the razed Quiché stronghold of Utatlán and named Chuv-lá, "Place of Caustic Leaves"; modern name is Spanish for "Place of the Nettles." Indians native to municipality are known as *maxeños,* a corruption of Tomás. The majority live in hills and woods, enter village only on market and fiesta days. Municipality so large and population so scattered that Indians returning from long journey fire rockets to announce return to neighbors.

Good hotels, bracing climate, beautiful scenery, varied sports— horseback riding, motoring, hiking, swimming—and excursions of interest in town and neighborhood make village one of chief tourist centers.

Principal local attractions are colonial church and chapel, El Calvario, and market. Church, built by Dominican Order, 1540, is visited by a continuous stream of devout Indians who worship pagan gods on the steps and portico and the Christian God inside. In its convent lived, until 1944, Father Ildefonso Rossbach, curate of the parish, widely known for his collection of jade and pre-Conquest objects, including many pieces of Zacualpa polychrome pottery, and for his own life and work. The padre came to Guatemala as a bookkeeper, but becoming interested in the Indians, resigned, and studied for priesthood in the United States. Returning to Guatemala in 1907, he served as parish priest until 1923, when he was made curate here with several widely separated parishes under his jurisdiction.

The market, one of the largest in the country, attracts from 800 to 1000 and more Indians, both *maxeños,* whose costumes of black wool, red headdresses and sashes, strikingly embroidered, are unique, and members of many highland tribes with a wide variety of costumes and wares, notably blankets and woolen goods.

Its fiestas are always attractions, particularly the Fair and celebration of St. Thomas Day, December 18-21, when from 5000 to 10,000 Indians gather for dances and religious ceremonies, Christian and pagan; Holy Week, the mid-October Harvest Festival, All Saints' Day, Nov. 1, and Corpus Christi (page 38).

In the immediate neighborhood are the ruins of Ziguan Tinamit (Village of the Ravines), original site of the settlement, and now called Patzac (On the Ruins). On the hill, La Democracia, are shrines of the pagan deities, Pocojil and Pascuala Abaj, where the annual ceremonies for rains and good crops are held. A good highway links the village with Santa Cruz, Department capital, and surrounding villages (see Santa Cruz).

* **Chimaltenango** (Santa Ana de), capital of Chimaltenango. E: 2246 meters (7369 feet). P: 14,736—ladino, Cakchiquel. F: July 26. MD: daily. From Guatemala City, 48 kms. (30 miles). h.

"On the Wall of the Shields," founded 1526 by Pedro de Portocarrera, one of Alvarado's officers. Its strategic location makes it active trade center for region twice considered as site for national capital. Colonial church (rebuilt, 1854) situated on continental divide; also fountain in plaza (duplicate of fountain in Chiapa de Indias, Mexico), half of whose waters flow to Atlantic, half to Pacific. National Agricultural School and government experimental station, 2 miles distant; near it, Aposento Swimming Pool and picnic grounds. Since colonial days, vicinity famous for bricks—called Lobo, because Spaniard of that name was first to realize properties of its clay—and for stockraising.

Four Cakchiquel villages within short drive or walk:

* 1. *El Tejar* (San Lorenzo) . . . 4 kms. (2½ miles). When survivors of destruction of first capital at Almolonga started building new capital at Panchoy, prices of tiles and bricks soared. Real Audiencia appointed two claypits or *barreros* where prices would be reasonable; El Tejar, then *de los Tejares,* one of them. First bricks made from model officially selected by Bernal Diaz in 1557 from Almolonga bricks, and all stamped with official seal of new capital. Vil-

lage still brick and tile center. Also site of good thermal springs. F: Jan. 20.

2. *Itzapa* (San Andrés) . . . 7 kms. (4⅜ miles). Founded in 1643 and renowned in colonial times for horse fairs to which traders came from all parts of Central America. Now agricultural center for corn, peppers, beans, fruit. Highway between this village and village of Patzún known as "Seven Mortal Sins" because of acute turns. Church and convent good examples of colonial architecture. F: Nov. 26-Dec. 1. MD: Fri. and Sun.

3. *Parramos* . . . 7 kms. (4⅜ miles). Attractive and clean village with typical straw-thatched huts and walled enclosures. *Cofradia* house, municipal building, and church in colonial style. Known for its basket craft and good beans. Women's textiles embroidered in red; men wear thick white overdress, reminiscent of habit of Dominican Order.

4. *Zaragoza* (Villa de) . . . 9 kms. (5⅝ miles). P: 8038. Especially interesting during annual fiesta, Oct. 11-13; always interesting for colors and designs of textiles.

Chiquimula (de la Sierra), capital of Chiquimula. E: 240 meters (704 feet). P: 35,614—ladino. F: Jan. 5-Aug. 12-17. MD: daily. From Guatemala City, 113 miles by train, 200 kms. (125 miles) by road, via Zacapa.

Since colonial days most important town in this region; now reached by three good highways; highway to Copán, Honduras, starts here. Thick-walled homes and haciendas approached by palm-lined avenues still retain colonial atmosphere. Near station, ruins of baroque colonial church and sugar mills from 1765 earthquake. Well-laid-out streets; some of the best schools in the country, including Protestant Mission School; trade from the cattle raised in the region, and fruits—mangoes and other tropical fruits —make it busy center at any time and more so in January when thousands of pilgrims pass through on way to Esquipulas.

Chiquimulilla, Santa Rosa. E: 330 meters (1083 feet). P: 25,453— ladino. F: May 1-5. MD: daily. From Cuilapa, 41 kms. (25⅝ miles).

Important Pacific seaboard town; industries, El Ahumado Salt Works, sawmills, cheese factory. Its tobacco rivals famous Hon-

duras leaf; rice also excellent. Chiquimulilla Canal—colonial waterway paralleling coast line—between this point and San José provides
communication for Departments of Jutiapa, Santa Rosa and Escuintla and opens up rich farming, cattle and commercial section.

> **Ciudad Vieja,** Sacatepéquez. E: 1524 meters (4917 feet). P: 8372—
> ladino, Tlascala. From Antigua, 5 kms. (3⅛ miles). First "per-
> manent" capital of Kingdom of Guatemala, pages 132-135. Fair,
> Dec. 8.

> **Coatepeque,** Quezaltenango. E: 484 meters (1595 feet). P: 28,839—
> ladino. F: Fair, Mar. 12-15. From Quezaltenango, 56 kms. (35
> miles); from Ayutla by train, 21 miles.

Trade center for Chuvá coffee region on Pacific; several fine
coffee-drying plants located here: modern machinery and methods.

> **Cobán** (Santo Domingo), capital of Alta Verapaz. E: 1320 meters
> (4331 feet). P: 45,924—ladino, largely German, and Kekchi. F:
> Holy Week; Fair and Saint's Day, Aug. 1-6. MD: daily. From
> Guatemala City, 250 kms. (156 miles). Airport. H and pension.

Most important town in this area; headquarters of government
and military, of Bishop of Verapaz and U. S. A. Protestant Missions.
Surrounded by large, rich fincas, tea plantations; much cardamon
seed, vanilla, sarsaparilla; also much cutting of hardwoods; active
manufacturing center for jute products. Substantial public buildings, schools, hospitals, homes, all with gardens, give town title of
City of Flowers. Charles V of Spain gave it title of Imperial City
of Cobán and coat of arms, said to be those on government building. Until recent development of roads and airlines, functioned
as almost independent and self-sustaining state, communicating, via
the Polochic and Dulce Rivers, with the Atlantic and Europe rather
than the capital.

Intermarriage between Germans and various Indian tribes of
region has produced distinct Indian type; not unusual to meet
Indian with fair hair and blue eyes. Indian women wear picturesque costume—soft white shadow-work blouses, full blue skirts,
quantities of silver chains and ornaments.

Original settlement founded by famous Dominican Father, Bartolomé de las Casas, about 1544, though claims are made for 1538, and named in honor of Indian chief, Cobaón. Village established by merging several Indian hamlets; now each hamlet a ward. Colonial church, 1650, well preserved; bears pagan symbol of Plumed Serpent on façade.

Most interesting building is El Calvario Church, situated on hill summit in outskirts. Tradition says that shortly after Conquest, old Indian hunter frequently encountered pair of tiger cubs on rocky ledge of hilltop, and wise men of tribe prophesied from that some momentous event to come. One day, instead of cubs, hunter found a beautiful figure of Christ Crucified on ledge and carried it to most important house in village. Again and again it was carried there as each time it returned supernaturally to the hill. At last in 1559, El Calvario was erected to house it, and the tiger cubs are symbolized in its decoration. The figure of Christ in the church now is the work of the colonial artist, Zuñiga. Steps ascending to the church form the rosary.

Many pre-Conquest sites in surrounding valleys have yielded interesting evidences of ancient civilizations. Mr. Irwin Dieseldorff of Cobán has made large collection over many years, including among his pottery some polychrome ware.

Year-round rainfall and fertile soil result in a region of luxuriant tropical vegetation, and excursions to near-by villages are made through beautiful country:

1. *San Cristóbal Verapaz*—Page 287.
2. *San Juan Chamelco* . . . 9 kms. (5⅝ miles). A Kekchi village of 19,686, whose church bell, made of gold and alloy, according to Indian legend, was left in the tower by Matalbatz (Chief of the Bats) when he was frightened away by the dawn. For years the Indians allowed no woman to approach it lest its clear tone be impaired. The church also contains much silver work, made from ore of neighboring mines. Textiles, good. F: June 24. MD: daily in afternoon.
3. *San Pedro Carchá* . . . 8 kms. (5 miles). Another Kekchi village, whose good clay deposits make it a pottery center. Situated on pre-Conquest site from which many rare clay pieces have been excavated. Colonial bridges over Cobán River here, also electric

power plant for Cobán. Craftsman who carves and rents masks for Indian dances has large collection worth seeing. Also interesting here are the primitive foot looms for shadow-work weaving still in use. Until 1867 San Pedro was a large, purely Indian town; then ladinos arrived; the Indians revolted, were subdued, and many left; their descendants are now found in distant parts of the country. F: June 29. MD: Tues.

4. *Tamahú* . . . 51 kms. (31⅞ miles). Small, neat village, and growing smaller as Indians refuse to marry outside clan. Tall, well built, very reserved; work on surrounding coffee fincas. Women's headdress—two braids wound and wound with red and crossed above forehead—and thermal springs, Agua de Zarza, Agua Salada, and Agua Azufrada, are chief sources of interest; each spring has different properties and temperatures. P: 5417—Pokonchi. F: Jan. 20-25; June 29. MD: Wed. and Sat.

5. *Tucurú* (San Miguel) . . . 64 kms. (40 miles). Another small Pokonchi village, like Tamahú, worth a stop if passing on way to River Dulce because of its Indian atmosphere and picturesque plaza, and for its costumes. The women wear a longish, three-piece blouse, heavily embroidered in the center section, and the same headdress as the women of Tamahú. The skirt, vivid red and finely woven, becomes rich rose from sun, washing and wear. Church has some interesting images which during Lent and Holy Week processions are dressed in Indian costume. MD: Th. and Sun.

Comalapa (San Juan), Chimaltenango. E: 2668 meters (8650 feet). P: 18,161—Cakchiquel. F: June 24, Dec. 12. MD: Sun A.M. From Chimaltenango, 19 kms. (11⅞ miles).

Reached by scenic highway and interesting for colonial and Indian atmosphere. Church and convent of St. John the Baptist, 1564, contains old paintings, carved and gilded altars, many silver ornaments, particularly hammered silver screens, the work of famous colonial artists. Name of town derived from Comalapám, "Village of Comales," the clay plates on which tortillas are made. Indians still observe tribal traditions. Textiles very good, notably blouses and head-ribbons.

Cotzal (San Juan), El Quiché. E: 1796 meters (5890 feet). P: 9483 —Ixil. F. June 24-25. From Santa Cruz, 76 kms. MD: Sat.

Arduous to reach, but repays effort. Spectacular views and colorful village, almost untouched by modern influences. Along road are interesting formations caused by lime deposits of Chajul and Cotzal Rivers. Men wear bright red coats trimmed with black braid in imitation of colonial Spanish officers; women's blouses are white, with bright birds in design. Colonial church dominates village. Rope-craft products chief industry here, as henequen grows plentifully; also extensive sheep raising.

* **Cuilapa** (or Cuajiniquilapa), capital of Santa Rosa. E: 899 meters (2916 feet). P: 14,832—ladino. F: Fair, Dec. 24-27. MD: daily, best on Sun. From Guatemala City, 64 kms. (40 miles). h.

New, well-built town, reconstructed since 1913 earthquake, when capital moved temporarily to Barberena. Active commercially because of neighboring coffee and tobacco regions and mahogany forests. During July and August, popular for pineapples. In early days of Republic, the scene of many battles between Guatemala and Salvador.

El Progreso, capital of Progreso. E: 519 meters (1703 feet). P: 4337 —ladino. F: Jan. 15. MD: daily. From Guatemala City, 54 miles by train; 102 kms. (63¾ miles) by road. h.

Until 1935, known by Indian name of Huastatoya, then made capital of Department. Historically important as center from which Serapio Cruz began insurrection that culminated in 1871 Revolution and establishment of Liberal Party in power. Center of fruit-growing section.

El Rancho (San Augustín), Progreso. E: 274 meters (900 feet). F: Mar. 19. MD: daily, at station. From El Progreso, 11 kms. (6⅞ miles). From Guatemala City, 62 miles by train; 113 kms. (70⅝ miles) by road.

Shipping point for various fruits of region—jocotes, mameys, mangoes, zapotes, avocados, coconuts, cacti fruits, oranges and cashew nuts. Junction where buses are secured for Departments of Alta and Baja Verapaz. Across river from station is convalescent hospital for tubercular patients of American Hospital in Guatemala

City; hot, dry climate, very beneficial. Hospital also is one of stations on route of Ambulance Clinic.

Escuintla (Nuestra Señora de la Concepción), capital of Escuintla. E: 338 meters (1109 feet). P: 49,221—ladino. F: Dec. 8-12. MD: daily. From Guatemala City, 48 miles by train; by road, 63 kms. (39⅜ miles). h.

The name is a contraction of Izcuintepeque, "Hill of the Dogs," given the pre-Conquest village by the Spanish because the Pipil Indians there owned so many *tepescuintle,* animals resembling dogs. For long this area was a scene of war, as the Pipil refused to permit Indians of other tribes to pass through to make peace and pay tribute to Alvarado. In days of the Republic, its thermal springs, Aguas Zarzas and Aguas Vivas, made the town a famous watering place for Guatemala City society. Today the springs are popular for swimming and picnicking.

Region of rich tropical vegetation and soil; surrounding coffee, sugar, and banana plantations make town active trade center. Fruits—mangoes, breadfruits, coconuts, oranges, and pineapples; essential oils and rubber are other products here.

Esquipulas, Chiquimula. E: 920 meters (3018 feet). P: 4011—ladino, Cholti. F: Throughout Lent and Jan. 15. (Pilgrimages, page 45). From Chiquimula, 57 kms. (23¼ miles). h.

Esquipulas is of interest at any time for its views from surrounding hills, its fertile valleys, and the massive Sanctuario which houses the Black Christ. During Lent and particularly on the third Friday, numerous pilgrims visit the shrine, but Jan. 15, the Day of Esquipulas, the Indian chief who ruled this region during the Conquest, is the great day of the year.

Near the church are the springs of Sesecapa (River of Air) which form the source of the Lempa River. On the outskirts are some good thermal springs. From Esquipulas, a highway (not too good for cars as yet) continues to Copán, Honduras; the trip can be made on horseback in one day.

Flores, capital of Petén. E: 133 meters (436 feet). P: 2755—ladino.
F: Jan. 15-17. MD: daily. Reached by air from Guatemala City.
h.

Located on island of San Andrés in Lake Petén-Itzá, is at present
accessible by air or long overland route from Belize, British Honduras; highway from Guatemala City now under construction.
Airport is located at Pueblo Nuevo on mainland, from which one
crosses to island in dugout canoes. An increasingly important trade
and export center for hardwoods and lumber from the vast Petén
forests, for chicle, rubber, and—if the current survey proves successful—for petroleum. Petén is also the location of innumerable
Maya sites and Flores the headquarters and starting point for archeological expeditions. Planes secured here for Paso Caballo, chicle
center, and Uaxactún, Maya site (page 302).

Until 1697, San Andrés Island was the last stronghold of the
Maya. In 1618, when Franciscan priests arrived, they found the
Indians worshiping a stone sculpture of a horse left on the island
by Cortes. When they ordered it destroyed, the Indians tried to
transport it to the mainland in a dugout canoe. A storm over-
turned the boat, and now the imaginative believe that on clear days
they can see the horse beneath the waters. In 1698 the island was
fortified by the Spanish and made a penal colony.

Gualán, Zacapa. E: 127 meters (416 feet). P: 34,742—ladino. F: San
Miguel Day, Sept. 29. From Zacapa, by train, 20 miles; by trail,
40 kms. (25 miles). Fair, April 3-6.

Town proper is one mile from station. Since 1800, important as
head of navigation on Motagua River; at that time required 18-20
days to bring merchandise 80 miles in piroguas (dugouts) from
mouth of river; later dredged for larger craft, but when Puerto
Barrios was established and railway begun, navigation was abandoned. A century later it became important as headquarters of
International Railways. Now is center of agricultural district and
shipping point for coffee, tobacco, beans, yuccas. Name signifies,
"abundance of guaje trees," a large tree of dense foliage whose sap
is used by Indians on cancer sores. Interesting cave, Cueva de
Doña Maria, 7 kms. (4⅜ miles) distant.

* **Guatemala City** (Nueva Guatemala de la Asunción), national and Department capital, Guatemala. E: 1750 meters (4910 feet). P: 210,627. MD: daily except Sun. From Puerto Barrios, 198 miles by train; from San José, 76 miles.

Fiestas

** National Holiday
* Local Bank Holiday

* Jan. 1	New Year
* Jan. 6	Day of the Kings (Epiphany)
Mar. 1	Opening of Congress
* Mar. 19	St. Joseph's Day
* May 1	Labor Day
* June 29	Day of St. Peter and St. Paul; annual review of the schools
** June 30	Anniversary of Liberal victory in 1871 Revolution; annual review of the Army
* July 4	Independence Day, U. S. A.
* July 14	Bastille Day, France
Aug. 3	Flag Day, celebrating anniversary of day Christopher Columbus sailed from Palos, Spain, 1492
Aug. 15	Day of Our Lady of the Ascension, patron saint of city
** Sept. 15	Independence Day
* Oct. 12	Columbus Day
Oct. 20	Anniversary of 1944 Revolution
** Nov. 1	All Saints' Day
* Dec. 8	Day of Immaculate Conception
** Dec. 25	Christmas
* Dec. 31	Bank Holiday

All Saturdays half holidays

Movable Dates

National Fair and Central American Exposition—third week in November, with Monday, Tuesday and Wednesday official holidays.

Carnival—from Saturday evening to Tuesday evening, preceding Ash Wednesday.

Holy Week, beginning with Palm Sunday, processions and ceremonies daily; Thursday and Friday, national holidays.

Corpus Christi—beginning on first Thursday after Pentecost with celebration in front of Cathedral, continuing on Sunday, ten days later, with similar observance at Santo Domingo Church, and thereafter on each succeeding Sunday, one or two churches in different sections of city hold celebrations and fairs until some time in August, a final celebration is held in Guarda Viejo.

Industries

Shoes, soap, candles, cotton textiles, cement, knitted goods, rayon piece goods, cosmetics, and pharmaceuticals.

For history, background and places of interest, see pages 233-253.

Numerous trips, long and short, may be made from the capital to places of interest. The following are suggestions of near-by excursions to Indian villages off the beaten track:

Chinautla (Santa Cruz) . . . 10 kms. (6¼ miles). A picturesque Pokomán village, isolated in a steep *barranca,* and divided in two by the Chinautla River. Famous for its pottery, particularly water jars, which can be seen in the making within most of the wattle-enclosed dooryards. Forty years ago, a favorite spa for Guatemala City society; now has a minute, modern, tiled swimming pool. F: first Sun. in Dec.; May 3.

Chuarrancho . . . 40 kms. (25 miles). Pre-Conquest Cakchiquel village, originally known as Chibatutuy; interesting for its faithful observance of traditions and for its textiles. F: June 29. MD: Thurs. and Sun.

San Antonio las Flores . . . 6 kms. (3¾ miles). Another pre-Conquest Cakchiquel village in picturesque setting. Men cultivate communal lands, supply wood to Guatemala City households; women weave very good textiles. F: June 13. MD: Thurs. and Sat.

San José Nacahuil . . . 20 kms. (12½ miles). Near Nacahuil volcano; soil surrounding village arid, but men prepare charcoal and cut wood from forests on communal lands; women make interesting, colorful and good textiles. Also Cakchiquel. F: Mar. 19. MD: Thurs.

Huehuetenango (Concepción), capital of Huehuetenango. E: 1890 meters (6201 feet). P: 17,032—ladino, Mam. F: Fiestas Julianas or Fiesta del Carmen, July 10-18. MD: Th. and Sun. From Guatemala City, 274 kms. (171¼ miles) via Quiché. H.

Prosperous town with good buildings, homes, hotels, parks; its race course famous for quality of horses. Bracing climate, beauti-

ful scenery, quantities of flowers. A busy trade center and handi-
craft market for textiles, pottery, shoes, tinwork, leatherwork, etc.
Colonial church retains old silver ornaments, screens and altar.
Name signifies "Place of the Old People."

Near by are ruins of pre-Conquest Mam city of Zaculeu. A scenic
highway is under construction to Barillas in Cuchumatanes Mountains. Five kms. (3⅛ miles) distant is the beautifully situated
Mam village of Chiantla where annually, on February 2, one of
the large pilgrimages of the country is made to the Virgin of the
Rosary in the colonial church built by the Dominican Order. From
this village horses and guides can be secured for trips to villages
perched high on crags of the Cuchumatanes. One day this will be
an exploited mining section; today it is interesting for the variety
of its birds.

Iztapa, Escuintla. From Guatemala City, 118 kms. (73¾ miles).
From Escuintla, 55 kms. (34⅜ miles).

A small, primitive, straw-thatched village on Rio Maria Linda
(Beautiful River), and a favorite week-end resort for Guatemala
City residents. Ocean and river bathing, tarpon and other deep-
sea fishing, boating and hunting, all excellent. Here in colonial
days Alvarado built and equipped his ships for his expedition to
Peru, and in the nineteenth century President Rufino Barrios tried
to establish a port; unsuccessful because of jealousy of San José.
Name means "River of Salt," because Pacific tides impregnate river
waters. Can be reached readily in dry seasons by car, but at any
time via the Chiquimulilla Canal from San José, a delightful experience in itself, as the launch winds in and out of mangrove jungles, alive with egrets, herons of all colors, including pink, and
brilliant butterflies.

Jacaltenango (la Purificación), Huehuetenango. E: 1372 meters
(4593 feet). P: 7740—Jacalteca. F: Carnival, Feb. 2; Holy Week;
May 3, The Year Bearer. From Huehuetenango, 72 kms. (45
miles) by trail.

"House of Water," largest village in this region; active trade
center for palm-leaf hats, baskets in various techniques, and weav-

ing. Its Year Bearer ceremonies (page 33), one of most interesting and faithfully followed of ancient pre-Conquest pagan rituals.

Jalapa, capital of Jalapa. E: 1380 meters (4528 feet). P: 50,376—ladino. F: Fair, Dec. 23-25. MD: daily. From Guatemala City, 45 miles by train to Jalapa station, 15 miles by bus to village; by road, 118 kms. (73¾ miles). h.

Because of isolated location, retains much of colonial culture and architecture. Trading center for coffee fincas and cattle haciendas; hospital, hotel, shops. In fertile valley, cereals, sugar, tropical fruits, beans, corn, potatoes and rice also grown. Famous for cheese. Within 2 kms. (1¼ miles) are medicinal waters of Jumay Pool; within 8 kms. (5 miles), cool springs, Los Chorros, for bathing.

* Jutiapa (San Cristóbal de), capital of Jutiapa. E: 892 meters (2927 feet). P: 53,236—ladino. F: Fair, Nov. 8-15; Saint's Day, July 25. MD: Th. and Sun. From Guatemala City, 123 kms. (76⅞ miles). h.

Near International Bridge over Tamasulapa River on Guatemala-Salvador highway. Commercial center for region; hotels, hospital, attractive park. Very hot climate. Name derived from Rio de Jutes, River of the Snails.

Several interesting side trips available: (1) by horseback to Moyuta and from there to pre-Conquest ruins on banks of Rio Paz (Peace River); (2) for ascent of volcano Moyuta; (3) to coffee finca, Santo Domingo Papalhuapa, near extinct crater of Obrajuela and site of another pre-Conquest ruin; (4) to Pozas Vivas, thermal springs, 4 kms., for swimming; (5) hunting on slopes of volcano Suchitán; (6) to Lake Atescatempa for good fishing, hunting and beautiful scenery.

Livingston, Izabal. E: 31 meters (102 feet). P: 16,396—ladino, Carib. F: Day of the Rosary, first Sun. in Oct.; civic fêtes, Dec. 24-Jan. 1. From Puerto Barrios, by launch, 15 miles.

Situated at mouth of Rio Dulce, is export point for coffee, bananas and other products of Verapaz and headquarters of the Verapaz Railway, whose steamers ply between Livingston and Puerto Barrios across Amatique Bay. Named for the Louisiana author of the Livingston Code. Is the starting or finishing point for scenic or fishing trips in Dulce and Polochic Rivers and Lake Izabal or overland transportation from Panzos on Polochic to Cobán. Until 1921, served as capital of Department.

* **Malacatan,** San Marcos. E: 365 meters (1198 feet). P: 14,966—ladino. F: Dec. 14. MD: Sun. From San Marcos, 53 kms. (33⅛ miles). h.

Fourteen miles from Mexican border, is first town reached in Guatemala on Pan American Highway; passports and customs inspection at El Carmen. Highway to San Marcos, a continuous flow of magnificent scenery, ranging from coastal plains to highest volcanoes in Central America and ever-changing vegetation. Between Pie de la Cuesta (Foot of the Hill) and San Marcos, altitude rises on 19 kms. (11⅞ miles) ascent from 3000 feet to 10,500.

Mataquescuintla, Jalapa. E: 1600 meters (5251 feet). P: 22,905—ladino. F: July 24-26. MD: Wed. From Jalapa, 45 kms. (28⅛ miles).

"Bagful of dogs" was important during colonial times for output from its silver and copper mines; now, regional trading center for cattle haciendas, lumber camps, and a fertile agricultural section; regaining importance through location on road from Guatemala City to Honduras (via Esquipulas).

Maya Sites—Page 299.

Mazatenango (San Bartolomé), capital of Suchitepequez. E: 380 meters (1249 feet). P: 29,714—ladino. F: Carnival, week preceding Ash Wednesday. MD: best on Sat. and Thurs. From Guatemala City, by train 115 miles; by road, via Escuintla, 208 kms. (130 miles). h.

Center of varied agricultural and industrial activities, essential oils, rubber, several factories, including one for extracting oil from zapote seeds, and a cotton gin. Extensive Costa Grande coffee fincas, cotton, banana and peanut plantations in district. Indian shawls, made in tied and dyed technique, are expensive but in great demand. Name means "Hill of the Deer." Interesting excursion:

Cuyotenango (7 kms.—4⅜ miles), known now for its fertile fields of coffee, cotton, corn and bananas, was originally a pre-Conquest Cakchiquel village established by Indians who came from the highlands to cultivate cotton and cacao here. Later, it was an important colonial town, and the flavor of that period still lingers in fluted doors, wooden grills at windows, fountains, and furnishings of homes.

*Mixco (Santo Domingo), Guatemala. E: 1696 meters (5564 feet). P: 11,746—Pokomán, ladino. F: Aug. 4; Fiesta de los Morenos, with many Indian dances, last week in Jan. MD: trade at Guatemala City. From Guatemala City, 15 kms. (9⅜ miles).

Name derived from Mixconco, "Place in the Clouds," because original Pokomán fortified capital was located on hilltop. After 1773 earthquake, gained a large ladino population in refugees from Antigua; also the printing press was brought here to publish Felipe Cadena's account of the disaster. Mixco itself was almost destroyed in the 1917-18 earthquakes, but now is a large and prosperous village engaged in supplying Guatemala City with fruits and vegetables, and site of a large soap factory. Until recently, when it became fashionable for ladino mothers to nurse their own babies, Mixco women were in demand as wet nurses; today they are house servants and nursemaids.

Momostenango, Totonicapán. E: 2220 meters (7283 feet). P: 27,161 —Quiché, ladino. F: Aug. 1-2; Ceremony of the Eight Monkey (page 35). MD: Best on Sun. From Totonicapán, 34 kms. (21¼ miles).

One of the largest cities in the country, famous for woolen blankets and woolen textiles, which are in demand from Mexico to Panama. Wool gathered from herds of sheep and goats on mountains, prepared, woven on primitive foot looms, shrunk and waterproofed in near-by sulfur springs, spread on streets to dry and for sale, gives unique appearance to town.

Substantial buildings, electricity, airport, many large colonial homes, colonial church and convent here. Church owns some interesting examples of colonial silver work, particularly monstrance, which bears inscription, "Diego Vicente, 1699." Vicente was an Indian who is said to have moved town from original site in Chuitzac Hills and with his sister, Francisca, to have developed industries and opportunities for the Quiché even under Spanish oppression. Of great energy, unusual education and wealth, he won the resentment of the Spaniards, but on a voyage to Spain secured land grants and titles personally from the King. He is still worshiped almost as a god in the region. The Quiché name for the town is Tzunn-ché, "Tree of Hummingbirds."

Several thermal springs on outskirts of city, the analysis of whose waters proves them to have medicinal qualities similar to those of Vichy, France, becoming popular with Guatemaltecos. Los Riscos, curious earth formations, resulting from erosion, interesting near-by sight. And for the Ceremony of the Eight Monkey, a movable ritual and one of the most ancient pagan ceremonies in America, tens of thousands of Indians and ladinos visit the city each year.

Nahualá, Sololá. E: 2478 meters (8129 feet). P: 20,991—Quiché. F: Nov. 25. MD: Sun. From Sololá, 30 kms. (18¾ miles).

Until recently this section was almost unknown, as Nahualá Indians permitted no outsider to enter; even now, no ladino may remain over night. Taciturn, independent, proud, they adhere strictly to their traditional customs and moral codes. Drinking, for example, is taboo; anyone who wishes to drink must go elsewhere and, on his return, confess his misdemeanor and receive twenty lashes in the village plaza. They are very jealous of their lands and delegations in full ceremonial costume are frequently seen in Guatemala City, come to interview the President in defense of their grants and titles. They cultivate large areas of communal lands to corn and also are large sheep raisers. For trade, they have two specialties, *marimbas* and *metates* (stones for grinding corn). Costumes most interesting, particularly the men's, which include a thick brown wool coat and short black and white aprons; officials wear hats shaped with beeswax.

Nahualá Indians populated Santo Tomás el Perdido (St. Thomas the Lost), chief of the villages known as Pueblos Chancatales which occupy the territory to the Pacific Coast, given them as grants by President Rufino Barrios and considered the best coffee lands in the country.

Although characteristics, customs, and dress of the Nahualá and Santa Catarina Indians are the same and their wise men always consult on weighty tribal matters, they are great rivals. Both have solid stone churches containing beautiful altars and hammered silver images of Santa Catarina which during troubled times were buried. Nahualá's figure is the better, but Santa Catarina's church bears the sign, "Here is the only real Santa Catarina." Both villages cling to the antiquated and outlawed custom of the church tithe, and three times a year, Christmas, Easter and St. Catherine's Day, each Indian pays the priest two pesos—about three and a half cents—for each herd of sheep he owns.

Nebaj (Santa Maria), El Quiché. E: 1920 meters (6299 feet). P: 15,087—Ixil. F: Aug. 15. MD: Th. and Sun. From Santa Cruz, 68 kms. (42½ miles).

Chajul, Cotzal and Nebaj are the only three Ixil villages in the country. Nebaj's costumes are also colorful and topped with square straw hats. Grows the best apples in Guatemala, but otherwise the village is without industry, as during coffee-picking seasons everyone moves to fincas on Pacific Coast.

Palín, Escuintla. E: 1126 meters (3695 feet). P: 9485—Pokomán. F: July 25, Oct. 3. MD: Sun. and Wed. From Escuintla, 18 kms. (11¼ miles).

The name is derived from *palinha*—"water that holds itself erect"—due to waterfalls near village. One, Catarata de San Pedro Martír, inspired a poem by Guatemala's best poet, Landivar; another supplies power for lighting Guatemala City. In the village plaza is the famous ceiba tree with a spread of 180 feet under which the market is held, a charming sight with Agua, Fuego and Acatenango in the background. Village particularly known for its pineapples and as the beginning of the *capok*-producing region. Women wear peculiar *huipiles* or blouses which hang loose from the shoulders, just reaching the waistline; their textiles, particularly ceremonial, are woven with a special technique.

Once the place was celebrated for its cancer cure, but Domingo Juarros, writing in 1808, says, "The Indians who suffer from this disease eat lizards. Though this does not entirely cure cancer, it brings immense relief. The Spaniards began to use this remedy in 1780."

Panajachel—See Atitlán (Lake) Villages.

* **Patzicia** (Santiago), Chimaltenango.   E: 2130 meters (6155 feet).
P: 11,942—Cakchiquel.   F: July 23-26.   MD: Wed. and Sat.   From Chimaltenango, 16 kms. (11¼ miles).

Established 1545 by converted Indian noble, and historically significant as setting for formulation of the Act of Patzicia, platform of the Liberal Party, during 1871 Revolution.   Now center of a prosperous corn and wheat area.   Name signifies "At the River of the Badgers."

* **Patzún** (San Bernardino), Chimaltenango.   E: 2180 meters (7152 feet).   P: 17,836—Cakchiquel.   F: Fair, May 13-20.   MD: Sun.   From Chimaltenango, 30 kms. (18¼ miles).   h.

"Beating Place," a colonial village surrounded by fertile wheat, corn and bean fields.   Large sawmill serves lumber industry.   Vivid red costumes of women make market a brilliant scene.   Colonial church has excellently carved doors, silver ornaments.

Puerto Barrios, capital of Izabal.   E: 2 meters (6½ feet).   P: 27,308—ladino.   F: July 18-20: Izabal Fair, Mar. 6-13.   From Guatemala City, 198 miles by train.   H.

Most important port, established in early 1880's on Bay of Amatique by President Rufino Barrios; safe, landlocked harbor, concrete pier, all modern equipment and facilities.   Terminal of International Railways and export point for all bananas (brought by special banana trains from all parts of country); all chicle (brought by plane from the Petén); also for coffee and other fruits.   Tropical Radio maintains station here; various vice-consulates and trade headquarters make it active commercially.   Population includes many North Americans; English spoken generally.   Very hot. (See fishing, page 228.)

Visible across Bay is Santo Tomás, a ladino town of 1000, including descendants of Belgian colony established there in 1843. Town laid out by Belgian engineer, but climate and other tropical conditions decimated colony; many returned to Belgium. Town originally founded in 1604 by Spaniards who brought some Carib survivors from Roatan Island after an expedition to wipe out pirates there; the pirates, in turn, sacked Santo Tomás.

* **Quezaltenango,** capital of Quezaltenango. E: 2334 meters (7690 feet). P: 48,891—ladino, Quiché. F: Virgin of the Rosary, first Sun. in Oct.; Fair, Sept. 15; Espiritu Santo, one month after Holy Thursday; first Friday in Lent; Holy Week. MD: daily. From Guatemala City, 199 kms. (128⅞ miles). H.

Commercially, politically, historically is second only to Guatemala City. Established as fortified, pre-Conquest city of Xelahu, meaning "Under the Ten" guardian mountains surrounding the site—Cerro Quemado (Burned Hill), Siete Orejas (Seven Ears), and Santa Maria and Zunil, volcanoes. Overpowered by Alvarado in 1524, renamed by his army, En la Muralla del Quetzal, "On the Hill of the Quetzal"; modern name signifies "Place of the Quetzal."

In 1835, local politicians instigated secession of highlands from Republic and made city capital of independent state, El Estado de los Altos. Strategic location near ports of San José and Champerico on the Pacific and the richest coffee regions in country made it leading trade center until 1902 earthquake and growth of Puerto Barrios. A railway, Ferrocarril de los Altos, constructed at great cost of money and life, was destroyed by rains in 1930-32; never rebuilt; the station is now a school. Good highways and plane service, however, link city with all parts of country.

Schools, hospitals, public buildings, homes, military barracks, radio station, vice consulates, modern shops, branch of Central Bank of Guatemala, hotels, clubs—German and Casino—make for a prosperous and growing city. Industrial center for highlands, with shoe, textile, and broom factories, wool, knit-goods and flour mills. Much wealth concentrated in city, and social life is lavish. Ladinos live in center of city; Indians, many of them rich too, in wards or *barrios*. Pumice stone from Cerro Quemado used in the construction of many homes.

The Bishop of the Highlands is stationed here and an imposing Cathedral is under construction. Contains the venerated image of El Padre Eterno (Eternal Father) enclosed in hammered silver case, made in early 1800's by three silversmiths who, condemned to death, were promised freedom if case were completed before date of execution; only opened on most significant occasions. Here too is image of Justo Juez (The Just Judge), by Juan de Aguirre, colonial artist, and another of Nuestra Señora del Rosario, patron saint of the city, with antique rosary of pearls and diamonds.

Fair, first Friday in Lent in front of El Calvario Church, draws thousands of highland Indians. Market large, and especially good for highland textiles and woolens. Indian costumes are favorites with Guatemaltecos and foreigners alike. Women wear heavily pleated skirts and three-piece *huipiles;* their head ribbons are ten yards long and finely woven.

Several pleasant drives about the city include: (1) la Democracia, residence section with many gardens and Temple of Minerva, built by President Estrada Cabrera (who was born here) and left uncompleted on his downfall; (2) mineral baths at Almolonga, Aguas Amargas, and Fuentes Georginas; (3) Park, Cerro Tecúm-Umám (7 kms.—4⅜ miles), by way of race course and gorgeous views; (4) to neighboring villages—

Cantel, San Juan Ostuncalco and *San Martín Sacatepéquez* (see this section), also

Chicalajá—Especially on Jan. 15-18 when Quiché hold miniature pilgrimage of Esquipulas in local church and fair; begins with the Dance of the Jester before the church and ends with Snake Dance on river bank.

Concepción Chiquirichapa—14 kms. (8¾ miles). A Mam and ladino village: P: 4639; very well-to-do and attractive, with annual fair and fiesta, Dec. 8.

Olintepeque—8 kms. (5 miles). Located on Rio Xequixel (River of Blood) where thousands of Quiché warriors died under Spanish swords and guns in great battle of the Conquest. Highway branches here for Huehuetenango. Women's blouses of dark blue with horizontal magenta stripes. M: Tuesday. F: June 24-August 29.

Salcajá (San Luís)—8 kms. (5 miles). Established 1524 by Alvarado and first hermitage in Central America erected here. Church boasts that its painting, La Conquistadora, was Alvarado's gift. Ladino families here very proud to trace ancestry back to Juan de Leon Carmona, one of the conquerors. This is the first village in Guatemala where tie and dye weaving was made; its *cortes*—women's skirts—are in demand. MD: Sun. F: Aug. 25.

Zunil (Santa Catarina)—9 kms. (5⅝ miles). Thermal springs, Fuentes Georgians, here; road to springs mounts slope of volcano, Zunil, where sweeping views are available of ravines and mountains for miles. Colonial church interesting for architecture, carved altars, antique art, silverware. F: Nov. 25.

Quezaltepeque (Santa Catarina), Chiquimula. E: 620 meters (2034 feet). P: 16,043—Chol, ladino. From Chiquimula, 32 kms. (20 miles). F: Nov. 9-13.

Beautifully situated on a ridge along the highway to Esquipulas. The large and important colonial trade center is now a quiet village whose pride is the excellent fish nets woven by Chol men. In pre-Conquest days, Indians of this section were so rich that they are said to have weighted their nets with gold nuggets. Colonial church has some good silver.

Quiché, El—See Santa Cruz.

Quiriguá, Izabal. E: 73 meters (240 feet). From Puerto Barrios, 60 miles; from Guatemala City, 138 miles, by train. h.

Banana belt station in Motagua Valley and location of United Fruit Company Hospital, one of the best in all tropics for treatment of tropical diseases. Indian village, half-mile distant, is of little interest.

Two miles east, however, is one of the most famous and accessible of the excavated Maya sites (see Maya sites, page 299). A rest house, run by Americans, and transportation to the site, are available to visitors. Reservations must be made in advance through United Fruit Company.

Rabinal (San Pablo), Baja Verapaz. E: 975 meters (3197 feet). P: 19,884—Quiché. F: June 29; Jan. 25-29. MD: daily. From Salamá, 26 kms. (14¼ miles).

Founded 1537 as first of Christian villages in peaceful conquest of this region by the Dominican priest, Bartolomé de las Casas. Renowned for its carved and painted gourd craft, unique musical instruments and colorful textiles and also as the scene of the last presentation in 1856 of the most famous of the Indian dance dramas, the Rabinal Achi. Indians also have profitable sources of revenue in their excellent oranges and in *nij,* a dye extracted from insects.

From quarries near by the stone was secured for building the great Quiché fortified capital before the Conquest, Utatlán. About two miles to the northwest are the ruins of another fortified pre-Conquest city, and on the hill of Cagagüitz is Xecoc, historic site of the Pokonchi, a branch of the Maya Quiché, said to have been founded as a temporary shelter during the migration from the north which brought the Quiché, Cakchiquel and Tzutuhil nations into Guatemala.

Retalhuleu, capital of Retalhuleu. E: 241 meters (890 feet). P: 21,374 —ladino. F: Dec. 6-12. MD: daily, best on Sunday. From Guatemala City, 128 miles by train; by road, 251 kms. (156⅞ miles). H.

Modern town with customs house, post office, airport, substantial public buildings, park, club—Casino Retalteco—and many coffee *beneficos* (drying and cleaning plants). Residents here very proud of their pure Spanish lineage. Colonial church, erected in early 1700's, in park; its silver ornaments the gifts of Indians in 1720. Distribution center for imported merchandise; trading center for cotton growers.

The town was established by the Spaniards, who merged the villages of San Antonio and Santa Catarina Sacatepéquez; the brook that ran between them now runs underground beside the church. Many of the original Indians refused to be merged and moved to a new site to found San Sebastián and raise fruits and vegetables for the Retalhuleu market. Their descendants still resent the Spaniard, and many times have risen against authorities. For some reason they are called San Cebolla (St. Onion). In their homes they wear no clothing above the waist; carry store-bought blouses and shirts to be put on when entering town. Women's ceremonial headdress is twenty yards long.

Sacapulas (Santo Domingo), El Quiché. E: 1230 meters (4036 feet). P: 10,889—Quiché. F: Jan. 15; Aug. 4; Holy Week. MD: Th. and Sun. From Santa Cruz, 50 kms. (31¼ miles).

Indian name for village, Tuhala (Vapor Baths); founded 1537, still retains Indian character. Inhabitants accepted Christianity readily; their chief, don Juan, honored by the King of Spain, is subject of many essays and stories in colonial literature. Colonial church and convent built in 1554. Bartolomé de las Casas had first residence here and was instrumental in having bridge built over Rio Negro, now in ruins.

The river runs through extensive salt deposits here which the Indians work most primitively by mixing mud with salt, draining and filtering mud away, drying residue over fires; salt is sold in round cakes for cattle and also for eye medicine.

Indians distinguished by amount of interesting silver jewelry they wear, not found elsewhere; silver chains have large colonial and Peruvian coins as pendants. Aristocrats wear as many silver or brass rings as possible, hang others on chains.

Salamá (San Mateo de), Baja Verapaz. E: 920 meters (3018 feet). P: 20,430—ladino, Nahuatl or Pipil. F: Fair, Sept. 16-21; Corpus Christi. MD: daily. From Guatemala City, by road, 180 kms. (112½ miles). h.

Picturesque town on Salamá River, in wide valley circled by mountains. Name signifies "base for corn-grinding stones and water." Large colonial church contains fourteen altars, examples of finest carved and gilded work in country; figure of Christ by Evaristo Zuñiga. (Main altar not included, is of no artistic value.) Also some good paintings, furniture and antique cabinets in vestry.

Climate hot, soil arid; olive oil and raincoats manufactured here; sugar cane, beans, corn and cattle raised.

Highway branches here for Rabinal and for San Miguel Chicaj (9 kms.—5⅝ miles), a Pokomán village of 2268, which holds colorful market daily at sundown and fiesta on Sept. 27-28.

San Augustín Acasaguastlán, El Progreso. E: 260 meters (770 feet). P: 15,638—ladino. F: Aug. 26-29; Holy Week. From El Progreso, 16 kms. (10 miles). From Guatemala City, reached by train to El Rancho and from there by bus.

History of this site vanishes in antiquity. Once a Maya city stood here, from whose ruins many rare objects are excavated, among them the Vasija de Acasaguastlán, a vase now in the Museum of the American Indian in New York City, famous as the most beautiful piece of Maya ceramics yet found. Later village called Acatzahuastlán, "Abundance of Thrushes," and in colonial times the village known as St. Augustine of the Royal Crown was established here as important trade center.

One of the earliest large colonial churches and convents still stands, interesting for its architecture and murals. On one of the bells is the date 1522, two years earlier than the Conquest. It is one of four brought to the colony in 1554 by priests charged with delivering supplies to churches in the New World. Villagers, however, are more proud of the fact that the most expert *chirimia* players in Guatemala are found here. Chief industry, raising vegetables.

Holy Week processions attract large audiences because of custom of casting leading citizens in chief roles. San Cristóbal Acasaguastlán (8 kms.—5 miles) has one of best colonial churches in Central America.

San Antonio Aguas Calientes, Sacatepéquez. E: 1524 meters (5000 feet). P: 3474—Pokomán. F: Jan. 20; June 13. From Antigua, 6 kms. (3¾ miles).

One of the most typical and attractive villages in the country. Textiles among the best, both for techniques and for color combinations. Tule mats woven by the men are also in great demand. Until recently the reeds grew in surrounding swamps, but these have been drained to reduce malarial fevers, and Indians must travel far for their materials. Both men and women cultivate industriously large communal areas of vegetables and fruit for Antigua and Guatemala City markets.

* **San Cristóbal,** Totonicapán. E: 2380 meters (7812 feet). P: 11,311
—Quiché. F: July 24-25. MD: Sun. and Wed. From Totonicapán, 14 kms. (8¾ miles).

Situated at junction of Sija and Salamá Rivers, is important commercial center. Textile weaving principal industry, the skirt lengths
for women of many villages being made here; some of them excellent examples of tie and dye work. Toys, pottery, light furniture
and coffins other industries; one of largest flour mills in country
here, and one of the two leading supply houses for dance costumes
and properties.

Very impressive seventeenth-century Franciscan church, once fortified, still serves, though convent badly damaged by earthquakes.
Contains portraits of many celebrated colonial personages; also
baroque altars and silver work. Original main altar now for safe-
keeping in vestry as Indians have habit of nailing paper and tinsel
streamers to altars on fête days.

Near town are thermal springs, Agua Tibia and San Bernardino.
A pleasant excursion can be made to San Andrés Xecul (4 kms.—
2½ miles), a Quiché village of 2594, whose fiesta, Nov. 28-30, market each Thursday, and burial mounds are of interest.

San Cristóbal Verapaz, Alta Verapaz. E: 1380 meters (4527 feet).
P: 20,996—Pokonchí, ladino. F: Fair, July 22-26. MD: Sun. and
Tues. From Cobán, 22 kms. (13¾ miles).

Active commercially, with business largely in hands of German
and Chinese merchants; largest shoe factory in country here: important also as fiber craft center: for coffee, candles and *achiote,* a
red paste used to color foods. Impressive municipal building and
large colonial church with good silver and antique figure of San
Joaquin. Lake Cristóbal on outskirts is favorite resort of Cobán
residents for fishing, boating, swimming, hunting in surrounding
forests and, in season, duck hunting.

According to legend, lake was created in 1590 as a result of difference of opinion between priest and Indians over pagan rites.
One version has it that when Indians proved adamant, an earthquake split the ground under their feet, entombed them, then
opening filled with water. Another says that the priest, terrified

by pagan practices, fled, hurling maledictions behind him. These were so heavy that they depressed the earth where they fell.

Pacaya, a special delicacy here, is traded all over the country for Holy Week.

San Felipe de Lara (or Fuerte de San Felipe), Izabal.

Now a handful of picturesque straw-thatched huts sleeping in the sun at the junction of Lake Izabal and the Rio Dulce, interesting only as a riverboat stop to see the ruins of the seventeenth-century Spanish fort. Founded in 1652 by Lara y Mongrovejo, named in honor of Felipe II of Spain, it was strongly fortified for the double purpose of preventing pirates from penetrating to the interior of the country and to protect the warehouses of merchandise waiting shipment for Spain. Here too was the colonial penal colony until the late eighteenth century. Near the ruins now stands an ancient cannon, dated 1496, all that remains of a galleon that sank off the mouth of the Rio Dulce.

San Francisco el Alto, Totonicapán. E: 2640 meters (8661 feet). P: 11,515—Quiché. F: Oct. 4-6. MD: Fri. From Totonicapán, 19 kms. (11⅞ miles).

Market, best in region; textiles, blankets particularly, very good. Cattle market in conjunction. Best market of year held on first Friday of Lent. Wheat and corn cultivated extensively. Colonial church has some interesting murals and silver, including 1702 lamp. Sweeping views of valley of Salamá and beyond, volcanoes Santa Maria, Tacaná and Tajumulco.

San Gerónimo, Baja Verapaz. E: 900 meters (2952 feet). P: 5463— ladino. F: Sept. 26-30. From Salamá, 10 kms. (6¼ miles).

Established by Dominican priests who erected massive church and convent, then by ingenious system of irrigation and aqueducts brought water over arid lands to supply miles of vineyards. Shortly they were distributors of wine to entire Kingdom and the name of the town became a synonym for good wine. When religious Orders were abolished, an Englishman took over the lands, planted them to sugar cane and, from 1845, brewed *aguardiente* that soon became as famous and widely used as the Dominicans' wine. An Indian revolt was pacified by returning to them the church and village lands. Now government maintains a Depositos de Licores (liquor depot) and bottling works here, but of vineyards and canefields nothing remains but miles of crumbling walls.

San José, Escuintla. E: 3 meters (10 feet). P: 11,263—ladino. F: Mar. 19. From Escuintla, by train, 28 miles, by highway, 53 kms. (33⅛ miles); from Guatemala City, 76 miles; by highway, 115 kms. (71⅞ miles). h.

Most important Pacific port; an open roadstead. Passengers and freight transferred from ships or dock to launches by mechanical cranes. Terminal of International Railways. Favorite week-end resort for swimming and deep-sea fishing. During Holy Week thousands camp on the magnificent beach of black sand. Launches secured here for 12 kms. (7½ miles) trip through Chiquimulilla Canal, which ends here, to Iztapa. (See Iztapa.)

* San Juan Ostuncalco, Quezaltenango. E: 2495 meters (8181 feet). P: 16,493—Mam, ladino. F: Feb. 2; June 24. MD: Sun. From Quezaltenango, 19 kms. (11⅞ miles).

Largest village in fertile region for grains and corn; market days attract wholesale traders from various parts of the country. Its chief pride is its musical reputation as the home of Miguel Espinosa, composer and pianist, and former home of Jesús Castillo, composer and authority on Indian music. Its *cofradias* (church organizations) own many curious musical instruments which are played on fête days. Also here is a silver figure of the Virgen del Rosario, celebrated for granting prayers.

San Juan Sacatepéquez, Guatemala. E: 1820 meters (5971 feet). P: 29,674—Cakchiquel. F: Jan. 15; Fair and Saint's Day, June 24. MD: daily. From Guatemala City, 30 kms. (18¾ miles).

Large village extending along highway, with mountain on one side and deep ravines on other, the slopes of both terraced and planted to carnations, violets, gladioli, and other flowers and vegetables which are sold on Guatemala City market. Village market here is brilliant sight with women in red costumes against background of green. Textiles, well woven, feature the double-headed eagle and horse. June 24 fiesta is worth seeing as all neighboring villages turn out and many return from distance. Church has some good hammered-silver altar screens.

San Lucas Sacatepéquez, Sacatepéquez. E: 2118 meters (6950 feet). P: 3702—Cakchiquel. F: Oct. 17-19. From Antigua, 16 kms. (12½ miles).

Pre-Conquest village, known as Ichanzuquit, "House of Mud," and mud from neighboring pools for long in demand as excellent and lasting black dye. Now vegetable raising for Guatemala City chief industry. Here decisive battle of 1871 Revolution fought on June 29; shaft in plaza commemorates Liberal victory.

* **San Marcos,** capital of San Marcos. E: 2371 meters (8612 feet). P: 15,468—ladino. F: Fair, Apr. 22-30. MD: Tues. From Guatemala City, 255 kms. (159⅜ miles); from Mexican border, 80 kms. (50 miles). H.

Modern town in rich coffee country; also profitable industry in extraction of sulfur from deposits on volcano Tajumulco. For years has carried on feud with town of San Pedro Sacatepéquez with which it is linked by broad tree-lined boulevard. Dispute now being settled by erection of municipal building, La Union, halfway between two. Near it is modern club, Valin T'Manek, (The Tiger and the Roaster), with tennis courts and hunting and fishing in surrounding forests and streams. President Reina Barrios born here. First revolt against Conservative Party from here. (President Rufino Barrios, born 14 miles distant, at San Lorenzo.) Good thermal springs, 10 kms. Pre-colombian museum.

San Martín Jilotepeque, Chimaltenango. E: 1800 meters (5905 feet). P: 32,036—Cakchiquel. F: Fair, Nov. 11. MD: best on Sun. From Chimaltenango, 20 kms. (12½ miles).

"Hill of the Corn Cob," a prosperous commercial town; beans chiefly cultivated now. Wholesale eggs and orchids, vegetables and some corn sold in Guatemala City. Is true Indian town, faithful to customs and dress, particularly to pagan ritual of corn-planting season. Women's blouses colorful, and workmanship excellent;

most women wear two, one as hood protection from sun. Road to Chimaltenango a scenic highway between aisles of trees, in spring covered with orchids in flower.

San Martín Sacatepéquez, Quezaltenango. E: 2460 meters (8071 feet). P: 8762—Mam. F: Nov. 11. MD: Fri. From Quezaltenango, 19 kms. (11⅞ miles).

Located in pocket of mountains, covered with volcanic ash; continually swept by high winds, in dry season by dust storms. Popularly known as Chile Verde, "Green Pepper," because of Indian preference for this food. Surrounding slopes cultivated to corn and beans.

Indians here picturesque and taciturn. Men wear red and white undergarments with large red cuffs on sleeves, heavy brown wool outer tunic that touches ground, and heavily embroidered headscarfs and sash.

Excursions: (1) To lake on summit of near-by Chicabal Mountain—one hour's ride (horses secured through Municipal office). Lake is gathering place for witch doctors on certain days of each year, especially before rainy season to ask for good crops. Fowl and small animals sacrificed and *aguardiente* sprinkled over lake waters. (2) To Pre-Conquest site, one mile distant; legend says settlement was destroyed by jaguars.

San Mateo Ixtatán, Huehuetenango. E: 2555 meters (8333 feet). P: 8705—Chuj. From Huehuetenango, 112 kms. (70 miles) by trail.

Communal salt works, sheep raising, spinning wool into thread for weaving *capixays*—warm capes—and wheat raising principal industries here. Women wear long white *huipiles;* older women have sun embroidered about neck; worn over tightly wrapped skirt.

San Pedro Sacatepéquez, Guatemala. E: 2100 meters (6890 feet). P: 6328—Cakchiquel. F: Jan. 15; Carnival and Fair, week before Ash Wednesday; Thurs. and Fri. of Holy Week; June 29 (with Indian dances). MD: Sun. and Fri. From Guatemala City, 20 kms. (12½ miles).

Weaving center for textiles of many villages; designs and symbols of own textiles, particularly ceremonial, varied and significant, including tree of life and small figures representative of ancestors in red and purple on white. Also lively trade center. About half the village lives on hillsides, cultivating corn and beans for Guatemala City. Church, reconstructed and cupolas added after 1917 earthquake, contains interesting silver lamps. This and other villages whose names end in Sacatepéquez, "Hill of Grass," were pre-Conquest settlements of the Sacatepéquez nation.

San Pedro Sacatepéquez, San Marcos. E: 2338 meters (7670 feet). P: 12,411—Mam. F: Dec. 27-29. MD: Thurs. and Sun. From San Marcos, 2 kms. (1¼ miles). F: June 27-29, with dances.

Prosperous commercial town, with business largely in hands of Germans, though village primarily Indian. Industrial School of Spinning and Weaving maintained here by government to keep indigenous arts alive; everything taught from the selection and preparation of wool for spinning to designing and weaving; many trade pieces made to order. Own textiles unique because of general use of clear yellow (see San Marcos).

San Raimundo (de las Casillas), Guatemala. E: 1564 meters (5165 feet). P: 7637—Cakchiquel. F: Jan. 22-26. MD: Th. and Sun. From Guatemala City, 30 kms. (18¾ miles); via San Juan, 42 kms. (26¼ miles).

Founded by Indians of San Juan Sacatepéquez, who were brought here by Spanish priest early in seventeenth century; is one of oldest villages in this region. The church, early seventeenth-century, contains some striking altars and old paintings. Women wear distinctive red or blue and white fringed scarf. Trade center for region.

Santa Catarina Ixtahuacán—See Nahualá.

Santa Cruz del Quiché, capital of El Quiché. E: 2017 meters (6117 feet). P: 4143—ladino, Quiché. F: Fiestas Elenas, Aug. 16-20. MD: best on Th. and Sun. From Guatemala City, via Sololá, 164 kms. (102½ miles).

Active commercial as well as government center. Market very colorful and well attended. Colonial church and cloisters, built by Dominican Order, with stone from Quiché stronghold, Utatlán. August fêtes, including fair, sports and Indian dances, commemorate occasion when ladino troops, facing annihilation, promised Santa Elena annual feast if lives were saved.

From here many short trips to source of Motagua River, known as "Where the Clouds Rest," and to Quiché villages—

Chiche . . . 11 kms. (6⅞ miles). P: 6990. F: Dec. 15-17. MD: Sat., with interesting cattle market. Many Indian burial grounds in vicinity. Good textiles.

Chinique . . . 17 kms. (10⅝ miles). F: Dec. 13; Pilgrimage and Fiesta de Esquipulas, Jan. 13-15. Good swimming in Baños del Chorro Blanco, ⅝ mile distant.

Jocopilas . . . 8 kms. (5 miles). F: June 29, with ritual dances. Archeological site.

Joyabaj . . . 52 kms. (32½ miles). Village consists of a single mile-long street paralleling highway that in colonial times was part of Royal Road to Mexico. F: Aug. 12-15, includes fair and cattle market and Indian dances—Snake, Deer, Conquest, and Moors (p. 105).

Lemoa . . . 9 kms. (5⅝ miles). Called San Sebastián frequently because of lake of that name near by; good fishing in rainy season.

San Andrés Sajcabaja . . . 42 kms. (26¼ miles) by trail. Name means "St. Andrew Where White Water Flows Beside White Stones." F: Nov. 30. Bag-weaving center.

Zacualpa . . . 40 kms. (25 miles). Interesting for burial mounds and ruins of pre-Conquest settlements. Many rare objects excavated here, especially polychrome ware; some reveal Peruvian influence. "Where They Make Fine Walls," meaning of name.

Santa Eulalia, Huehuetenango. E: 2589 meters (8497 feet). P: 9187 —Chuj, ladino. F: Feb. 2. From Huehuetenango, 84 kms. (52½ miles) by trail.

Trade center for region and weaving center, particularly for heavy *capixays*. Chiefly interesting for its beautiful vistas and preservation of ancient pagan rites. In secret place is hidden the *holom-konop,* "Head of the Village," a carved wooden image worshiped by witch doctors and pagan priests. Here too is the cave where the witch doctors gather annually after the Ceremony of the Year Bearer (page 33) to forecast events for the entire region for the coming year.

Santa Maria Chiquimula, Totonicapán. E: 2000 meters (6562 feet). P: 10,291—Quiché, ladino. F: Jan. 15. MD: Sun. and Tues. From Totonicapán, 20 kms. (12½ miles) by trail.

Village proper very small because Indians live in thatched huts in woods. Village homes appear odd in their combination of adobe walls and colonial porches. Work communal fields. Particularly known for bread which is sold throughout district. Costumes very interesting.

Santa Maria de Jesús, Sacatepéquez. E: 1981 meters (6500 feet) P: 6288—Quiché. F: Aug. 25. From Antigua, 10 kms. (6¾ miles).

On slopes of Agua, commands view of valley and volcanoes. Ceremonial costumes unique; men wear ragged suits and top hats. One of the last villages to abandon the loin cloth. In colonial days the chief industry was supplying ice to the capital, the men gathering it before dawn from the high slopes of Agua; today they manufacture fireworks, cultivate peaches, and weave textiles.

Santiago Sacatepéquez, Sacatepéquez. E: 2021 meters (6633 feet). P: 6437—Cakchiquel. F: July 25-26; Aug. 15. MD: Sun. From Antigua, 22 kms. (13¾ miles).

Repeatedly destroyed and rebuilt after earthquakes. Supplies vegetables and fruits to Guatemala City. July 25 celebration in honor of St. James includes masked Indian dances and variety of typical festivities.

* Sololá (Asunción de), capital of Sololá. E: 2103 meters (6899 feet). P: 18,338—Cakchiquel. F: Aug. 13-14; week preceding Holy Week and Holy Week. MD: Fri. From Guatemala City, 118 kms. (73¾ miles). h.

Location of real grandeur, high on ridge above Lake Atitlán, circled by mountains. Especially worth seeing on market day when from 600 to 800 or more Indians gather, including wholesale traders from all parts of country. Holy Week ceremonies also elaborate and impressive.

Substantially built town with good buildings, including government distillery. Famous for onions, garlic, and anise seed, which are cultivated for miles around, and for woolen goods.

Stands on ancient pre-Conquest site of Tecpán-Atitlán, the symbol of whose ruling house, the Clan of the Bats, is embroidered between shoulders of men's woolen coats. Church and convent erected in 1541 by Franciscan Order. Clan customs still observed, particularly homage to elders and officials. Name signifies "Weeping Willow."

For the superb views alone three small villages near Sololá are worth visiting. In addition, each is clean and attractive and possesses a colonial church with many interesting carved-wood or silver pieces.

Concepción Quichelaj—8 kms. (5 miles). Must be reached from Sololá on horseback. Typical Cakchiquel village of 907. Baroque church, 1621. F: Dec. 12. E: 6500 ft.

San José Chacayá—4 kms. (2½ miles), but on highway. P: 774—Cakchiquel. F: Jan. 15; Mar. 19.

Santa Lucia Utatlán—12 kms. (7½ miles), also on highway. P: 6034 —Quiché. E: 2488 meters. MD: Thurs. Scene of many colorful fiestas, especially processions and ceremonies during Holy Week; on Dec. 13, and on various saints' days as each *cofradia* celebrates in honor of the image for which it is responsible. Markets also colorful.

Sumpango, Sacatepéquez. E: 1565 meters (5235 feet). P: 8750—Cakchiquel. F: Aug. 26-29. From Antigua, 12 kms. (7½ miles). h.

"Place of the Skull Rack," a busy village devoted to cultivation of corn and manufacture of soap and candles. Particularly interesting during fiesta when large fair with Indian dances and other characteristic festivities held. Costumes, notably those for ceremonial wear, striking and colorful though not woven here.

Tactic, Alta Verapaz. E: 1450 meters (4765 feet). P: 8474—Pokonchi. F: Aug. 12-15. MD: Sun. and Thurs. From Cobán, 35 kms.
(21⅞ miles).

Lively trade and weaving center, supplying textiles to villages
for miles around, also candles and soap. Costumes vivid, with
three-piece blouses, heavily embroidered in red, green, blue; brilliant red skirts. Only village in Guatemala whose houses have
small clay animals, symbols of ancient protectors of mankind, and
pagan cross on roof ridge. Colonial church has some paintings
showing Byzantine influence and interesting altars.

Tecpán (Guatemala), Chimaltenango. E: 2284 meters (7493 feet).
P: 24,133—Cakchiquel. F: Dec. 8; Oct. 1-8; May 3. MD: Thurs.
From Chimaltenango, 36 kms. (22½ miles). H.

Two miles distant from Iximché, "Court of the Royal House of
Goathemalán," where Alvarado established his first headquarters;
Tecpán was founded by Franciscan Order and colonial church
erected that still retains its painted beams, silver altars and original
paintings and images of the Mater Dolorosa and Jesús Nazareno.
Market day interesting for number of highland tribes represented.
Tecpán costumes distinctive, especially those of officials; women
wear loose, heavy brown blouses. Village circled by fertile wheat,
corn and fruit country. Several flour mills, one of largest in the
country here.

Tiquisate, Suchitepéquez. E: 220 feet. P: about 5000. 11 miles from
Rio Bravo station.

Anciently a pre-colombian center; today center for *Compania de
Guatemala,* subsidiary of United States Fruit Company. Modern
community, connected with Guatemala City and Ayutla by International Railways. Good hospital. Archeological museum. English
and Spanish spoken.

Todos Santos Cuchumatán, Huehuetenango. E: 2470 meters (8154
feet). P: 7677—Mam. F: Nov. 1-2. From Huehuetenango, 40
kms. (25 miles) by trail.

Magnificent setting in Cuchumatanes Mountains; isolation explains preservation of traditions, rites and costumes; Tzolkin Cal-

endar of 260 days still in use. Near village, archeological site of Tojcunanchen, where witch doctors and pagan priests gather for rites and prognostications. Mam Indians here, distinctive type, taller than average, very dignified and shy.

Men tend sheep, spin and weave woolens; women make pottery, weave cotton textiles. Costumes of both striking for bright colors and curious effects in combinations of Indian and sixteenth-century Spanish dress and in manner of wearing. When working in cold altitudes, men wear overdress of long-haired black monkey skin.

* **Totonicapán** (San Miguel), capital of Totonicapán. E: 2504 meters (8215 feet). P: 33,199—Quiché, ladino. F: Sept. 25-Oct. 2; July 25-26; Holy Week. MD: Tues. and Sat. From Guatemala City, 170 kms. (104¼ miles). h.

In beautiful valley, surrounded by hills and mountains, is largest and most important town of this region. Divided into wards— the Quiché Indians in one, Tlascala in another, and ladinos in between. In pre-Conquest times, this was the artistic and scientific center of Maya-Quiché nation.

Now known for its pottery, particularly glazed ware, pine furniture, textiles (ceremonial headribbons a specialty) and woolen goods. Each craft has its own guild and head man. Here too is Miguel Chuj's warehouse for dance costumes and properties, the largest in Central America. Wheat, corn, beans, grown extensively; great herds of sheep and goats graze on hillsides.

On outskirts are old colonial silver mines and battlefields of 1871 Revolution.

Tzanjuyú—See Atitlán Villages, Panajachel.

Yampuc—See Ayampuc.

Zacapa (San Pedro), capital of Zacapa. E: 225 meters (738 feet). P: 54,527—ladino. F: Dec. 1-10; June 29. MD: Sun. From Guatemala City, 95 miles by train; 172 kms. (107½ miles) by road. H.

Zacapa station is junction for railway branch to Salvador. Hotel here serves luncheon to trains between Guatemala City and Puerto Barrios. Motor buses at station for transportation to town two miles distant and to thermal springs, Baños de Santa Marta (1 mile), popular for their rheumatic cures and good swimming.

Town proper is active commercial center for prosperous region of cattle raisers and tobacco growers. Large tobacco market here and factory for making fireworks from saltpeter deposits. Zacapa cheese is famous. White marble mines near by. Climate hot, but dry and healthful.

Six kms. (3¾ miles) distant is ladino town of Estanzuela, established in late eighteenth century and still celebrated for the fine drawn work resembling filet made by the women. Craft originally introduced by Spanish nun of colonial times and erroneously called Zacapa work.

XXIII

MAYA SITES

FROM Palenque in Mexico, just across Guatemala's northern border, to Copán in Honduras, just below her southern, archeological sites of ancient Maya, Quiché and other pre-Conquest civilizations make Guatemala a source of limitless interest and treasure for the world. No estimate of their number has yet been reached, but the Department of Petén alone is known to have hundreds of sites hidden in the depths of its unbroken forests. Even of the sites known, only the surface has been scratched.

Until recently, professional or amateur might dig and do what he would with his findings. Now a law prohibits all but authorized and scientifically trained and equipped expeditions to undertake studies and excavations and the removal of objects found from the country.

The Carnegie Institution of Washington for the past fifteen years has been engaged in investigations in Guatemala, not only in the field of archeology, but in ethnology, sociology, anthropology, geography, languages, and is making available the results of its studies. The University Museum of the University of Pennsylvania has also undertaken excavations, chiefly at the Maya site of Piedras Negras in Petén.

Visitors to Guatemala will find the Archeological Museum in Guatemala City an invaluable introduction to the cultural history of America in general and to the civilization of the Maya in particular. Here is a collection of ceramics, stelae, monuments, jade, and other artifacts that compare in interest and beauty with those of any archeological museum in the world.

Of the known sites, those of pre-Conquest Quiché have been mentioned in connection with the towns and villages of their locations (pages 254-298). Of the Maya, the outstanding sites for importance, interest, and accessibility in the three geographical cultures into which they have been divided, follow:

HIGHLAND

Kaminal-Juyú, Guatemala City

Long known to archeologists but only recently excavated, this site includes about 200 mounds, once part of a ceremonial center of the Old Empire period; the name itself means "Valley of the Dead." The ceramics in the mounds excavated reveal characteristics similar to those found at Uaxactún in Petén and Teotihuacán in Mexico.

The first mound excavated consists of eight small superimposed pyramids, one side revealing three tombs that contained skeletons of men of high rank, to judge by the jade ornaments and other objects buried with them. Figurines like those found at the crossroads of ancient Maya commercial and immigration routes; a solid block of jadeite weighing 168 pounds; mosaic looking-glasses and mother-of-pearl have been uncovered here.

Scientifically, the mounds are of utmost importance, according to the Carnegie Institution, because this is one of the few sites in the highlands to contain multiple pyramidal structures, thus proving that the sophisticated architecture common to the lowland Maya was known also to the highland.

Nebaj, El Quiché

Here, in 1947, Carnegie Institution explorations uncovered twenty mounds on a ceremonial site believed to be the center of an important Mayan population. The first mound yielded treasures in clay and jade, estimated to date from the 9th century A.D. and an alabaster jar of about 1200. These, now on exhibit in the Archeological Museum in Guatemala City, have excited expectations of even rarer riches to be revealed when the remaining mounds are catalogued.

LOWLAND

Quiriguá (Quiriguá, page 283)

One of the most interesting and accessible of all Maya sites, extending some two miles along the north shore of the Motagua

River, colonized, it is believed, by Maya from Copán, since the stone carving of both show similar characteristics in their craftsmanship and sophistication. This site had scarcely a century of active existence before its inhabitants migrated to the north.

Among the numerous stelae found here, one (Stela E), 35 feet in height, is believed to be the largest stone ever quarried by the Maya. Another (Stela H) is one of the two found to date in all the Maya area which has inscriptions arranged in diagonal patterns instead of the usual perpendicular columns. Sandstone quarries near at hand reveal the source of their materials, but not the methods by which they were able to transport huge stones through jungles.

Copán, Honduras

By plane from Guatemala City or by highway, via Chiquimula.

On the northern bank of the Copán River are ruins of one of the largest cities of the Old Empire and one of the most important centers of Maya civilization. Temples, pyramids, a ball court, hieroglyphic stairway, and stelae are still in good condition. The only gold object in an Old Empire site was found here. Its ceramics are exceedingly important and will become more so with the years and further knowledge. The Carnegie Institution has done much work here, excavating and reconstructing the site.

Santa Lucia Cotzumalguapa

Named for a small Pacific Coast village in the Cotzumalguapa area. Ruined temples, pyramids and carved boulders in the forms of animals are found here in great numbers. Carvings, decorations and ceramics reveal two styles: one related to the art of the Maya, the other to that of the Pipil Indians. Carved faces of this region are characterized by an appearance of blindness. The explanation may lie, according to Dr. T. T. Waterman, who investigated this site, in the fact that this region is one of the three known in the world where the parasite, *Philaria,* has been found, an organism which, when introduced to the head by the bite of a fly, causes blindness.

Petén

Palenque, Mexico

By plane from Guatemala City.

Although not in Guatemala now, this site is a unit and one of the most important and magnificent units of the chain of Maya sites. It is particularly famous for its bas-relief on stone tablets and for its stucco work, both in high and low relief. The ruins are still in a fair state of preservation.

Piedras Negras (Black Stones)

By plane from Flores, Petén, or by river boat from the seaport of Alvaro Obregón, Mexico.

In this hilly region of the Usumacinta River, these pyramidal mounds remained undiscovered until 1935, although many archeologists had traveled the trail that leads directly over them. Except for one room with a vaulted roof, they are now largely a mass of débris. They are principally famous for the sculptured monuments which compose one of the longest and most complete series of dated stelae (almost 500 years), as one seems to have been erected at the end of every five-year period. Excavations of some structures indicate that the site was settled some time before the carving of the first monument. The site in its later aspects reveals a typical Maya city with ornate masonry, edifices covered with plaster and stucco ornamentation, probably brightly painted. The masonry indicates, too, that the city came to a violent end long before the Conquest.

More than forty monolithic stelae, some of them weighing eight tons or more, also tablets, thrones, lintels and other sculptures were found here by the expedition of the University of Pennsylvania. According to the standards of modern art, the sculptures of Piedras Negras are among the most artistic of the whole Maya region, less barbaric than those of Copán, less flamboyant than those of Quiriguá.

Uaxactún

By plane from Flores or Guatemala City.

Another of the most important Maya sites and one with the longest consecutive record of occupation yet discovered; endured almost

600 years. The earliest dated stela—and also the latest—of the Old Empire Period was found here. The masonry of the city is still visible.

Compared with other Maya centers of the same period, its stone work is poor, but its architecture is fine, revealing maturing stages of sophistication; its ceramics are magnificent and provide the best sequence yet found from the archaic period to the peak of Maya civilization. One of the finest frescoes known was uncovered here, a reproduction of which is in the Archeological Museum. Its jades, though neither in quality or craftsmanship as excellent as highland jades, are very representative of the Petén. Two archeologists, O. G. Ricketson and Dr. Franz Blom, believe that one of the groups formed an astronomical observatory.

Tikal

By plane to Uaxactún, then five hours by mule.

Of all the sites yet known, this is the one to see if opportunity permits, says one archeologist. The largest city of the Old Empire, it is a breath-taking spectacle as after days of riding through dense jungle one emerges to confront a series of five temples, ranging in height from 185 to 210 feet, palaces, monuments, altars and other structures soaring above the green. Discovered in 1848 by Colonel Modesto Mendez.

NOTES

1. *Area and Boundaries*—Guatemala includes 42,456 square miles, with Mexico as the northern boundary, British Honduras and 200 miles of Caribbean Sea and Honduras as the eastern, El Salvador as the southern, and 70 miles of Pacific Ocean as the western.

2. *Climate*—Although geographically located in the tropics, Guatemala's tropical climate is limited to the coastal lowlands. These, ranging in altitude from sea level to 800 meters (about 2500 feet), are known as the *tierra caliente* (hot country), with temperatures from 77 to 86 degrees Fahrenheit (25-30° C.). The highlands, or *tierra templada*, from 800 to 1500 meters (2500-5000 feet), average a temperature of 68 degrees F. (20° C.), the source of Guatemala's slogan, "Land of Eternal Spring." In the mountains, or *tierra fria*, above 1500 meters, the temperature averages 59 degrees F. (15° C.). The year is divided into two seasons, dry from November to May; rainy from May through October.

3. *Mountains*—Four main mountain ranges roll through the country, their slopes frequently cut with steep and narrow *barrancas* or ravines from several hundred to one and two thousand feet deep. The Cordilleras of the Andes, known as the Sierra Madre, run from northwest to southeast; the Sierra de Chamá-Santa Cruz range runs through Alta Verapaz to Amatique Bay on the Caribbean Sea, with a spur, the Cockscomb Range, running through Petén into British Honduras; the Merendon Mountains pass from east to northeast, forming part of the boundary between Guatemala and Honduras; and the Sierra de las Minas (really a spur of the Cordilleras) begin in the highlands and run northeast—with frequent changes of name—to the Bay of Amatique. The highest peaks are found among the Cuchumatanes Mountains in the Cordilleras on the Pacific Coast, some exceeding 13,000 feet.

4. *Volcanoes*—Though many of the 33 volcanoes within Guatemala's borders are still active, only Santa Maria and Fuego are continuously erupting. The most prominent and accessible are:

Volcano	Department	Elev. meters [1]	Last Eruption
Tacaná	San Marcos	4064	1855
Tajumulco	San Marcos	4210	
Cerro Quemado	Quezaltenango	3179	1785-1818
Zunil	Quezaltenango	3533	
Santa Maria	Quezaltenango	3768	1902-1928
San Pedro	Sololá	3024	
Santo Tomás	Sololá	3505	
Santa Clara	Sololá	2847	
Atitlán	Sololá	3525	1524-1843
Tolimán	Sololá	3130	1823-1852
Acatenango	Chimaltenango	3960	1925
Agua	Sacatepéquez	3752	
Fuego	Sacatepéquez	3835	1526-1932
Pacaya	Escuintla	2544	1565-1775
Tecuamburro	Santa Rosa	1946	
Suchitán	Jutiapa	2042	1469 (Indian record)
Ipala	Chiquimula	1670	
Quezaltepeque	Chiquimula	1200	

5. *Rivers*—Thirty-seven rivers drain Guatemala; 18 flow into the Pacific, 12 into the Caribbean Sea or Atlantic, 7 into the Gulf of Mexico. Of these the largest and longest is the Usumacinta of Petén, frequently called the Nile of Central America because it flows through land dotted with Maya ruins, but its name means "River of Monkeys." Contains numerous rapids around which portages must be made. The Rio Dulce, shortest and most beautiful river, is the only one navigable throughout its entire length, 22½ miles. The Sarstoon in Verapaz is the only one on which large river boats can be used. Following are the more important rivers, 60 miles or more in length, navigable by small river boats:

FLOWING INTO THE PACIFIC OCEAN

River	Department	Length Kms.	Length Miles	Navigable Kms.	Miles
Suchiate	San Marcos	150	93¾	60	37½
Salamá	Quezaltenango	135	84⅜		
Nahualate	Quezaltenango	150	93¾	25	15⅝
Esclavos	Santa Rosa and Jutiapa	120	75	15	9⅜
Paz	Jutiapa	100	62½		

[1] For elevation in feet, see Mountain Climbing, page 225.

Flowing into the Caribbean Sea

Motagua	.....Quiché, Guatemala, Verapaz,				
	Zacapa, Izabal	400	250	150	93¾
Polochic	......Alta Verapaz	240	150	50	31¼
Cahabon	.....Alta Verapaz	300	185	70	43¾
Sarstoon	......Alta Verapaz	120	75	48	30

Flowing into the Gulf of Mexico

Usumacinta	...Petén	780	485	780 (portages)
San Pedro	....Petén	300	185	150	93¾
Santa Isabel	...Petén	350	218¾	250	154¼
Salinas	.......Huehuetenango, Quiché	400	250	220	135
Lacantún	.....Huehuetenango, Quiché	300	185	150	93¾

6. *Lakes*—Guatemala has numerous lakes, especially during the rainy season, and the craters of several volcanoes have in addition their own lagoonlike lakes of cold volcanic waters.

Atitlán (Abundance of Water) surpasses them all in scenic grandeur, historical and legendary interest, and must be included among the most beautiful lakes of the world. Its perfection is the despair of artists and photographers, who call it "Lake Chromo." In length 26 kms. (16¼ miles), width 18½ kms. (11½ miles), depth 320 meters (1049 feet) or more, it has no known outlet. Every afternoon, the *chocomil,* a high wind, makes boating tricky for small craft and is the source of many of the lake's legends.

Amatitlán (Under the Amatle Tree), 12 kms. long (7½ miles), 5 kms. wide (3⅛ miles), and 40 meters (131 feet) deep, is another lovely lake whose outlet is the Michatoya River. Petén-Itza (Island Lake, or *Hatunnah,* as the Indians call it) is the largest of the Petén's many lakes; 36 kms. (22½ miles) long, 16 kms. (10 miles) wide; 80 feet above sea level. Izabal or Golfo Dulce, 48 kms. (30 miles) long, 24 kms. (15 miles) wide, and 18 meters (59 feet) deep, is the largest lake in the country, its outlet, the Rio Dulce. Güija, one half in the Department of Jutiapa, the other half in El Salvador, is 29 kms. (18⅛ miles) long, 10 wide (4¼ miles), 18 meters (59 feet) deep. Atescatempa, also in Jutiapa and on Pan American Highway, is only eight or ten feet deep, but is popular with both Salvadoreans and Guatemaltecos for its tall trees, beautiful scenery, and myriad egrets and waterfowl. During Lent, Indians fish day and night from dugouts here, and their women dry the fish over open fires. In 1897, without warning, the lake disappeared; a few years ago it as unexpectedly returned.

7. *Animals*—Guatemala makes up in the variety and numbers of birds, butterflies and small animals for its lack of large and spectacular wild beasts. Its lions are pumas, agile as tree climbers and a constant menace to cattle; its tigers are jaguars or leopards. Monkeys in numbers of species, coyotes, mountain cats, tapir, peccary, wild boar, fox, armadillos, tiny bears, deer, rabbits, weasels, opossum, porcupine, moles and *tepeizcuinte* (a species of dog) are plentiful.

Two species are unusual. One of these is the *danta,* a large animal of the tropical sections whose brownish color and long snout give it resemblance to a donkey. Before the Conquest introduced the horse, it was held in high esteem. Its figure in stylized symbols, included in many textile designs, is today often mistaken for a horse. Though it does not live in water, it frequents isolated waterways and lakes, browsing on shore grasses and, if hunted, takes refuge in the water, where it stands at bay, facing its attackers.

The second is the *manatí* or sea cow, found in tropical waters, particularly those of Lake Izabal. From ten to twelve feet long, with the mouth of a cow and eyes the size of a pea, a neck short and larger than its head, a fin at either side of the belly, tapering toward a broad 20-inch-long tail, it is not a beautiful animal. It lives near the shores where tall grasses are plentiful, and to be caught must be harpooned from dugout canoes. Large *manatís* weigh up to 1200 pounds. Because the flesh is white and toothsome and the hide in demand for whips, straps, walking sticks and other articles, it has been hunted so persistently that it is in danger of extinction. Now a law prohibits capturing or killing a *manatí* for some years.

Of snakes, Guatemala has 87 different species; 45 are non-poisonous, 20 are poisonous but "only dangerously so," and 22 are mortally poisonous. Of the last, the most feared are the rattlesnake, the bushmaster, fer de lance, water moccasin, and palm viper, of which there are many varieties.

8. *Birds*—In proportion to its size, Guatemala is one of the richest countries in the world in bird life. More than 900 species have been classified; of these only 190 are migratory visitors from the north.

Among the many species indigenous to the country are several varieties of turkeys. One, known as the Petén, ocellated or golden turkey (*Pavo dorado*), can be found only around the borders of Lake Yaxha and La Libertad in the Petén. It has the very bad habit of harboring beneath its wings a parasite whose bite causes the ears of its victim to rot. Other varieties are the horned turkey (*Pavo de cacho*), found only on the volcanoes Fuego and Zunil, and the *callaya,* whose habitat is in Alta Verapaz.

The *quetzal* also confines itself to the high altitudes of Verapaz and is becoming increasingly rare. Its plumage is gorgeous, of brilliant green and blue, the breast of iridescent red. Its tail, from two to three feet long, hangs gracefully in the form of a question mark. Because it was believed to die in captivity, it was long ago chosen as the symbol of Guatemala's love of liberty. That theory, however, and another, that the *quetzal's* nest has openings on two sides to protect its beautiful tail, have recently been disproved. In pre-Conquest times, the plumage of these birds was used in the headdresses of Indian chiefs; today it is forbidden to kill or capture them.

The *oropendula,* a large oriole, frequents the hot climates and can be seen in numbers along the River Polochic. It builds a long, hanging nest from the branches of dead trees, some trees having from 50 to a 100, tenement-house fashion, with scores of birds flying in through the top and out at the bottom constantly.

Nightingales are seldom seen but frequently heard in the highlands of Verapaz. The golden bill or *pico de oro* prefers the temperate areas. Parrots, parrakeets and macaws in all varieties and colors abound in the lowlands.

One of the most curious birds is the *cuchuchito* which has a call like a small dog's bark. It can set an entire Indian village afire with foreboding, as it is believed that its call forecasts earthquake, war, death or other major disaster.

Similar beliefs are attached to the calls of some of the many varieties of owls that make their homes in the forests. An Indian dreads to hear one near his own roof-tree because "When the owl sings, an Indian dies." One variety is known as the Guide of the Lion (*Guia del León*) as a result of its habit of flitting ahead from tree to tree, emitting short, sharp notes whenever a puma or tropical lion is stalking his prey at night.

Among the common varieties of birds are two species of linnet, the *guarda barranca* (Guardian of the Ravine) and the *pito real* (Royal Whistler). Their beautiful songs can be heard in all parts of the country where the altitude is between 5000 and 7000 feet. About eight varieties of thrush make their permanent homes in Guatemala, and many others from the north winter there. The best-known and loved is the *cenzontle* ("Bird of 400 Voices" is the Indian's pet name for it). Though an insignificant brown in appearance, it has a song of such range and variety that it is said to be the inspiration for Indian music (page III). As *cenzontles* live happily in captivity, they are much sought as pets. Godinez, a cross-roads center on the highway to Lake Atitlán, is a popular bird market; here *cenzontles, guarda barrancas,* and many other birds are displayed for sale in cages hanging from rafters of porches and corridors.

Of the migratory birds, one of the most interesting is the *azacuán,* a species of falcon. They fly north in great numbers in April and May, returning in late October when the rains are over. From this derives the Indian belief that the *azacuáns* are charged by the gods with the responsibility of opening and shutting the springs for the rains. In their migrations they cover an enormous range, going as far south as the Argentine, as far north as Canada.

Immense quantities of waterfowl, including egrets, gray, white and pink herons or *garzas,* cranes, wild duck, abound on the lakes and marshes. The Chiquimulilla Canal between San José and Iztapa is one of their favorite haunts and easily accessible to bird lovers.

The only collection of Guatemala birds—and it is not complete—is on exhibition in the museum of the School of Pharmacy and Natural Science of the National University in Guatemala City. The best book on the subject is *Distribution of Bird Life in Guatemala,* by Ludlow Griscom, published in 1932 by the American Museum of Natural History.

9. *Butterflies*—Except that one flies by day, the other by night, the Spanish language makes no differentiation between butterflies and moths; all are known as *mariposas.* Of the diurnal butterflies from 1000 to 1200 varieties have been found in the country; of the nocturnal, from 1500 to 2000 different species. No complete classification has ever been made and no book on the subject is available. The best information is contained in the English translation of the *Macro-Lepidoptera of the World,* by the German scientist Zeitz, and the best collection is in the possession of Alberto Fuentes Novella in Guatemala City.

Mariposas in the greatest numbers and most beautiful varieties are found in the lowlands, in altitudes ranging from 300 to 1000 feet, and especially in Alta Verapaz, around Cobán, and Izabal along the borders of the Polochic River and Lake Izabal. The forests about Escuintla and Retalhuleu on the Pacific slopes and about Quiriguá on the Caribbean are also favorite haunts. Throughout the year butterflies can be seen, but the best season extends from April through August.

Of the *morpho,* most beautiful butterfly in the world, Guatemala possesses five varieties: *morpho octavia,* a pale violet or green mother-of-pearl color with brown spots; *morpho polyphemus,* white mother-of-pearl; *morpho montezuma* and *morpho peleides,* both a brilliant peacock blue, and *morpho justitia,* a neutral brown. Of the *caligo* butterfly, two species are found, the *caligo mennon* or owl butterfly, so called because the design on the underside of the wings resembles the face of an owl, and the *caligo uranus,* a light mauve with underwings edged in yellow ochre.

Among the rare *mariposas* indigenous to Guatemala are the *Agrias Rodriguezi,* a choice specimen sought by many collectors, and the *Anaxita Drucei.* Most prized and rare of all is the *Copiopterix Bang Hassi,* which flies abroad only between one and five in the morning. Only six specimens exist in collections, two in the museum of zoology in Berlin, two in London, and two in the private collection of Alberto Fuentes Novella. And we must not forget the *Tysania agripina,* largest butterfly in the world, with a wingspread of ten to eleven inches.

10. *Vegetation*—Because of its varied climates, Guatemala's flora is almost limitless in scope and variety, with palms and pines, chrysanthemums and orchids growing side by side. Except in the *tierra fria,* flowers can grow the year round, with the result that dahlias, cosmos, asters, grow tree-high, geraniums and begonias hedge-high. To determine which are trees and which plants is a confusing matter to a layman. Flowers bloom the year round, but the best time to see trees in blossom is during March and April. To list even the most commonly seen trees, plants and flowers is impossible, but following are a few of special interest in each group.

10A. TREES

Amatle (Ficus sp.: Moraceae)—Of the numerous varieties in Guatemala, *Ficus Glaucescens* is most popular; used as the favorite shade tree in village plazas.

Aguacate (Persea gratissima: Lauraceae)—Large tree with thick foliage; its fruit—the avocado—of high vitamin value. Soap and shampoo manufactured from it.

Arbol de Pan (Artocarpus communis: Moraceae)—The breadfruit tree, found in profusion in lowlands, its fruit edible when roasted, fried or boiled.

Balsamo (Myroxylon Pereirae: Leguminosae)—A tall tree whose gum, erroneously called Balsamo del Peru, is of high medicinal value; wood used for many purposes.

Ceiba (Ceiba Pentandra L.: Rombacaceae)—Distinguished by its straight trunk, which often rises 80 feet or more in height, and its feathery leaves. Considered sacred by the Indian, it is never felled, even when land is cleared for sowing. Valuable commercially for its *kapok* or tree cotton, one tree giving as much as 100 pounds. Table oil secured from seed, one ton of seeds yielding from 50 to 60 gallons of oil.

Conacaste or *Guanacaste* (Enterolobium cyclocarpum: Mimosaceae)—Giant of the forest, ranging from 90 to 130 feet in height. Its leaves close at night. Wood excellent for dugout canoes, its bark for pulmonary infusions and its seeds for soap.

Ebano (Maba salicifolia: Ebenaceae)—Ebony or blackwood, much in demand for furniture.

Guayacán (Lignum vitae: Zygophyllaceae)—Small purple flowers cover crooked branches. Wood too hard for construction purposes but used for bearings.

Jacaranda (Jacaranda mimosaefolia; Bignoniaceae)—Recognizable by its tall, slender trunks, and in season by lilac flowers which completely cover its branches.

Laurel (Nectandra sp.: Lauraceae)—Several varieties flourish in Guatemala, none of them similar to those of the north or the European Laurel nobilis. Wood provides cheap lumber for construction work.

Liquidambar (Liquidambar orientalis: Hamamelidaceae)—One of the most beautiful trees in tropical forests, growing at altitudes from 2400 to 4500 feet. Wood is exported for furniture and veneers; sometimes used for medicinal purposes.

Madre Cacao (Gliricidia sepium: Fabaceae)—"Mother Cacao," this tree derives its name through its use as a shade tree on cacao plantations. Its poisonous roots drive away ants and other insect pests. In flowering season, covered with small, delicate pink blossoms.

Madroño (Calycophyllum candidissimum: Rubiaceae)—A showy tree of the forest with thick glossy leaves and large clusters of white flowers.

Morro (Crescentia alata and Crescentia Cujete: Bignoniaceae: Calabash)— Grows in humid lowlands, its spreading branches covered with orchids. Its gourds widely used in gourd craft (page 68).

Matilisguate (Tabebuia pentaphylla: Bignoniaceae)—Tall tree of light yellow wood used extensively for cabinet work. Sheds its leaves when in flower with pink, white or yellow blossoms.

Palo Jiote or *Indio desnudo* (Bursera simaruba: Burseraceae)—Crooked trunk and scaly reddish bark used as a sudorific: its gum is source of copal resin.

Pinabete (Abies religiosa: Pinaceae)—Large tree found abundantly in the highlands. Its wood is used in the construction of Indian hand looms.

Pumpumjuche (Pachira macrocarpa: Bombacaceae)—Tall tree of the lowlands; large fruit considered to have medicinal properties.

Quina or *cinchona* (Cinchona officinalis: Rubiaceae)—Many varieties in Guatemala, the most attractive covered with bright red berries; each known by the different color of quinine extracted from it; several U. S. firms engaged in quinine extraction.

Roble (Quercus sp.: Fagaceae)—Many species of this tall and beautiful tree in Guatemala; its wood used in construction and cabinets; its bark by tanneries.

San Juan (Vochysia guatemalensis: Vochysiaceae)—Wood used for dugout canoes in Lake Izabal region.

Tamarindo (Tamarindus indica: Caesalpinaceae)—Tall tree whose fruit makes a delicious cooling or medicinal drink.

Taray (Eysenhardtia polystachia: Papilionatae)—Its light wood used in construction; its bark as medicine.

Tecomasuche (Cochlospermum vitifalium: Cochlospermaceae)—Distinguished by large yellow flowers and small gourdlike fruit much used for medicinal purposes.

10B. MEDICINAL PLANTS

For generations the Indians have turned to the plant life of Guatemala for their medicines and their craft materials. The secrets of their medical potions are guarded by the witch doctors with such success that some of the plants used are still unknown.

Albahaca (Ocimum basilicum: Labiatiae or Menthaceae)—"Sweet basil" of our grandmothers; used as a condiment and also as a rub for fever victims.

Alcotán (Cissampelos Pareira: Menispermaceae)—Leaves used as a diuretic.

Algalia (Hibiscus abelmoschus: Malvaceae)—Seeds contain oil; mashed for use against malaria, snake and poisonous insect bites.

Barrajo (Cassia alata: Caesalpinaceae)—A shrub whose leaves are used as a medicine to combat fevers and whose stalks when boiled are applied to insect bites.

Calzoncillo (Passiflora mexicana: Passifloraceae)—A diuretic.

Cañafistula (Cassia fistula: Caesalpinaceae)—In combination with tamarind, used as a blood purifier; also as a mild purge.

Floripundia or Florifundia. (Datura candida: Solanaceae)—Tall plant with huge, white, bell-like flowers and overwhelming odor; used as soporific and also to reduce swellings.

Hierba del Cancer (Alcalypha alopecuroides: Euphorbiaceae)—Several varieties in Guatemala; used on cancerous sores and infections.

Ixbut (Euphorbia Lancifolia: Euforbiaceae)—Long used to induce flow of milk in nursing mothers; now used by farmers on cows. U. S. firm investigating possibilities in commercial production.

Mejorana (Salvia mocinoy: Labiataceae)—Used for pulmonary affections and as a tonic; said to be excellent for chronic colds.

Pericon (Tagetes lucida: Compositaceae)—An herb, growing wild all over the country; during April, May and June, covered with yellow flowers. Used for digestive troubles, particularly dysentery. Must be cut before rains set in or, as the Indians believe, before June 24, the Feast of San Juan, as after that day the devil rolls in it.

Poliga (Polygala senega: Polygalaceae)—Roots used as a purge and against rheumatism and hydrophobia.

Ruda (Ruta chalapensis: Rutaceae)—Used for heart trouble.

Sanguinaria (Alternanthera repens: Amaranthaceae)—Used in cases of dysentery, digestive disorders, venereal diseases and "female weakness."

Simaruba (Simaruba officinalis: Simarubaceae)—A dysentery cure.

Suquinay (Vernonia patens: Compositaceae)—From leaves a medicine made for dysentery and digestive disorders.

Tuna (Opuntia sp.: Cactaceae)—Gum used in cases of hydrophobia and dysentery.

10C. INDUSTRIAL PLANTS

Ajonjolí (Sesamum orientale: Pedaliaceae)—Seeds used for flavoring tamales and on rolls; oil extracted from seeds and residue fed as *afrecho* or bran to cattle.

Arrayán (Myrica cerifera: Myrtaceae—Bay)—For soap and candles.

Cacahuete—peanut. (Arachis hypogaea: Papilionatae)—Essential and table oils; paint fixer.

Cacao volador (Virola guatemalensis: Myristicaceae)—Found abundantly in Suchitepequez; oil extracted from fruit.

Chian (Hyptis suaveolens: Menthaceae)—Paint dryer.

Copal (Hymenaea verrucosa: Caesalpinaceae)—Resin made into small round cakes which are used extensively by Indians as redolent incense during religious rites.

Higuerillo (Recinus communis: Euphorbiaceae)—Oil in seeds a source of castor oil; also used in lamps.

Piñon (Japropha Curcas: Euphorbiaceae)—Soap and lamp oil made from seeds.

10D. FIBROUS PLANTS

Huiscoyol (Bactris horrida)—From its strong fibers Indians make needles for weaving hats and mats.

Maguey (Agave sisalana sp. pl.: Amaryllidaceae)—Many varieties; fibers used in various ways by fiber craft (p. 72).

Palmeras (Palmaceae)—Innumerable varieties of palm abound in Guatemala, their fibers used in mat, hat and basket weaving (p. 71).

Paxte (Tillandsia usneoides: Bromeliaceae)—"Spanish moss," used for upholstering (Luffa cylindrica or acutangula: Cucurbitaceae); fruit used as substitute for sponges and in fiber-craft articles.

Pita floja (Furcraea gigantea: Amaryllidaceae)—Fine quality fiber used in all fiber crafts.

Ramie (Boehmeria nivea: Urticaceae)—Supplies an excellent quality of vegetable silk.

10E. ORCHIDS

As new specimens are still being found, no estimate of the number of species existing in Guatemala can be made safely, but orchids make up a conspicuous family in the country's flora. Most of the species known, however, would not be recognized by the casual traveler, as they are classed as "botanical" orchids. Many species of Bromeliads which grow in large numbers on branches of trees, frequently with a more showy inflorescence than the orchids growing beside them, are mistaken for orchids.

One of the loveliest varieties in Guatemala—and one that fulfills all the popular ideas of what an orchid should be—is the *Candelaria* (*Cattleya Skinneri*) so called because its graceful clusters of mauve flowers appear at the time of the feast of the Candelaria or Candlemas. This orchid has been used to some extent in breeding more showy commercial orchids.

Another fine orchid of Guatemala is the gold and brown *Odontoglossum grande* which appears in great profusion in the markets during late summer. The largest orchid both in size of plant and flower is the *Sobralia macrantha,* a magnificent purple orchid that often measures as much as eight inches across. This is the terrestial orchid that frequently grows taller than a man and may be seen along roadsides, particularly near Quezaltenango.

Visitors to Aurora Park in Guatemala City can see numbers of orchids growing on the cypress and walnut trees. The graceful sprays of small white flowers flecked with brown are *Oncidium Leuchochilum* which blossoms from November to April or May. Numerous species of *Stanhopea,* characterized by fantastic shapes and often powerful odors, appear during late spring and summer.

Alta Verapaz is particularly famous for the variety and beauty of its orchids. The *Monja Blanca,* or White Nun (Lycaste Skinneri, var. Alba), national flower of Guatemala, comes from here.

The "Little Nuns" or Monjitas, in a wide range of colors—yellow, pink, mauve, white—which the visitor is most apt to see in season, are another of the numerous branches of the *Lycaste* found in Guatemala.

10F. DYE PLANTS

Mora del Campo or
   Nance Morado........Brysonima cotinifolia: Malpighiaceae
Sacatinta ....Fuchsia parviflora-Zuco: Onagraceae
Jiquilite ....Indigofera suffruticosa: Fabaceae
Nacascolo or *dividivi*.....Caesalpinia coriaria: Caesalpinaceae. (Frequently confused with *Nascacolo*—Pithecolobium pachypus: Mimosaceae)
Nance ....Brysonima crassifolia L.: Malpighiaceae
Aliso ....Alnus acuminata: Betulaceae
Camotillo ....Curcuma tinctoria: Zingiberaceae
Achiote ....Bixa Orellana L.: Bixaceae
Curcuma ....Curcuma longa L.: Escitaminaceae
Campeche ....Haemtoxylon campechianum: Caesalpinoideae
Tempate ....Jatropha Curcas L.: Euphorbiaceae
Chinchinegritos ....Lantana camara L.: Verbenaceae
Palo de mora ....Maclura tinctoria: Moraceae
Palo Amarillo ....Chlorophora tinctoria: Moraceae

11. PRESIDENTS SINCE 1871

General Miguel Garcia Granados 1871
General Justo Rufino Barrios 1873-1885
General José Maria Orantes (Acting President) 1882-1883
General Alejandro M. Sinibaldi ....1885 (100 hours)
General Manuel Lisandro Barillas 1885-1892
General José Maria Reina Barrios 1892-1898
Don Manuel Estrada Cabrera 1898-1920
Don Carlos Herrera 1920-1921
General José Maria Orellana 1921-1926
General Lazaro Chacón 1926-1930
Don Baudillio Palma ....1930 (100 hours)
General don Manuel Orellana 1930-1931
Don José Maria Reina Andrade 1931
General don Jorge Ubico 1931-1937
   Reelected 1937-1943
   Overthrown ....June 30, 1944
General Federico Ponce Vaides, Acting President until October 20, 1944; overthrown by revolution, October 20, 1944.
Acting triumvirate: Major Arana, Captain Arbenz, and Jorge Toriello, acting until March 15, 1945.
Dr. Juan José Arévalo Bermejo, elected President, 1945-1951.

12. TRANSPORTATION

Steamships

Atlantic Coast (Puerto Barrios)
  United Fruit Company Line, weekly from New York, Philadelphia,
    Baltimore and New Orleans.
  Hamburg-American Line—monthly from Europe.
Pacific Coast (San José)
  Grace Line, from Seattle and San Francisco to Panama.
  French Line, Italian Line, Johnson Line and Danish East Asiatic Line,
    from San Francisco, monthly.

Railways

International Railways
  From Puerto Barrios to Guatemala City, daily, morning and evening.
    Branch at Zacapa for El Salvador.
  From Guatemala City to Ayutla on Mexican border daily.
    Branch at Santa Maria for San José.
    Branch at Las Cruces for Champerico.
    Branch at Ayutla for Ocos.
Verapaz Railway
  From Pancajché to Panzos. From Panzos, riverboat available to Liv-
    ingston and Puerto Barrios, by way of Polochic River and Lake
    Izabal.

Airways

Daily service north and south by Pan-American World Airways.
International service throughout the Continent.

Highways

International or Pan-American Highway—Enters Guatemala on Mexi-
    can border at Talisman, Department of San Marcos; extends to
    Guatemala City (324 kms.—202½ miles) and continues to San
    Cristóbal on border of Salvador (182 kms.—113¾ miles).
National Highways—Link Guatemala with the capitals of all Depart-
    ments but Petén and Izabal, for which highways are now under
    construction. Also network of side roads and trails.
  (See Road Map, between pages 256-257.)

13. COMMUNICATION

Cables

All American Cables and Tropical Radio Companies link Guatemala with all parts of the world; stations in Guatemala City, Puerto Barrios, San José.

Telephone

National Telephone System, with lines to all Central American Republics; long-distance communication through Tropical Radio Company in Guatemala City, via Miami with North America and Europe.

Telegraph

National Telegraph System, with lines to all Central American Republics.

Mails

Guatemala is a member of the Pan-American Postal Union. Airmail: 9 cents (for about ⅓ ounce) requires three different stamps. Regular mail for local and United States requires three-cent stamp plus one-cent reconstruction stamp.

Radio

National Radio System
  Guatemala City—Station TGW (1520 kcs.) long wave.
                Station TGWA (9685, 11,760, 15,170, 17,800 kcs.) short wave.
  Quezaltenango—TGQ (1420 kcs.) long wave.
                TGQA (6100 kcs.) short wave.

BIBLIOGRAPHY: FOUR KEYS TO GUATEMALA

Star (*) indicates books of interest to the general reader.

English

1. * Ancient Civilizations of Mexico and Central America
    By Herbert J. Spinden: American Museum of Natural History, New York, 1917
2. Biologia Centrali Americana (English Translation)
    By A. P. Maudsley: London, 1902
3. Comparative Study of the Maya and Lacandones
    By Alfred Marston Tozzer: Archeological Institute of America, New York, 1907
4. Conquest of Guatemala
    Edited by Sedley Mackey: The Cortes Society, New York, 1924
5. Discovery and Adventures in Central America
    By Thomas Gann: Duckworth, London, 1927
6. Glimpse of Guatemala
    By Anne C. and A. P. Maudsley: Murray, London, 1899
7. * Guatemala Textiles
    By Lilly de Jongh Osborne: Tulane University, 1935
8. * Guide Book to Ruins of Quiriguá
    By Dr. Sylvanus G. Morley: Carnegie Institution of Washington, 1935
9. History of the Maya
    By Eric Thompson and Thomas Gann, 1937
10. * Incidents of Travel in Central America, Chiapas and Yucatan
    By John L. Stephens: Harper Brothers, 1841-42
11. Kaminal Juyú
    By Dr. A. V. Kidder: Carnegie Institution of Washington, 1937
12. Maya Cities
    By Thomas Gann: Duckworth, London, 1927
13. On Certain Antiquities in Western Guatemala
    By T. T. Waterman: Pan-American Union, 1924
14. Reprints from Indian Notes
    By S. K. Lothrop: Museum of the American Indian, New York, 1926-27
15. Some Spanish Entradas—A Revision
    By Doris Zemurray Stone: Tulane University, 1932
16. States of Central America, The
    By E. G. Squier: Harper Brothers, New York, 1858

17. Thomas Gage, the English American
    Published, Routledge and Sons, London, 1648; Broadway Travellers, 1928
18. Uaxactún, Guatemala (Group E—1926-1931)
    Oliver and Edith B. Ricketson: Carnegie Institution of Washington, 1937
19. Year Bearer's People, The
    By Oliver La Farge and Douglas Byers: Middle American Research Institute of Tulane University, 1931
20. Zacualpa
    By S. K. Lothrop: Carnegie Institution of Washington, 1936

Spanish

21. Anales de la Sociedad de Geografía é Historia de Guatemala
    15 Volumes: Guatemala City, 1924-38
22. Chilam Balam de Chumayel
    By Antonio Mediz Bolio: Imprenta Lehman, Costa Rica, 1930
23. Compendio de la Historia de la Ciudad de Guatemala
    By Domingo Juarros: Ignacio Beteta Edition, Guatemala, 1808
24. Cronica de la Provincia del Santissimo Nombre de Jesús de Guatemala
    By Francisco Vasquez: Biblioteca Goathemala, Guatemala, 1937
25. Diccionario Geográfico de la República de Guatemala
    By Emilio Descamps: Tipografia San Antonio, Guatemala, 1937
26. Elementos de Botánica General
    By Ulises Rojas: Tipografia Nacional, Guatemala, 1936
27. El Señor Crucificado de Esquipulas
    By church authorities, Esquipulas, Guatemala
28. Fray Bartolomé de las Casas
    By Carlos Gutierrez: Imprenta de Fortanet, Madrid, 1878
29. Geografía de la Republica de Guatemala
    By José Victor Mejia: Tipografia Nacional, Guatemala, 1927
30. Guajxaquip Bats
    By Antonio Goubaud Carrera: Anales, Sociedad de Geografía é Historia, Guatemala, 1935
31. Historia de la America Central
    By José Milla: El Progreso, Guatemala, 1879
32. Historia de la Literatura de Centro America
    By Leonardo Montalván: Tipografia Nacional, El Salvador, 1931
33. Historia de la Provincia de El Itza
    By Juan de Villagutierre Sotomayor: Biblioteca Goathemala, Guatemala, 1933
34. Historia de la Provincia de San Vicente de Chiapas y Guatemala
    By Francisco Ximinez: Biblioteca Goathemala, Guatemala, 1930

35. Historia de los Veintiún Años
    By Ramon Salazar: Tipografia Nacional, Guatemala, 1928
36. Historia General de Chiapas y Guatemala
    By Antonio de Remesal: Biblioteca Goathemala, Guatemala, 1933
37. Huehuetenango
    By Adrian Recinos: Sanchez y de Guise, Guatemala, 1913
38. Isagoge Historicia Apologetica de las Indias Occidentales, especial de
    la Provincia de San Vicente de Chiapa y Guatemala
    By Unknown Author: Biblioteca Goathemala, Guatemala, 1930
39. La America Central ante la Historia
    By Antonio Batres Jauregui: Sanchez y de Guise, Guatemala, 1920
40. * La Metrópoli Colonial Centro Americana y el Departmento de Sacate-
    péquez
    By Jorge Aguirre Matheu: Tipografia Azmitia, Antigua, 1936
41. * La Nueva Guatemala de la Asuncion
    By Pedro Perez Valenzuela: Guatemala, 1934
42. La Romántica Ciudad Colonial
    By Victor Miguel Diaz: Tipografia Nacional, Guatemala, 1924
43. Las Bellas Artes en Guatemala
    By Victor Miguel Diaz: Diario de Centro America, Guatemala, 1934
44. Libro de Actas del Ayuntamiento de la Ciudad de Guatemala
    Issued by Museo de Guatemala, Guatemala, 1856
45. Libro Viejo de la Fundación de Guatemala
    Issued by Biblioteca Goathemala, Guatemala, 1936
46. Memorial de Tecpán-Atitlán (Anales de los Cakchiqueles)
    By Francisco Hernandez Arana Xahila: translated by J. Antonio
    Villacorta: Tipografia Nacional, Guatemala, 1936
47. Monografia del Departmento de Guatemala
    By J. Antonio Villacorta: Tipografia Nacional, Guatemala, 1926
48. Popul-Buh (Manuscrito de Chichicastenango)
    Author unknown: translated by J. Antonio Villacorta and Flavio
    Rodas: Sanchez y de Guise, Guatemala, 1927
49. Recordación Florida del Reyno de Guatemala
    By Francisco Antonio Fuentes y Guzmán: Biblioteca Goathemala,
    Guatemala, 1933
50. Verdadera y Notable Relacion del Descubrimiento y Conquista de la
    Nueva España y Guatemala
    By Bernal Diaz del Castillo: Imprenta Benito Cano, Madrid, 1796

French

51. Le Livre Sacré et les Myths de l'Antiquité Americaine
    By Brasseur de Bourbourg: Arthus Betrand, Paris, 1861
52. Le Totemisme des Lacandones
    By Jacques Soustelle: Maya Research Incorporated, Vol. II, No. 4,
    1935

53. Nouvelle-Relations: Les Voyages de Thomas Gage
    By Thomas Gage: Amsterdam, Holland, 1720

German

54. Aus dem Hochlande der Maya
    By F. J. Lenz: Berlin, 1928
55. Die Mittelamericanischen Vulkane
    By Karl Sapper: Niemeyer, Berlin, 1930
56. * Zur Etnologie und Ethnographie der Nordlichen Mittelamerika
    By Franz Termer: Universität Wurzburg, Germany, 1930

Recommended for General Reading

Books included above which are marked with a star and

Boy with the Parrot
    By Elizabeth Coatsworth: Macmillan, New York, 1930
Civilization of the Maya, The
    By Eric Thomson: Chicago University Press, 1936
Indian Tales from Guatemala
    By Marie H. Jessup and L. B. Simpson: Scribner, New York, 1937
Maria Paluna
    By Blair Niles: Longmans, Green, 1934
Santiago de los Caballeros de Guatemala
    By Dorothy Popenoe: Harvard University Press, 1933

INDEX

INDEX

325